IRAN'S WORLD

BREAKING OUT OF THE MOUNTAIN FORTRESS

STRATFOR
221 W. 6th Street, Suite 400
Austin, TX 78701

Printed in the United States of America

ISBN: 1463748833
EAN-13: 9781463748838

Publisher: Grant Perry
Project Coordinator: Robert Inks
Designer: TJ Lensing

CONTENTS

Introduction   ix

A Note on Content   xv

CHAPTER 1: THE GEOPOLITICS OF IRAN   1

Geography   1

The Broad Outline   6

Geopolitical Imperatives   12

The Current Situation   13

CHAPTER 2: THE INTERNAL STRUGGLE   17

Iran: A Presidential Election and Metamorphosis   17

The Iranian Election and the Revolution Test   31

Crisis as Opportunity for the Islamic Revolutionary
    Guards Corps   38

The Factionalization of the Iranian State   40

Long-Term Consequences of Iran's Intra-Elite Struggle   43

CHAPTER 3: CONVENTIONAL AND UNCONVENTIONAL CAPABILITIES   47

Hezbollah's Iranian Connection   47

Iran: Entangled in the Web of Iraq's Shiite Factions   51

Iran and the Strait of Hormuz, Part 1:
A Strategy of Deterrence   53

Iran and the Strait of Hormuz, Part 2:
Swarming Boats and Shore-Based Missiles   58

Iran and the Strait of Hormuz, Part 3:
The Psychology of Naval Mines   64

Iranian Proxies: An Intricate and Active Web   69

Iranian Intelligence and Regime Preservation   75

CHAPTER 4: THE IRANIAN NUCLEAR DILEMMA   99

Decoupling the Nuclear and Iraq Issues   99

Misreading the Iranian Situation   101

The Complications of Military Action Against Iran   108

Two Leaks and the Deepening Iran Crisis   110

Iran: Sanctions and Smuggling   117

Attacks on Nuclear Scientists in Tehran   123

CHAPTER 5: IRAN AND ITS ALLIES   131

Red October: Russia, Iran and Iraq   131

Iran: Militant Proxies in the Shadows   138

Russia, Ahmadinejad and Iran Reconsidered   140

Hypothesizing on the Iran-Russia-U.S. Triangle 148

Et Tu, Moscow? 155

Syria, Iran: Estranged Allies Collide in Lebanon 158

Syria, Hezbollah and Iran: An Alliance in Flux 162

CHAPTER 6: HISTORIC OPPORTUNITIES IN THE MIDDLE EAST 169

Overdoing Chalabi 169

Iran and the Saudis' Countermove on Bahrain 176

Iraq, Iran and the Next Move 179

The U.S. Withdrawal and Limited Options in Iraq 186

Iran Sees an Opportunity in the Persian Gulf 191

Bahrain and the Battle Between Iran and Saudi Arabia 195

History Repeats Itself in Eastern Arabia 201

CHAPTER 7: THE U.S.-IRANIAN STRUGGLE 205

The Region After Iraq 205

A Positive Iranian Influence in Iraq? 211

Iran's View of the Surge 214

The NIE Report: Solving a Geopolitical Problem
with Iran 216

The Real Struggle in Iran and Implications for
U.S. Dialogue 221

A Defensive Buildup in the Gulf 227

Thinking About the Unthinkable: A U.S.-Iranian Deal 234

Iran and the United States, Grasping for Diplomacy 242

Rethinking American Options on Iran   245

U.S.-Iran Negotiations Redux   252

The U.S.-Saudi Dilemma: Iran's Reshaping of Persian
    Gulf Politics   255

ILLUSTRATIONS

Iran	viii
Physiography of Iran	xvi
Population Density	4
The Iranian Land Bridge	5
Petroleum Facilities	7
The Persian Empire	9
Ethno-Religious Distribution	11
Iranian Political Power Structure	19
Hezbollah-MOIS Organizational Relationship	49
Topography and Bathymetry of the Strait of Hormuz	57
Iran's Executive Branch and Intelligence Services	83
Persian Gulf Energy	192

IRAN

INTRODUCTION

An understanding of what drives Iranian behavior cannot begin with the newspaper headlines of the past decade. Alarmist press reports on Iran's drive toward nuclear weapons, vitriolic statements by the country's leadership, attacks by Iranian militant proxies and the regime's impossibly complex power struggles would spin the reader into a frenzy trying to figure out the true nature of Iranian intentions and capabilities. The key to dissecting this poorly understood country is to begin, simply, with its geography and history.

Iran is essentially a mountain fortress, a landscape that makes it easy for its residents to repel foreign invaders but difficult for it to expand, and similarly difficult to control politically and develop from within. The country's mountain barriers have allowed a distinct Persian culture to develop, but only around half of modern Iran's 77 million people are ethnically Persian, giving a host of minorities the power to strain the country's central authority. This dynamic explains why Iran has long maintained an expansive and powerful security and intelligence apparatus to maintain internal control, while also compensating for deficiencies in conventional military power when dealing with threats from abroad. The rough terrain makes internal transport extremely costly, which means that while abundant energy resources can allow the country to get by economically, Iran can never prosper like its sparsely populated, oil-rich Arab adversaries.

The historic foundation of Persian power does not sit within modern Iran's borders. Indeed, the Persians developed their civilization from the fertile plains of Mesopotamia in modern-day Iraq. Historically, if the Arab power that controls the region between the

Tigris and Euphrates rivers is weak and fractured, Iran has an opportunity to expand beyond its borders and enrich itself. If the power in this land is strong and under Sunni control, however, Iran's biggest threat will emanate from there.

The U.S. move to topple Iraqi ruler Saddam Hussein in 2003 presented just such a historic opportunity for Iran. If Iran is able to consolidate Shiite influence in Iraq — which already demographically favors the Shia — it both avoids another nightmare scenario like the 1980-1988 Iran-Iraq war and provides Tehran with abundant resources and a foothold in the Arab world with which to project influence. An understanding of Iran's Iraq imperative explains why Iran had covert assets positioned to fill the power void in Iraq immediately after Saddam Hussein fell from power. Iran had seized the opportunity and, much to the displeasure of the United States, would do everything within its power to hold onto it.

Therein lies the strategic dilemma for the United States. Stability in the Middle East is contingent on an Iraq-Iran balance of power. The United States shattered that balance of power by removing Iraq's Baathist regime, thinking it could rapidly rebuild a government to continue counterbalancing Iran. What it failed to anticipate was that Iran already had the pieces in place to ensure any post-Hussein government in Baghdad would be dominated by Shiites and thus operating under heavy Iranian influence. Tehran may not have the capability to transform a highly fractious country like Iraq into an Iranian satellite, but it does have the ability to prevent Iraq from re-emerging as a counterbalance to Iran. The most recent illustration of this dynamic is the current U.S. struggle in Baghdad to negotiate an extension for U.S. troops to remain in Iraq. If the United States fully withdraws from Iraq, it leaves Iran as the most powerful military force in the Persian Gulf region. Iran has every intention of ensuring that the United States is unable to reconfigure a blocking force in Iraq that could undermine Iran's regional potential.

To reinforce its strategy, Iran maintains a threat over the energy-vital Strait of Hormuz, through which 40 percent of the world's seaborne oil trade passes each day. As long as Iran can hold an iron grip over this crucial sea gate, it is a power to be reckoned with in the Persian Gulf region. Iran's covert capabilities in the region also are extremely unnerving for Sunni powers like Saudi Arabia. The Saudi royals are already coping with the uncomfortable reality of having to concede Iraq to the Shia, and by extension, Tehran, so long as the United States remains incapable of developing a coherent strategy to block Iran. But when Shiite-led demonstrations erupted in Bahrain in the spring of 2011, Iran succeeded in engineering the potential for long-simmering Shiite unrest to ignite and spread from Bahrain to the Shiite-concentrated, oil-rich Eastern Province in the Saudi kingdom. This prompted a hasty and rare military intervention by Gulf Cooperation Council forces in Bahrain and is also now apparently pushing a very reluctant Saudi Arabia toward a truce with Iran until it can get a better sense of U.S. intentions.

Though fairly confident in its position in Iraq, Iran still has a major challenge ahead: to reach an accommodation the United States that would essentially aim to recognize Iran's expanded sphere of influence, expand Iranian energy rights in Iraq, ensure the impotence of the Iraqi armed forces and provide the Iranian regime with an overall sense of security. Iran has an interest in coercing its U.S. adversary into such a negotiation now, while it still has the upper hand and before regional heavyweights like Turkey grow into their historical role of counterbalancing Persia. The United States has a strategic interest in rebuilding a balance of power in the region when it can afford to, but its immediate interest in this region is in ensuring the flow of oil through the Strait of Hormuz, containing the jihadist threat and reducing its military presence — goals that do not stray far from those of Iran, much to Saudi Arabia's concern. Given this dynamic, STRATFOR has focused much of its analysis over the past decade on the drivers behind a potential U.S.-Iranian accommodation.

In examining the ebb and flow of U.S.-Iranian negotiations, there are two key misconceptions to bear in mind. The first misconception is that nuclear weapons are the fundamental issue for Iran. Iran naturally has an interest in enhancing its security through a nuclear deterrent, but the distance between a testable nuclear device and deliverable nuclear weapon is substantial. Iran has used its nuclear ambitions as a sideshow to delay and distract its adversaries while focusing on its core imperative in Iraq. When a country trying to develop a nuclear weapons capability — a process usually done in extreme secrecy — feels the frequent need to announce to the world its progress on uranium enrichment, it raises the question of what other purposes an Iranian nuclear bogeyman may be serving.

The second misconception is that Iran's clerical regime is extremely vulnerable to a democratic uprising. The failure of the so-called Green Revolution in 2009 was not surprising to us, but what did catch our attention is the manner in which Iranian President Mahmoud Ahmadinejad used his renewed political mandate in 2009 to launch a political offensive against the corrupt clerical elite. The power struggle has intensified to the point that the country's supreme leader, lacking the charisma of the founder of the Islamic republic, is now directly intervening in trying to contain the president. The most striking aspect of this power struggle is not the idea of a single firebrand leader under attack from the country's most senior clerics but the fact that such a leader would not be attacking the clerical establishment unless it was already perceived as weakening and undergoing a crisis in legitimacy. Ahmadinejad, a mere politician, should therefore not be the main focus in monitoring the development of this power struggle. The far more important issue is the underlying faction that he represents and the delegitimization of the country's clerical elite. Iran's internal pressures are unlikely to distract the country from meeting its imperatives in Iraq, but with time, the discrediting of the clerics is likely to create an opening in the country for the military — as opposed to the pro-democracy youth groups — to assert itself in the political affairs of the state.

The articles contained in this book are STRATFOR's featured analyses of Iran's historical roots and modern goals and challenges. From the core geopolitics and military realities of the state to the internal struggles of the Islamic republic to Iran's complex web of foreign relationships, the goal of this compilation is to cut through the media hype and get to the core question of what has driven Iranian behavior in the past and, more important, what will frame Iranian options in the future as it seeks to reshape the balance of power in one the world's most active energy arteries.

Reva Bhalla, Director of Analysis
STRATFOR
Austin, Texas
Aug. 22, 2011

A NOTE ON CONTENT

STRATFOR presents the following articles as they originally appeared on our subscription Web site, www.STRATFOR.com. These pieces represent some of our best analyses of Iran's domestic politics and international relations since June 2002, organized under chapter headings and presented in the order in which they were published. Since most of the articles were written as individual analyses, there may be overlap from piece to piece and chapter to chapter, and some of the information may seem dated. Naturally, many of the observations herein are linked to a specific time or event that may be years removed from Iran's situation today. However, STRATFOR believes bringing these pieces together provides valuable insight and perspective on a significant global player.

PHYSIOGRAPHY OF IRAN

RUSSIA

KAZAKHSTAN

UZBEKISTAN

Caspian Sea

GEORGIA

ARMENIA

AZERBAIJAN

TURKMENISTAN

KARAKUM DESERT

ELBURZ MOUNTAINS

Tehran ★

DASHT-E KAVIR
(SALT-DESERT)

ZAGROS MOUNTAINS

IRAN

AFGHANISTAN

IRAQ

DASHT-E LUT

KUWAIT

Shatt al-Arab Waterway

PAKISTAN

Persian Gulf

Strait of Hormuz

CENTRAL
MAHRAN RANGE

BAHRAIN

QATAR

Gulf of Oman

SAUDI ARABIA

U.A.E.

OMAN

0 mi   200

0 km   400

YEMEN

Copyright STRATFOR 2011   www.STRATFOR.com

CHAPTER 1: THE GEOPOLITICS OF IRAN

July 14, 2008

Geography

To understand Iran, you must begin by understanding how large it is. Iran is the 17th largest country in world. It measures about 636,300 square miles (1,648,000 square kilometers). That means that its territory is larger than the combined territories of France, Germany, the Netherlands, Belgium, Spain and Portugal — Western Europe. Iran is the 16th most populous country in the world, with about 70 million people. Its population is larger than the populations of either France or the United Kingdom.

Under the current circumstances, it might be useful to benchmark Iran against Iraq or Afghanistan. Iraq is about 167,200 square miles, with about 25 million people, so Iran is roughly four times as large and three times as populous. Afghanistan is about 251,750 square miles, with a population of about 30 million. One way to look at it is that Iran is 68 percent larger than Iraq and Afghanistan combined, with 40 percent more population.

More important are its topographical barriers. Iran is defined, above all, by its mountains, which form its frontiers, enfold its cities and describe its historical heartland. To understand Iran, you must understand not only how large it is but also how mountainous it is.

Iran's most important mountains are the Zagros. They are a southern extension of the Caucasus, running about 900 miles from the

1

northwestern border of Iran, which adjoins Turkey and Armenia, southeast toward Bandar Abbas on the Strait of Hormuz. The first 150 miles of Iran's western border is shared with Turkey. It is intensely mountainous on both sides. South of Turkey, the mountains on the western side of the border begin to diminish until they disappear altogether on the Iraqi side. From this point onward, south of the Kurdish regions, the land on the Iraqi side is increasingly flat, part of the Tigris-Euphrates basin. The Iranian side of the border is mountainous, beginning just a few miles east of the border. Iran has a mountainous border with Turkey, but mountains face a flat plain along the Iraq border. This is the historical frontier between Persia — the name of Iran until the early 20th century — and Mesopotamia ("land between two rivers"), as southern Iraq is called.

The one region of the western border that does not adhere to this model is in the extreme south, in the swamps where the Tigris and Euphrates rivers join to form the Shatt al-Arab waterway. There the Zagros swing southeast, and the southern border between Iran and Iraq zigzags south to the Shatt al-Arab, which flows south 125 miles through flat terrain to the Persian Gulf. To the east is the Iranian province of Khuzestan, populated by ethnic Arabs, not Persians. Given the swampy nature of the ground, it can be easily defended and gives Iran a buffer against any force from the west seeking to move along the coastal plain of Iran on the Persian Gulf.

Running east along the Caspian Sea are the Elburz Mountains, which serve as a mountain bridge between the Caucasus-Zagros range and Afghan mountains that eventually culminate in the Hindu Kush. The Elburz run along the southern coast of the Caspian to the Afghan border, buffering the Karakum Desert in Turkmenistan. Mountains of lesser elevations then swing down along the Afghan and Pakistani borders, almost to the Arabian Sea.

Iran has about 800 miles of coastline, roughly half along the eastern shore of the Persian Gulf, the rest along the Gulf of Oman. Its most important port, Bandar Abbas, is located on the Strait of Hormuz. There are no equivalent ports along the Gulf of Oman, and the Strait of Hormuz is extremely vulnerable to interdiction. Therefore, Iran is not a major maritime or naval power. It is and always has been a land power.

The center of Iran consists of two desert plateaus that are virtually uninhabited and uninhabitable. These are the Dasht-e Kavir, which stretches from Qom in the northwest nearly to the Afghan border, and the Dasht-e Lut, which extends south to Balochistan. The Dasht-e Kavir consists of a layer of salt covering thick mud, and it is easy to break through the salt layer and drown in the mud. It is one of the most miserable places on earth.

Iran's population is concentrated in its mountains, not in its lowlands, as with other countries. That's because its lowlands, with the exception of the southwest and the southeast (regions populated by non-Persians), are uninhabitable. Iran is a nation of 70 million mountain dwellers. Even its biggest city, Tehran, is in the foothills of towering mountains. Its population is in a belt stretching through the Zagros and Elburz mountains on a line running from the eastern shore of the Caspian to the Strait of Hormuz. There is a secondary concentration of people to the northeast, centered on Mashhad. The rest of the country is lightly inhabited and almost impassable because of the salt-mud flats.

If you look carefully at a map of Iran, you can see that the western part of the country — the Zagros Mountains — is actually a land bridge for southern Asia. It is the only path between the Persian Gulf in the south and the Caspian Sea in the north. Iran is the route connecting the Indian subcontinent to the Mediterranean Sea. But because of its size and geography, Iran is not a country that can be easily traversed, much less conquered.

The location of Iran's oil fields is critical here, since oil remains its most important and most strategic export. Oil is to be found in three locations: The southwest is the major region, with lesser deposits along the Iraqi border in the north and one near Qom. The southwestern oil fields are an extension of the geological formation that created the oil fields in the Kurdish region of northern Iraq. Hence, the region east of the Shatt al-Arab is of critical importance to Iran. Iran has the third largest oil reserves in the world and is the world's

POPULATION DENSITY

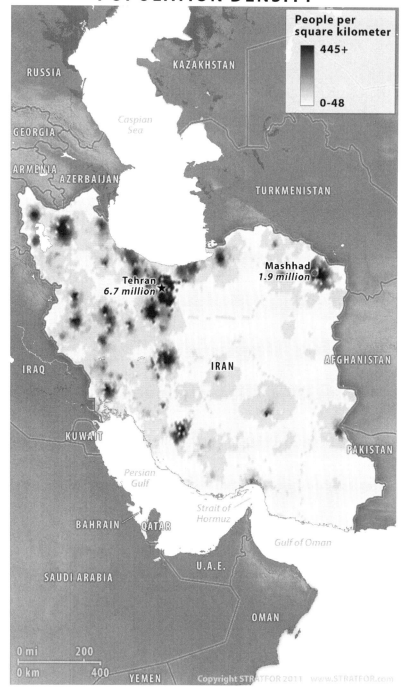

People per square kilometer

445+

0-48

RUSSIA

KAZAKHSTAN

Caspian Sea

GEORGIA

ARMENIA

AZERBAIJAN

TURKMENISTAN

Mashhad
1.9 million

Tehran
6.7 million

IRAN

AFGHANISTAN

IRAQ

KUWAIT

PAKISTAN

Persian Gulf

Strait of Hormuz

BAHRAIN QATAR

Gulf of Oman

U.A.E.

SAUDI ARABIA

OMAN

0 mi   200
0 km   400

YEMEN

Copyright STRATFOR 2011   www.STRATFOR.com

THE IRANIAN LAND BRIDGE

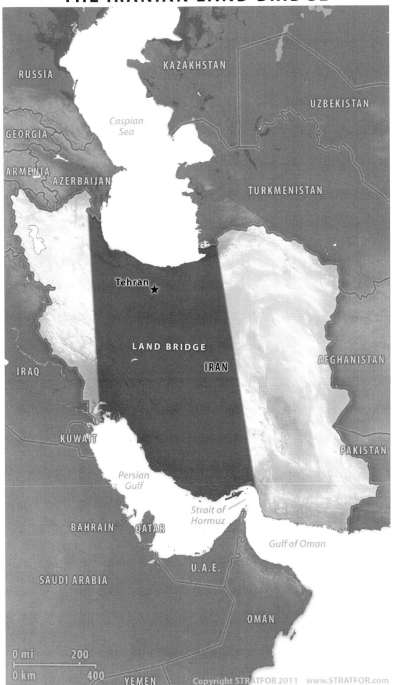

fourth largest producer. Therefore, one would expect it to be one of the wealthiest countries in the world. It isn't.

Iran has the 28th largest economy in the world but ranks only 71st in per capita gross domestic product (as expressed in purchasing power). It ranks with countries like Belarus or Panama. Part of the reason is inefficiencies in the Iranian oil industry, the result of government policies. But there is a deeper geographic problem. Iran has a huge population mostly located in rugged mountains. Mountainous regions are rarely prosperous. The cost of transportation makes the development of industry difficult. Sparsely populated mountain regions are generally poor. Heavily populated mountain regions, when they exist, are much poorer.

Iran's geography and large population make substantial improvements in its economic life difficult. Unlike underpopulated and less geographically challenged countries such as Saudi Arabia and Kuwait, Iran cannot enjoy any shift in the underlying weakness of its economy brought on by higher oil prices and more production. The absence of inhabitable plains means that any industrial plant must develop in regions where the cost of infrastructure tends to undermine the benefits. Oil keeps Iran from sinking even deeper, but it alone cannot catapult Iran out of its condition.

The Broad Outline

Iran is a fortress. Surrounded on three sides by mountains and on the fourth by the ocean, with a wasteland at its center, Iran is extremely difficult to conquer. This was achieved once by the Mongols, who entered the country from the northeast. The Ottomans penetrated the Zagros Mountains and went northeast as far as the Caspian but made no attempt to move into the Persian heartland.

Iran is a mountainous country looking for inhabitable plains. There are none to the north, only more mountains and desert, or to the east, where Afghanistan's infrastructure is no more inviting. To the south there is only ocean. What plains there are in the region lie to the west, in modern-day Iraq and historical Mesopotamia and Babylon. If Iran

PETROLEUM FACILITIES

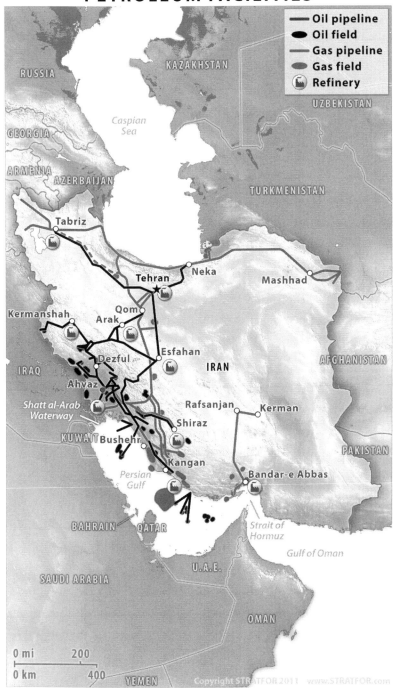

could dominate these plains, and combine them with its own population, they would be the foundation of Iranian power.

Indeed, these plains were the foundation of the Persian Empire. The Persians originated in the Zagros Mountains as a warrior people. They built an empire by conquering the plains in the Tigris and Euphrates basin. They did this slowly, over an extended period at a time when there were no demarcated borders and they faced little resistance to the west. While it was difficult for a lowland people to attack through mountains, it was easier for a mountain-based people to descend to the plains. This combination of population and fertile plains allowed the Persians to expand.

Iran's attacking north or northwest into the Caucasus is impossible in force. The Russians, Turks and Iranians all ground to a halt along the current line in the 19th century; the country is so rugged that movement could be measured in yards rather than miles. Iran could attack northeast into Turkmenistan, but the land there is flat and brutal desert. The Iranians could move east into Afghanistan, but this would involve more mountain fighting for land of equally questionable value. Attacking west, into the Tigris and Euphrates river basin, and then moving to the Mediterranean, would seem doable. This was the path the Persians took when they created their empire and pushed all the way to Greece and Egypt.

In terms of expansion, the problem for Iran is its mountains. They are as effective a container as they are a defensive bulwark. Supporting an attacking force requires logistics, and pushing supplies through the Zagros in any great numbers is impossible. Unless the Persians can occupy and exploit Iraq, further expansion is impossible. In order to exploit Iraq, Iran needs a high degree of active cooperation from Iraqis. Otherwise, rather than converting Iraq's wealth into political and military power, the Iranians would succeed only in being bogged down in pacifying the Iraqis.

In order to move west, Iran would require the active cooperation of conquered nations. Any offensive will break down because of the challenges posed by the mountains in moving supplies. This is why the Persians created the type of empire they did. They allowed

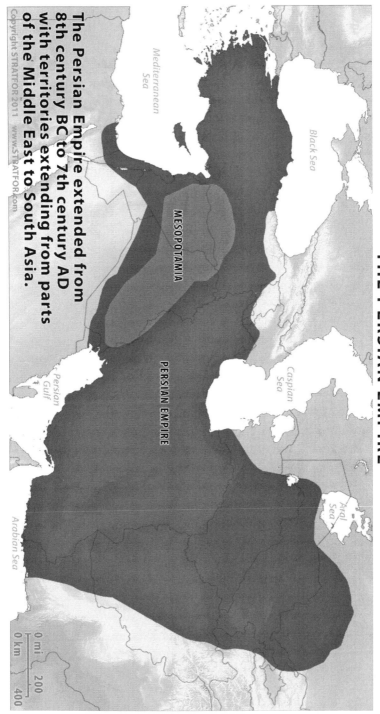

THE PERSIAN EMPIRE

The Persian Empire extended from 8th century BC to 7th century AD with territories extending from parts of the Middle East to South Asia.

MESOPOTAMIA

PERSIAN EMPIRE

Mediterranean Sea

Black Sea

Caspian Sea

Aral Sea

Persian Gulf

Arabian Sea

0 mi   200   400
0 km

conquered nations a great deal of autonomy, respected their culture and made certain that these nations benefited from the Persian imperial system. Once they left the Zagros, the Persians could not afford to pacify an empire. They needed the wealth at minimal cost. And this has been the limit on Persian/Iranian power ever since. Recreating a relationship with the inhabitants of the Tigris and Euphrates basin — today's Iraq — is enormously difficult. Indeed, throughout most of history, the domination of the plains by Iran has been impossible. Other imperial powers — Alexandrian Greece, Rome, the Byzantines, Ottomans, British and Americans — have either seized the plains themselves or used them as a neutral buffer against the Persians.

Underlying the external problems of Iran is a severe internal problem. Mountains allow nations to protect themselves. Completely eradicating a culture is difficult. Therefore, most mountain regions of the world contain large numbers of national and ethnic groups that retain their own characteristics. This is commonplace in all mountainous regions. These groups resist absorption and annihilation. Although a Muslim state with a population that is 55 to 60 percent ethnically Persian, Iran is divided into a large number of ethnic groups. It is also divided between the vastly dominant Shia and the minority Sunnis, who are clustered in three areas of the country — the northeast, the northwest and the southeast. Any foreign power interested in Iran will use these ethno-religious groups to create allies in Iran to undermine the power of the central government.

Thus, any Persian or Iranian government has as its first and primary strategic interest maintaining the internal integrity of the country against separatist groups. It is inevitable, therefore, for Iran to have a highly centralized government with an extremely strong security apparatus. For many countries, holding together its ethnic groups is important. For Iran it is essential because it has no room to retreat from its current lines and instability could undermine its entire security structure. Therefore, the Iranian central government will always face the problem of internal cohesion and will use its army and security forces for that purpose before any other.

ETHNO-RELIGIOUS DISTRIBUTION

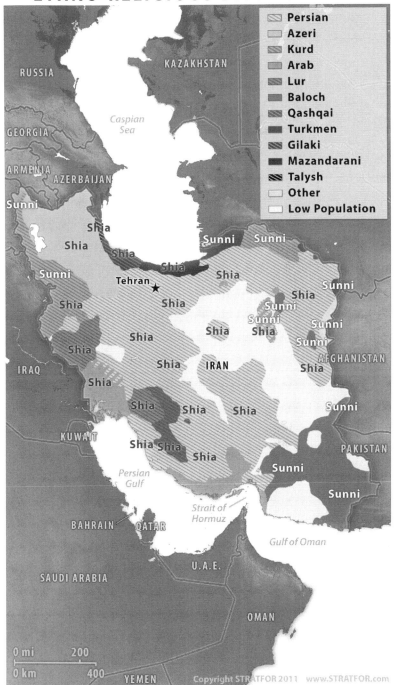

Legend:
- Persian
- Azeri
- Kurd
- Arab
- Lur
- Baloch
- Qashqai
- Turkmen
- Gilaki
- Mazandarani
- Talysh
- Other
- Low Population

Copyright STRATFOR 2011   www.STRATFOR.com

Geopolitical Imperatives

For most countries, the first geographical imperative is to maintain internal cohesion. For Iran, it is to maintain secure borders, then secure the country internally. Without secure borders, Iran would be vulnerable to foreign powers that would continually try to manipulate its internal dynamics, destabilize its ruling regime and then exploit the resulting openings. Iran must first define the container and then control what it contains. Therefore, Iran's geopolitical imperatives are:

1. Control the Zagros and Elburz mountains. These constitute the Iranian heartland and the buffers against attacks from the west and north.

2. Control the mountains to the east of the Dasht-e Kavir and Dasht-e Lut, from Mashhad to Zahedan to the Makran coast, protecting Iran's eastern frontiers with Pakistan and Afghanistan. Maintain a line as deep and as far north and west as possible in the Caucasus to limit Turkish and Russian threats. These are the secondary lines.

3. Secure a line on the Shatt al-Arab in order to protect the western coast of Iran on the Persian Gulf.

4. Control the divergent ethnic and religious elements in this box.

5. Protect the frontiers against potential threats, particularly major powers from outside the region.

Iran has achieved four of the five basic goals. It has created secure frontiers and is in control of the population inside the country. The greatest threat against Iran is the one it has faced since Alexander the Great — that posed by major powers outside the region. Historically, before deep-water navigation, Iran was the direct path to India for any Western power. In modern times, the Zagros remain the eastern anchor of Turkish power. Northern Iran blocks Russian expansion.

And, of course, Iranian oil reserves make Iran attractive to contemporary great powers.

There are two traditional paths into Iran. The northeastern region is vulnerable to Central Asian powers while the western approach is the most-often used (or attempted). A direct assault through the Zagros Mountains is not feasible, as Saddam Hussein discovered in 1980. However, manipulating the ethnic groups inside Iran is possible. The British, for example, based in Iraq, were able to manipulate internal political divisions in Iran, as did the Soviets, to the point that Iran virtually lost its national sovereignty during World War II.

The greatest threat to Iran in recent centuries has been a foreign power dominating Iraq —Ottoman or British — and extending its power eastward not through main force but through subversion and political manipulation. The view of the contemporary Iranian government toward the United States is that, during the 1950s, it assumed Britain's role of using its position in Iraq to manipulate Iranian politics and elevate the shah to power.

The 1980-1988 war between Iran and Iraq was a terrific collision of two states, causing several million casualties on both sides. It also demonstrated two realities. The first is that a determined, well-funded, no-holds-barred assault from Mesopotamia against the Zagros Mountains will fail (albeit at an atrocious cost to the defender). The second is that, in the nation-state era, with fixed borders and standing armies, the logistical challenges posed by the Zagros make a major attack from Iran into Iraq equally impossible. There is a stalemate on that front. Nevertheless, from the Iranian point of view, the primary danger of Iraq is not direct attack but subversion. It is not only Iraq that worries them. Historically, Iranians also have been concerned about Russian manipulation and manipulation by the British and Russians through Afghanistan.

The Current Situation

For the Iranians, the current situation has posed a dangerous scenario similar to what they faced from the British early in the 20th century. The United States has occupied, or at least placed substantial forces, to the east and the west of Iran, in Afghanistan and Iraq. Iran is not concerned about these troops invading Iran. That is not a military possibility. Iran's concern is that the United States will use these positions as platforms to foment ethnic dissent in Iran.

Indeed, the United States has tried to do this in several regions. In the southeast, in Balochistan, the Americans have supported separatist movements. It has also done this among the Arabs of Khuzestan, at the northern end of the Persian Gulf. And it has tried to manipulate the Kurds in northwestern Iran. (There is some evidence to suggest that the United States has used Azerbaijan as a launchpad to foment dissent among the Iranian Azeris in the northwestern part of the country.)

The Iranian counter to all this has several dimensions:

1. Maintain an extremely powerful and repressive security capability to counter these moves. In particular, focus on deflecting any intrusions in the Khuzestan region, which is not only the most physically vulnerable part of Iran but also where much of Iran's oil reserves are located.

2. Manipulate ethnic and religious tensions in Iraq and Afghanistan to undermine the American positions there and divert American attention to defensive rather than offensive goals.

3. Maintain a military force capable of protecting the surrounding mountains so that major American forces cannot penetrate

4. Move to create a nuclear force, very publicly, in order to deter attack in the long run and to give Iran a bargaining chip for negotiations in the short term.

The heart of the Iranian strategy is, as it has always been, to use the mountains as a fortress. So long as it is anchored in those mountains, it cannot be invaded. Alexander succeeded and the Ottomans had limited success (little more than breaching the Zagros), but even the

Romans and British did not go so far as to try to use main force in the region. Invading and occupying Iran is not an option.

For Iran, its ultimate problem is internal tensions. But even these are under control, primarily because of Iran's security system. Ever since the founding of the Persian Empire, the one thing that Iranians have been superb at is creating systems that both benefit other ethnic groups and punish them if they stray. That same mindset functions in Iran today in the powerful Ministry of Intelligence and Security and the elite Islamic Revolutionary Guards Corps (IRGC). (The Iranian military is configured mainly as an infantry force, with the regular army and IRGC ground forces together totaling about 450,000 troops, larger than all other service branches combined.)

Iran is, therefore, a self-contained entity. It is relatively poor, but it has superbly defensible borders and a disciplined central government with an excellent intelligence and internal security apparatus. Iran uses these same strengths to destabilize the American position (or that of any extraregional power) around it. Indeed, Iran is sufficiently secure that the positions of surrounding countries are more precarious than that of Iran. Iran is superb at low-cost, low-risk power projection using its covert capabilities. It is even better at blocking those of others. So long as the mountains are in Iranian hands and the internal situation is controlled, Iran is a stable state, but one able to pose only a limited external threat.

The creation of an Iranian nuclear program serves two functions. First, if successful, it further deters external threats. Second, simply having the program enhances Iranian power. Since the consequences of a strike against these facilities are uncertain and raise the possibility of Iranian attempts at interdiction of oil from the Persian Gulf, the strategic risk to the attacker's economy discourages attack. The diplomatic route of trading the program for regional safety and power becomes more attractive than an attack against a potential threat in a country with a potent potential counter.

Iran is secure from conceivable invasion. It enhances this security by using two tactics. First, it creates uncertainty as to whether it has an offensive nuclear capability. Second, it projects a carefully honed image of ideological extremism that makes it appear unpredictable. It makes itself appear threatening and unstable. Paradoxically, this increases the caution used in dealing with it because the main option, an air attack, has historically been ineffective without a follow-on ground attack. If just nuclear facilities are attacked and the attack fails, the Iranian reaction is unpredictable and potentially disproportionate. Iranian posturing enhances the uncertainty. The threat of an air attack is deterred by Iran's threat of an attack against sea-lanes. Such attacks would not be effective, but even a low-probability disruption of the world's oil supply is a risk not worth taking.

As always, the Persians face a major power prowling at the edges of their mountains. The mountains will protect them from main force but not from the threat of destabilization. Therefore, the Persians bind their nation together through a combination of political accommodation and repression. The major power will eventually leave. Persia will remain so long as its mountains stand.

CHAPTER 2: THE INTERNAL STRUGGLE

Iran: A Presidential Election and Metamorphosis
June 11, 2009

Iran will hold a presidential election June 12 in which the country's ultraconservative president, Mahmoud Ahmadinejad, will face powerful challengers in trying to secure a second term. To a significant degree, the results of the election could determine the outcome of the Obama administration's efforts to diplomatically engage the Islamic republic. Limits to the power of the Iranian presidency, and the fact that policymaking in Tehran is a function of consensus among various stakeholders, underscore the complexity of the Iranian political structure and how it functions.

The Islamic Republic of Iran was founded in the aftermath of the country's 1979 revolution, which deposed the Shah of Iran. The new republic is a kind of hybrid between a Western parliamentary democracy and a Velayat-e-Faqih (a state ruled by a jurist, a concept developed in the 18th century). In Iran, this hybrid is a peculiar system that includes clerics as well as politicians and technocrats, and over the years it has evolved into a complex web of institutions and players stretching between the supreme leader and the president, the two most prominent posts in the country's political hierarchy.

Key Institutions

Supreme Leader

At the apex of the Iranian system, and undoubtedly the most powerful individual, is the supreme leader. This position has thus far been held by two individuals. The first was the founder of the Islamic republic, Ayatollah Ruhollah Khomeini, who held the post from 1979 until his death in 1989. He was succeeded by his key aide and a former two-term president, Ayatollah Ali Khamenei, who has been supreme leader for the past two decades. The supreme leader is directly elected not by the public, but by the Assembly of Experts (AoE), which also has the power to hold him accountable and to remove him. Nevertheless, the supreme leader enjoys vast powers, as he serves as the supreme commander of the country's armed forces and appoints the leadership of the country's most powerful political institutions, such as state broadcasting, the Joint Staff, Islamic Revolutionary Guards Corps (IRGC), Guardians Council (GC), Judiciary, Expediency Council (EC) and Supreme National Security Council (SNSC). All SNSC decisions require the supreme leader's approval. Despite this overwhelming authority, the supreme leader does not call the shots alone; rather, he rules by consensus.

According to the Iranian Constitution, if the supreme leader dies, resigns or is removed, a council consisting of the president, the head of the judiciary and a member of the GC takes over temporarily until the AoE selects a new leader. While this is only an interim arrangement, many Iranian power brokers, including Ayatollah Ali Akbar Hashemi Rafsanjani, former president and current EC chairman, have proposed that the office of the supreme leader be replaced by a council of jurists, a move that would require a change to the constitution. This would not be unprecedented; shortly before he died, Khomeini ordered a change to the constitution so that it would no longer require the supreme leader to be a marjaa taqleed (a senior cleric who has reached a level of scholarship so that he can be emulated by laypeople, a requirement in Shiite Islam).

IRANIAN POLITICAL POWER STRUCTURE

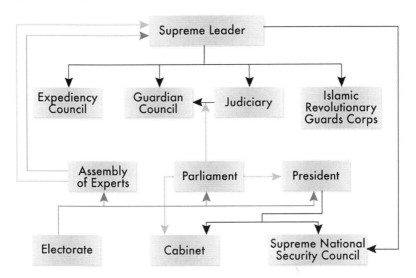

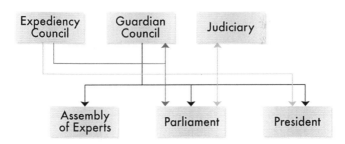

Appoints
Elects
Confirms/Rejects Appointments/Impeachment Authority
Approves Decision
Vets Candidates/Veto Power
Arbitrates Between
Oversight Authority

President

While the supreme leader exercises far greater authority, the Iranian president also wields considerable power given that he is head of the executive branch and makes all key government appointments (i.e., to the Cabinet and the SNSC). Because the country's premier intelligence service, the Ministry of Intelligence and Security, and the regular armed forces under the Ministry of Defense are headed by Cabinet members, the president has a lot of say in security matters. Popularly elected every four years, a president can serve two consecutive terms and is the one taking the lead on policymaking, with other institutions providing guidance and oversight. The fact that former President Mohammad Khatami, a reformist, was able to pursue policies that did not sit well with the conservative establishment, while his successor, Ahmadinejad, is able to resist strong opposition to his policies from fellow conservatives, speaks volumes about the power that rests within the office of the presidency.

Guardians Council

The authority to vet presidential candidates as well as those seeking membership in parliament and the AoE makes the GC one of the most powerful institutions in the Iranian state. It can approve or reject parliamentary legislation if it deems it not in keeping with the constitution. As the ultimate interpreter of the constitution, the GC also serves as the country's constitutional court.

The GC is a 12-member body consisting of six theologians appointed by the supreme leader and six jurists appointed by the judiciary chief but confirmed by parliament. Members serve six-year terms on a phased basis so that six members change every three years. Since 1988, the GC has been led by Ayatollah Ahmad Jannati, a key ultraconservative and supporter of the current president. The GC has earned notoriety because of its moves to disqualify thousands of reformist candidates seeking to run in parliamentary elections. In the case of the presidential election, the GC has been more lenient (largely because there is only one position up for grabs, and there usually are not many serious hopefuls).

Judiciary

The Iranian state's judicial branch consists of an elaborate web of different courts and is headed by a judiciary chief who must be a mujtahid (a cleric qualified to interpret religious texts and issue rulings) and is appointed by the supreme leader to serve a five-year term. The current judiciary chief is Ayatollah Mahmoud Hashemi Shahroudi, who has held the position since 1999. His current term expires this year, but he could be reappointed to a third term.

The judiciary chief has a tremendous amount of power. He directly reports to the supreme leader and, in turn, appoints the Supreme Court chief justice and the public prosecutor, both of whom also have to be mujtahids. Even the minister of justice, who plays a key role as a legal interlocutor among the three branches of government, is chosen by the president from a list of candidates proposed by the judiciary chief. Furthermore, the judiciary chief gets to nominate the six jurists who form the powerful 12-member GC (although they have to be approved by parliament).

While the judiciary chief enjoys vast powers, two key functions do not fall under his purview. First, the Special Clerical Courts, which try clerics accused of violating the law, operate separately from the judicial system and are under the direct control of the supreme leader. Second, the judiciary is not the ultimate authority to interpret the constitution, a power exercised by the GC.

Parliament

The legislative branch of Iran's government consists of a 290-member unicameral parliament known as the Majlis, whose members are elected by popular vote every four years. The Majlis has the power to approve laws, ratify international treaties and impeach the president. But the powers of the Majlis are greatly circumscribed by the GC with its oversight powers, which has led to tensions between the two institutions — especially during the years when Khatami was president (1997-2005), when reformists were in control of the Majlis and the presidency.

While the conservatives regained control of the Majlis in the 2004 elections, the election of Ahmadinejad the following year led to problems between the legislative and executive branches. Very early on, the Majlis began opposing the president by objecting to several of his Cabinet prospects, rejecting three consecutive nominees to head the Oil Ministry. In subsequent years, the Majlis became a key arena for opposition to many of Ahmadinejad's maverick policies. Though an intraconservative rift between hard-liners and pragmatists noisily played out, the parliament was unable to play a major role in checking the power of the president until after the 2008 elections. Rival conservative factions competed for seats, with the conservative bloc opposed to Ahmadinejad gaining some 50-odd seats and former national security chief Ali Larijani (a bitter opponent of the president) being elected Majlis speaker. Under Larijani's leadership, the Majlis is playing a far more assertive role in keeping a check on the government's policies through the revival of certain parliamentary committees. These include the national security and foreign policy committee and those related to the economy and energy sectors. In other words, the Majlis is fairly malleable in accordance with the political rivalries of the day.

Expediency Council

When it was created in 1989, the original purpose of the EC was to arbitrate in disputes between the Majlis and the GC in the event the Majlis was unable to satisfy the GC's objections on a given piece of legislation. In addition, the EC has served as a strategic advisory body to the supreme leader. At the time of its formation, the EC had a dozen or so members, but since then its composition has increased threefold.

Rafsanjani has headed the EC since its creation, first as president of the country and then as a formal chairman of the EC. The EC also has a secretary, a position held by former IRGC chief Mohsen Rezaie, a retired major general who is a candidate in the current presidential race. After Rafsanjani lost his bid for a third term in the 2005 presidential election, Khamenei, in keeping with his power of delegation, gave Rafsanjani oversight over all branches of government as head of the EC, which further enhanced the council's power. More recently, the EC has focused more on strategic planning and oversight than on arbitration.

Assembly of Experts

Not to be confused with an earlier body that went by the same name and drafted the constitution of the Islamic republic in 1979, the AoE, founded in 1983, is perhaps the most powerful institution in the country, given that it elects the supreme leader, monitors his performance and can even remove him. It consists of 86 clerics, vetted by the GC and then directly elected by the public to eight-year terms, who meet twice a year. The current AoE was elected in December 2006. In September 2007, Rafsanjani, who had long held the deputy chairmanship of the AoE, was elected chairman after the death of his predecessor, Ayatollah Ali Meshkini, who had led the assembly since its inception.

Supreme National Security Council

Created in 1989 as a successor to the original Supreme Defense Council, the SNSC brings together the civil and military elite of the Islamic republic to deal with national security affairs. The SNSC is led by a president-appointed secretary who is also the country's de facto national security chief. The SNSC chief has played the role of lead negotiator in talks with the West over Iran's controversial nuclear program.

Members of the SNSC include the president, parliamentary speaker, judiciary chief, head of the Supreme Command Council of the Armed Forces, chiefs of the army and the IRGC, head of planning and budgetary affairs, two representatives of the supreme leader and the ministers of foreign affairs, interior and intelligence.

In accordance with the constitution, the responsibilities of the SNSC include (roughly translated): crafting defense and national security policies within guidelines provided by the supreme leader; implementing those policies through the coordination of political, intelligence, social, cultural and economic activities; and utilizing the intellectual and material resources of the country in order to deal with domestic and foreign threats.

Islamic Revolutionary Guards Corps

Separate from the regular armed forces, the IRGC is an elite, ideologically driven military institution with its own ground, air, naval, intelligence, strategic and special operations forces that reports directly to the supreme leader. It was created in the aftermath of the revolution with the initial mission of protecting the nascent Islamic republic and its leadership. Since its pivotal role in the 1980-1988 war with Iraq, and given its political, economic and social influence, the IRGC has become far more powerful than the regular military, which serves under the Ministry of Defense.

Though primarily geared toward external threats, the IRGC has a significant domestic law enforcement role through its control of the Baseej, a paramilitary force. The IRGC also controls the country's defense industry and is believed to be running major civilian enterprises in various other sectors, including energy. Because of its economic clout, the IRGC has emerged as the second-most powerful group in the country after the clerical elite.

The IRGC's most important role is serving as Iran's main instrument for projecting power beyond its borders in accordance with Tehran's regional ambitions. Its main approach is the cultivation of nonstate proxies primarily in (but not limited to) the Arab world, such as Hezbollah in Lebanon and Shiite groups in Iraq. The IRGC has a dedicated unit for this purpose, the Quds Force, which the United States has accused in recent years of being the principal Iranian entity supporting a variety of terrorist groups from North Africa to Southwest Asia.

Prominent Players

Ayatollah Ali Khamenei

An ethnic Azeri from his father's side, Khamenei, 70, has climbed to the highest post in the Islamic republic. At the time he became supreme leader, Khamenei was neither a marjaa nor an ayatollah; he was given the title of ayatollah almost overnight. At the time of Khomeini's death, the problem was that the senior-most ayatollahs were unacceptable to the clerical leadership of the Islamic republic because they did not subscribe to the republic's founding principle, the "rule of the jurist," which dictates that the most learned jurist among the Shiite clergy should govern. Since Khamenei had served two terms as president, the clerical leadership rallied behind him, and he succeeded Khomeini when the AoE elected him supreme leader. While not enjoying the same status as his predecessor, the current supreme leader has successfully held the position by carefully balancing the state's various factions.

Ayatollah Ali Akbar Hashemi Rafsanjani

Being a key player in the Islamic republic since the days of its founding, Rafsanjani, 75, has held several positions that have allowed him to consolidate both political and economic power. He was a student under Khomeini and quickly became a key player in his revolutionary movement. After the shah was overthrown in 1979, Rafsanjani was part of the Revolutionary Council that served as the interim ruling body of the new Islamic republic.

In 1980, Rafsanjani also was elected as the first speaker of the Majlis, a position he held until 1989. After Khamenei became supreme leader, Rafsanjani succeeded him as president and served two terms, during which he was also head of the EC. In 1998, he assumed the formal chairmanship of the EC, and after years of being deputy head of the AoE, he was elected chairman of the assembly in 2007.

Rafsanjani's three-decade career as a politician and a pragmatic conservative has allowed him to work with rival factions within the Iranian political establishment and navigate his way to becoming the No. 2 man in the clerical regime. Rafsanjani's moderate political views have also manifested themselves on the foreign policy front, where he has played a key role over the years in back-channel negotiations with the United States. Although he is in position to succeed Khamenei as supreme leader, Rafsanjani's tarnished public image due to allegations of corruption and the accumulation of massive wealth will likely be an obstacle.

Ayatollah Ahmad Jannati

As chairman of the GC since 1988, Jannati, 83, has emerged as a key stakeholder in the system. He has been at the forefront of policy-making by leading the group that decides who can hold public office and what kind of legislation will become law. A key supporter of Ahmadinejad, Jannati is perhaps the most senior hard-line cleric in the Iranian political establishment.

Ayatollah Mahmoud Hashemi Shahroudi

Judiciary chief Shahroudi, 61, who was appointed head of the judiciary in 1999, has an unusual background. He is of Iraqi origin and at one point was a leader in the Supreme Council for Islamic Revolution in Iraq when the party was still based in Tehran in the 1980s. (Now known as the Islamic Supreme Council of Iraq, it is Iraq's largest Shiite political party and the one most closely aligned with Iran.) More recently, Shahroudi became a mentor to radical Iraqi Shiite leader Muqtada al-Sadr in the latter's quest to reach ayatollah status. Though a cleric and head of a very conservative institution, Shahroudi has pragmatist leanings, as evidenced by his move to impose a 2002 moratorium on stoning as a form of capital punishment. Last November, in a rare statement on political issues, Shahroudi came out and praised the U.S.-Iraqi security agreement a day after it was signed. His senior position and his tempered ideological position suggest that he could, at some point, become supreme leader.

Ali Larijani

The son of a prominent ayatollah, Larijani, 51, is perhaps Iran's most influential nonclerical political figure after the president. All four of his brothers occupy key positions in the state, with one being a member of the GC. Larijani served as minister of culture and Islamic guidance during Rafsanjani's presidency and later served as head of state broadcasting. He competed in the 2005 presidential race but did not perform well — it was his first run for elected office and there were many stronger, more experienced candidates.

After Ahmadinejad was elected president, Larijani was appointed head of the SNSC and, as such, handled all four key Iranian foreign policy portfolios: the nuclear issue, Iraq, Lebanon and the Palestinian conflict. In late 2007, he abruptly resigned as SNSC chief after serious disagreements with Ahmadinejad over policy issues, but Khamenei quickly appointed him as one of his two representatives on the SNSC.

Though a technocrat and a pragmatic conservative, Larijani enjoys great influence among the clerical establishment because of his background and family ties, which is why he successfully ran for parliament in 2008 from Qom, the headquarters of the Iranian clerical establishment. Larijani was quickly elected speaker by the new Majlis, a position he has used to energize the parliament as a policymaking body. Given his background and connections, Larijani is expected to play an increasingly critical role as a senior Iranian official in the coming years.

Mahmoud Ahmadinejad

Undoubtedly the most controversial of all Iranian leaders — both at home and abroad — Ahmadinejad, 52, is a member of the ultra-conservative group that seeks the return of the hidden 12th Shiite Imam, the Mahdi. He is the protege of one of the most hard-line clerics, Ayatollah Mohammad Taghi Mesbah Yazdi, a member of the AoE who is seeking to defeat the old clerical elite surrounding Rafsanjani and assume the leadership of the clerics. Ahmadinejad's hard-line policies have their roots in Mesbah Yazdi's mentorship.

Despite having been the main driver behind the intraconservative rift that has widened over his domestic and foreign policies (worsening economic conditions and bellicose foreign-policy rhetoric), Ahmadinejad continues to enjoy support from key hard-line institutions such as the GC, IRGC and Baseej, as well as from a significant segment of the clerical establishment. Though he disapproves of the way Ahmadinejad has stirred the pot on the domestic front, even Khamenei is not willing to completely abandon the president, because of the support he enjoys from these powerful quarters and because Khamenei, in many ways, sees Ahmadinejad as a means of securing his own position as supreme leader. While facing strong opposition, Ahmadinejad could still end up securing a second term, especially because of the support he has from the country's rural poor.

Mir Hossein Mousavi

Mir Hossein Mousavi, 68, a current EC member who served as the Islamic republic's prime minister from 1981 to 1989 (when the post was abolished), has emerged as the most promising contender in the current presidential race. If Ahmadinejad is defeated, it will be at the hands of Mousavi, who ideologically straddles the gap between pragmatic conservatives and reformists. Blending his credentials as a former regime insider with a reformist manifesto, Mousavi has garnered the support of conservatives who are opposed to Ahmadinejad and is riding a wave of anti-Ahmadinejad sentiment across the country.

Mousavi is remembered for his effective governance during the 1980-1988 war with Iraq, which did considerable damage to the Iranian economy. Though he reportedly has had a problematic relationship with Khamenei that goes back to the days when Mousavi was prime minister and Khamenei was president, the two have recently mended their relations. All things being equal, Khamenei would prefer to have Ahmadinejad win. Should that not happen, he could live with a Mousavi presidency by resorting to his traditional approach of playing different factions and institutions off one another.

Mohammad Ali Jafari

Maj. Gen. Jafari, 52, is the commander of the IRGC and was appointed to the post by Khamenei in September 2007, replacing Maj. Gen. Yahya Rahim Safavi, who was made top military adviser to Khamenei. Initially affiliated with the Baseej, Jafari moved to the IRGC during the Iran-Iraq war and served as commander of IRGC's land forces from the early 1990s to 2005. He also has served as a deputy to Supreme National Security Council Secretary Larijani and participated in talks between Iran and the International Atomic Energy Agency and in negotiations between Tehran and Washington on Iraq.

Jafari is the founder and former head of the IRGC's Strategic Research Center, which was created in 2005 to develop new defense and military strategies in the light of the U.S. military interventions in Iraq and Afghanistan. Jafari also is the architect of the IRGC's asymmetrical warfare strategies and has spearheaded the transfer of the lessons and experiences of the Iran-Iraq War to younger IRGC commanders. Given his experience, skills and age, and the fact that his immediate two predecessors headed the corps for 10 and 16 years, respectively, Jafari will likely serve as commander of the IRGC for years to come.

The Net Effect of Systemic Complexity

The Islamic republic's political system was intended to be one in which the masses were not as alienated as they were under the shah, and one that would be dominated by the clerics. Trying to maintain a balance between these objectives has resulted in a state structure that has become increasingly convoluted and has exacerbated tensions among rival political personalities, factions and institutions.

Though the supreme leader is the one with the most power, he clearly depends on support from other key stakeholders in the system to maintain his position at the apex. Likewise, policymaking has been a function of the supreme leader's ability to pull all the various forces together and achieve consensus. Although linking institutions together in a complex system was meant to facilitate policymaking, over time it has become a hurdle.

It is because of this very complexity that the forthcoming presidential vote — perhaps the most important in the history of the Islamic republic — will be significant, but only to a point. Despite being subordinate to the supreme leader, the Iranian president wields a certain degree of power, which is why the outcome of the vote is important. But presidential power is only one part of a complex equation. Making policy on major issues — from developing a nuclear capability to dealing with United States — is not driven by one figure or one institution in the state. Although not a democracy, the Iranian political system does have checks and balances, and these have been skillfully manipulated by various stakeholders to serve their individual and collective interests.

That, coupled with the polarization of the political elite, will make it difficult for the collective leadership of Iran, regardless of the outcome of the presidential election, to formulate coherent foreign policy in the post-election period on crucial matters the state must confront. The Obama administration's move to seek a U.S.-Iranian rapprochement imposes time limits on Tehran to respond on the various issues in dispute.

Washington likely realizes that it is not about to get Tehran to come to the table anytime soon, but it continues to extend overtures, which raises the question: To what end? The Obama administration is aware of the complexity of the Iranian political landscape, which is divided between those who are in favor of negotiating with the Americans and those who are reluctant. Therefore, by extending an unprecedented offer of negotiations, Washington has triggered a crisis in Tehran, which could tie up the system to such an extent that Iran's regional ambitions are stymied, at least for a time.

The United States understands that it is not in a position to effect regime change in Iran. Therefore, it is pursuing the novel approach of inducing behavioral change through peace overtures. Despite the fractious nature of the Iranian establishment, regime change — even from within — is unlikely. Instead, what we can expect to see as a result of Iran's increasingly complex political system is a gradual metamorphosis of the Islamic republic into a state where clerics, who have held sway since 1979, will have less leverage and will have to share more power with elected officials and the military. With the clerical establishment decreasingly cohesive, pragmatic conservative and reformist forces aligning against the hard-liners and the IRGC becoming more powerful, the Islamic republic seems to be nearing a true crossroads.

The Iranian Election and the Revolution Test
June 22, 2009

Successful revolutions have three phases. First, a strategically located single or limited segment of society begins vocally to express resentment, asserting itself in the streets of a major city, usually the capital. This segment is joined by other segments in the city and by segments elsewhere as the demonstration spreads to other cities and becomes more assertive, disruptive and potentially violent. As resistance to the regime spreads, the regime deploys its military and security forces. These forces, drawn from resisting social segments and isolated from the rest of society, turn on the regime and stop following the regime's orders. This is what happened to the Shah of Iran in 1979; it is also what happened in Russia in 1917 or in Romania in 1989.

Revolutions fail when no one joins the initial segment, meaning the initial demonstrators are the ones who find themselves socially isolated. When the demonstrations do not spread to other cities, the demonstrations either peter out or the regime brings in the security and military forces — who remain loyal to the regime and frequently personally hostile to the demonstrators — and use force to suppress the rising to the extent necessary. This is what happened in Tiananmen Square in China: The students who rose up were not joined by others. Military forces who were not only loyal to the regime but hostile to the students were brought in, and the students were crushed.

A Question of Support

This is also what happened in Iran this week. The global media, obsessively focused on the initial demonstrators — who were supporters of Iranian President Mahmoud Ahmadinejad's opponents — failed to notice that while large, the demonstrations primarily consisted of the same type of people demonstrating. Amid the breathless reporting on the demonstrations, reporters failed to notice that the uprising was not spreading to other classes and to other areas. In constantly interviewing English-speaking demonstrators, they failed to note just how many of the demonstrators spoke English and had smartphones. The media thus did not recognize these as the signs of a failing revolution.

Later, when Ayatollah Ali Khamenei spoke Friday and called out the Islamic Revolutionary Guard Corps, the media failed to understand that the troops — definitely not drawn from what we might call the "Twittering classes," would remain loyal to the regime for ideological and social reasons. The troops had about as much sympathy for the demonstrators as a small-town boy from Alabama might have for a Harvard postdoc. Failing to understand the social tensions in Iran, the reporters deluded themselves into thinking they were witnessing a general uprising. But this was not St. Petersburg in 1917 or Bucharest in 1989 — it was Tiananmen Square.

In the global discussion last week outside Iran, there was a great deal of confusion about basic facts. For example, it is said that the urban-rural distinction in Iran is not critical any longer because according to the United Nations, 68 percent of Iranians are urbanized. This is an important point because it implies Iran is homogeneous and the demonstrators representative of the country. The problem is the Iranian definition of urban — and this is quite common around the world — includes very small communities (some with only a few thousand people) as "urban." But the social difference between someone living in a town with 10,000 people and someone living in Tehran is the difference between someone living in Bastrop, Texas and someone living in New York. We can assure you that that difference is not only vast, but that most of the good people of Bastrop and the fine people of New York would probably not see the world the same way. The failure to understand the dramatic diversity of Iranian society led observers to assume that students at Iran's elite university somehow spoke for the rest of the country.

Tehran proper has about 8 million inhabitants; its suburbs bring it to about 13 million people out of Iran's total population of 70.5 million. Tehran accounts for about 20 percent of Iran, but as we know, the cab driver and the construction worker are not socially linked to students at elite universities. There are six cities with populations between 1 million and 2.4 million people and 11 with populations of about 500,000. Including Tehran proper, 15.5 million people live in cities with more than 1 million and 19.7 million in cities greater than 500,000. Iran has 80 cities with more than 100,000. But given that Waco, Texas, has more than 100,000 people, inferences of social similarities between cities with 100,000 and 5 million are tenuous. And with metro Oklahoma City having more than a million people, it becomes plain that urbanization has many faces.

Winning the Election With or Without Fraud

We continue to believe two things: that vote fraud occurred, and that Ahmadinejad likely would have won without it. Very little direct evidence has emerged to establish vote fraud, but several things seem suspect.

For example, the speed of the vote count has been taken as a sign of fraud, as it should have been impossible to count votes that fast. The polls originally were to have closed at 7 p.m. local time, but voting hours were extended until 10 p.m. because of the number of voters in line. By 11:45 p.m. about 20 percent of the vote had been counted. By 5:20 a.m. the next day, with almost all votes counted, the election commission declared Ahmadinejad the winner. The vote count thus took about seven hours. (Remember there were no senators, congressmen, city council members or school board members being counted — just the presidential race.) Intriguingly, this is about the same time it took in 2005, though reformists that claimed fraud back then did not stress the counting time in their allegations.

The counting mechanism is simple: Iran has 47,000 voting stations, plus 14,000 roaming stations that travel from tiny village to tiny village, staying there for a short time before moving on. That creates 61,000 ballot boxes designed to receive roughly the same number of votes. That would mean that each station would have been counting about 500 ballots, or about 70 votes per hour. With counting beginning at 10 p.m., concluding seven hours later does not necessarily indicate fraud or anything else. The Iranian presidential election system is designed for simplicity: one race to count in one time zone, and all counting beginning at the same time in all regions, we would expect the numbers to come in a somewhat linear fashion as rural and urban voting patterns would balance each other out — explaining why voting percentages didn't change much during the night.

It has been pointed out that some of the candidates didn't even carry their own provinces or districts. We remember that Al Gore didn't carry Tennessee in 2000. We also remember Ralph Nader, who also didn't carry his home precinct in part because people didn't want to spend their vote on someone unlikely to win — an effect probably felt by the two smaller candidates in the Iranian election.

That Mousavi didn't carry his own province is more interesting. Flynt Leverett and Hillary Mann Leverett writing in Politico make some interesting points on this. As an ethnic Azeri, it was assumed that Mousavi would carry his Azeri-named and -dominated home province. But they also point out that Ahmadinejad also speaks Azeri, and made multiple campaign appearances in the district. They also point out that Khamenei is Azeri. In sum, winning that district was by no means certain for Mousavi, so losing it does not automatically signal fraud. It raised suspicions, but by no means was a smoking gun.

We do not doubt that fraud occurred during the Iranian election. For example, 99.4 percent of potential voters voted in Mazandaran province, a mostly secular area home to the shah's family. Ahmadinejad carried the province by a 2.2 to 1 ratio. That is one heck of a turnout and level of support for a province that lost everything when the mullahs took over 30 years ago. But even if you take all of the suspect cases and added them together, it would not have changed the outcome. The fact is that Ahmadinejad's vote in 2009 was extremely close to his victory percentage in 2005. And while the Western media portrayed Ahmadinejad's performance in the presidential debates ahead of the election as dismal, embarrassing and indicative of an imminent electoral defeat, many Iranians who viewed those debates — including some of the most hardcore Mousavi supporters — acknowledge that Ahmadinejad outperformed his opponents by a landslide.

Mousavi persuasively detailed his fraud claims Sunday, and they have yet to be rebutted. But if his claims of the extent of fraud were true, the protests should have spread rapidly by social segment and geography to the millions of people who even the central government asserts voted for him. Certainly, Mousavi supporters believed they would win the election based in part on highly flawed polls, and when they didn't, they assumed they were robbed and took to the streets.

But critically, the protesters were not joined by any of the millions whose votes the protesters alleged were stolen. In a complete hijacking of the election by some 13 million votes by an extremely unpopular candidate, we would have expected to see the core of Mousavi's supporters joined by others who had been disenfranchised. On last Monday, Tuesday and Wednesday, when the demonstrations were at their height, the millions of Mousavi voters should have made their appearance. They didn't. We might assume that the security apparatus intimidated some, but surely more than just the Tehran professional and student classes possess civic courage. While appearing large, the demonstrations actually comprised a small fraction of society.

Tensions Among the Political Elite

All of this is not to say there are not tremendous tensions within the Iranian political elite. That no revolution broke out does not mean there isn't a crisis in the political elite, particularly among the clerics. But that crisis does not cut the way Western common sense would have it. Many of Iran's religious leaders see Ahmadinejad as hostile to their interests, as threatening their financial prerogatives, and as taking international risks they don't want to take. Ahmadinejad's political popularity in fact rests on his populist hostility to what he sees as the corruption of the clerics and their families and his strong stand on Iranian national security issues.

The clerics are divided among themselves, but many wanted to see Ahmadinejad lose to protect their own interests. Khamenei, the supreme leader, faced a difficult choice last Friday. He could demand a major recount or even new elections, or he could validate what happened. Khamenei speaks for a sizable chunk of the ruling elite, but also has had to rule by consensus among both clerical and non-clerical forces. Many powerful clerics like Ali Akbar Hashemi Rafsanjani wanted Khamenei to reverse the election, and we suspect Khamenei wished he could have found a way to do it. But as the defender of the regime, he was afraid to. Mousavi supporters' demonstrations would have been nothing compared to the firestorm among Ahmadinejad supporters — both voters and the security forces — had their candidate been denied. Khamenei wasn't going to flirt with disaster, so he endorsed the outcome.

The Western media misunderstood this because they didn't understand that Ahmadinejad does not speak for the clerics but against them, that many of the clerics were working for his defeat, and that Ahmadinejad has enormous pull in the country's security apparatus. The reason Western media missed this is because they bought into the concept of the stolen election, therefore failing to see Ahmadinejad's support and the widespread dissatisfaction with the old clerical elite. The Western media simply didn't understand that the most traditional and pious segments of Iranian society support Ahmadinejad because he opposes the old ruling elite. Instead, they assumed this was like Prague or Budapest in 1989, with a broad-based uprising in favor of liberalism against an unpopular regime.

Tehran in 2009, however, was a struggle between two main factions, both of which supported the Islamic republic as it was. There were the clerics, who have dominated the regime since 1979 and had grown wealthy in the process. And there was Ahmadinejad, who felt the ruling clerical elite had betrayed the revolution with their personal excesses. And there also was the small faction the BBC and CNN kept focusing on — the demonstrators in the streets who want to dramatically liberalize the Islamic republic. This faction never stood a chance of taking power, whether by election or revolution. The two main factions used the third smaller faction in various ways, however. Ahmadinejad used it to make his case that the clerics who supported them, like Rafsanjani, would risk the revolution and play into the hands of the Americans and British to protect their own wealth. Meanwhile, Rafsanjani argued behind the scenes that the unrest was the tip of the iceberg, and that Ahmadinejad had to be replaced. Khamenei, an astute politician, examined the data and supported Ahmadinejad.

Now, as we saw after Tiananmen Square, we will see a reshuffling among the elite. Those who backed Mousavi will be on the defensive. By contrast, those who supported Ahmadinejad are in a powerful position. There is a massive crisis in the elite, but this crisis has nothing to do with liberalization: It has to do with power and prerogatives among the elite. Having been forced by the election and Khamenei to

live with Ahmadinejad, some will make deals while some will fight —
but Ahmadinejad is well-positioned to win this battle.

————————————

Crisis as Opportunity for the Islamic Revolutionary Guards Corps
July 27, 2009

The domestic political crisis in Iran triggered by the June 12 presidential election grew more complex on Sunday. President Mahmoud Ahmadinejad fired Gholam Hossein Mohseni Ejei, the head of the Ministry of Intelligence and Security (MOIS), Iran's premier intelligence service. Earlier in the day, Iranian media had reported that Ahmadinejad sacked the ministers of culture and labor as well, but a more recent report from Press TV said he had reversed those decisions. Meanwhile, the Fars News Agency reported that the culture minister resigned, saying he could not continue serving because the current government is marred by "weakness."

Mohseni Ejei was MOIS chief throughout Ahmadinejad's first term (and, like the president, hails from the ideological group headed by Iran's most conservative cleric, Ayatollah Mohammad Taqi Mesbah-Yazdi). His sacking was described by the Mehr news agency as the result of a quarrel with Ahmadinejad over the appointment of First Vice President Esfandiar Rahim Mashaie.

Ahmadinejad, already dealing with the controversy surrounding his re-election, complicated matters when he appointed Mashaie — one of his own close friends and the father-in-law of his son — last week. Supreme Leader Ayatollah Ali Khamenei and others within the president's ultra-conservative faction, who had backed Ahmadinejad strongly against the pragmatic conservative camp during the post-election crisis, bitterly opposed the selection because of comments Mashaie made last year, when he said Iran was a friend of the Israeli people. Ahmadinejad resisted calls to remove Mashaie — even initial demands from Khamenei — until the supreme leader forced Mashaie's resignation as first vice president. However, Ahmadinejad reappointed him as an adviser and head of the presidential office.

The domestic political scene in Iran is one of pandemonium. Ahmadinejad, who has yet to be sworn in for his second presidential term, is caught between opponents and allies. The situation is hampering Iran's efforts to deal with crucial foreign policy matters. The Obama administration is beginning to move away from its initial approach of diplomatically engaging the Islamic republic and toward the possibility of military action if Iran is not willing to play ball. U.S. President Barack Obama has set a September deadline for Tehran to respond to the offer of talks on the nuclear issue. And U.S. Secretary of State Hillary Clinton said in the past week that the internal strife has rendered Tehran incapable of making a decision on the foreign policy front.

Meanwhile, Israel has been engaged in naval activity in the Red Sea, and top U.S. security officials — including Defense Secretary Robert Gates and National Security Adviser James Jones — will be meeting with Israeli officials for talks this week. While the Iranian political establishment is caught in an unprecedented internal tug-of-war, the only response from Tehran to the growing external threat came from the military. Maj.-Gen. Mohammad Ali Jaafari, commander of the elite Islamic Revolutionary Guards Corps (IRGC), on Saturday threatened to strike at Israel's nuclear facilities if Israel attacked his country.

While Iran's military leadership thus far has supported the supreme leader and the president in the political turmoil, it is likely worried over the civilians' inability to defuse the crisis, especially when external matters are pushing Iran toward a decisive moment. The IRGC's initial thinking after the election was that with its support, Khamenei and Ahmadinejad would be able to contain the unrest and consolidate their power. But with infighting between the president and his allies affecting the country's intelligence service — at a time when the state needs to be able to secure itself from external threats — the generals in the IRGC are bound to be worried as never before.

We have noted previously that, even though the IRGC's power is second to that of the clerics, the elite military corps sees itself as the guarantor of national security, and it has been enhancing its power. With the clerical establishment being weakened by the ongoing internal fracas, and with external threats mounting, the military could use this situation to assume a greater role in decision-making. By no means are we forecasting a military coup in Iran; rather, it appears that the military likely will become the strongest stakeholder in the Islamic republic.

If an Iran dominated by clerics was tough to deal with, expect great challenges if the IRGC begins calling the shots.

The Factionalization of the Iranian State
August 20, 2009

Iran's June 12 presidential election, which granted Iranian President Mahmoud Ahmadinejad a second term and threatened to rip the clerical establishment apart, illustrated just how complex Iranian politics can become.

The Iranian political system is a labyrinth of competing institutions made up of elected, quasi-elected and appointed officials. It is difficult to brand the Islamic republic as a pure theocracy, democracy or even an oligarchy. In reality, it is a blend of all three, where power traditionally has been concentrated in the hands of the religious elite and the right to rule comes from a mixture of divine right and the people.

Prior to 2005, when Ahmadinejad was elected to his first term as president, the political landscape in the country was roughly divided between reformists (who had risen to power during two-term President Mohammed Khatami's time in office) and conservatives, who dominated the clerical political establishment. During Ahmadinejad's presidency, however, a fissure opened up among the conservatives that pitted the so-called pragmatic conservatives, led by Ayatollah Ali Akbar Hashemi Rafsanjani, against an emergent ultraconservative faction led by Ahmadinejad. This split intensified in the final years of Ahmadinejad's last term but turned vicious after the June presidential vote.

Supreme Leader Ayatollah Ali Khamenei has long attempted to remain above the fray of Iran's factional politics, preferring to play the various blocs off each other to maintain his own position at the apex of the Iranian political system. But the fallout from the election was so severe that Khamenei had little choice but to directly intervene. The supreme leader took a calculated risk in coming out in support of Ahmadinejad and the hard-liners. This move prompted Rafsanjani's pragmatic conservative camp to align temporarily with the reformists in a united front against the firebrand president.

Ahmadinejad entered his second term on shaky ground and chose to test his limits by trying to pack his government with loyalists. The president ended up alienating members of his own hard-line camp, including Khamenei, when on July 16 he attempted to appoint his close friend and relative, Esfandiar Rahim Mashaie, as his first vice president — an extremely controversial move given Mashaie's past remarks on how the Islamic republic was a "friend" to the Israeli people. Ahmadinejad quickly buckled under pressure from his fellow hard-liners and canceled the appointment. However, he made Mashaie his chief of staff and top adviser, thus drawing attention to a growing unease between the president and the supreme leader.

Khamenei has continued to defend Ahmadinejad against powerful figures like Rafsanjani, but the supreme leader also understands that he needs to place limits on the president's power. With Rafsanjani already heading up two of Iran's most powerful institutions, there was a need for a third political front to rise up that would remain loyal to Khamenei's wishes, but act as a counter to both Ahmadinejad and Rafsanjani. This third faction is led by Iran's current speaker of parliament, Ali Larijani, whose clan now controls two of the three branches of the Iranian government — the legislature and the judiciary.

In addition to encouraging the rise of factions within the regime, Khamenei has taken a number of other key steps to protect his position and alter the power balances within the state. A number of non-clerical politicians like Ahmadinejad and technocrats like Larijani have risen up to diffuse the powers of the religious elites. At the same time, the military — though under the control of Khamenei and ideologically subservient to the clerics — has emerged as a powerful stakeholder in the system with a growing say in national security and foreign affairs and control over the Iranian economy.

After the clerics, Iran's security establishment, dominated by the Islamic Revolutionary Guard Corps (IRGC), is the strongest force within the Iranian power structure. The IRGC is closely watching how the ongoing political knife fight among the elites plays out and is realizing that figures like Khamenei and Ahmadinejad are going to have to increase their reliance on the security apparatus to remain afloat politically, given the growing splits within the political establishment. The IRGC is already well on its way to exploiting this political fracas to enhance its position within the decision-making process. And should present trends continue, the IRGC could emerge as the lead group calling the shots through figurehead clerical and non-clerical politicians.

A complex metamorphosis is under way in the Islamic republic and has been accelerated by the outcome of the June 12 election. The increasing complexity of the system has undermined the use of ideological labels, such as "pragmatic conservatives" and "ultraconservatives" in keeping track of the political ebb and flow. A more useful method of making sense of this struggle is to examine the political institutions in relation to each faction's influence. The supreme leader remains at the apex of the maze, and beneath him, Ahmadinejad, Larijani and Rafsanjani are the principal political figures to watch.

Long-Term Consequences of Iran's Intra-Elite Struggle
July 19, 2011

The head of Iranian intelligence, Heidar Moslehi, briefly spoke July 15 ahead of the regular sermon delivered at the main Friday prayer congregation at Tehran University. Moslehi, a cleric who holds the rank of hojjat ol-eslam (junior to the ayatollah), said the Ministry of Intelligence and Security was well prepared to thwart any plots hatched by foreign intelligence services hostile to the Islamic republic. Moslehi claimed that the ministry was particularly focused on identifying and neutralizing efforts to undermine the country via cultural, economic and social means.

STRATFOR would usually attach little significance to Moslehi's remarks. But considering the venue and Moslehi's place at the center of an increasingly bitter and very public power struggle between President Mahmoud Ahmadinejad and Supreme Leader Ayatollah Ali Khamenei, the intelligence chief's statements cannot be dismissed as routine. Moslehi is a key opponent of the president, and having him deliver a pre-sermon lecture in the current context is part of Khamenei's efforts to push Ahmadinejad into a corner.

Origins of the Struggle

Moslehi is the latest in a host of key officials throughout the Iranian political establishment (clerical, judicial, parliamentary and military) to come out and issue statements against the president's intransigence toward the supreme leader. After Ahmadinejad's controversial re-election in June 2009, Khamenei more or less tolerated the president's assertiveness until April 2011, when he reinstated Moslehi after Ahmadinejad forced the intelligence head to resign a few days earlier. Ahmadinejad's refusal to accept the reinstatement led Khamenei to rally the entire political establishment against the president. No longer favored by Khamenei, Ahmadinejad came to represent the biggest threat to the supreme leader's position.

Every week since, some key official or another has come out chastising the president. Additionally, a number of individuals from the presidential camp have been arrested. But because he went out of his way to support Ahmadinejad's re-election in 2009, and because he fears that any moves to get rid of the president would further destabilize the political system already weakened by intra-elite infighting, Khamenei prefers to contain Ahmadinejad's moves by building pressure from other institutions until the expiration of the president's second (and likely final) term in office.

Khamenei recognizes that Ahmadinejad, a non-cleric, has no significant future role within the Islamic republic. Nonetheless, Khamenei and the clerics fear that Ahmadinejad can do a lot to undermine their power in the next two years. Furthermore, Ahmadinejad is trying to exploit the key fissure within the Iranian political system: the one between its republican and clerical parts.

Ahmadinejad, who has a significant support base within the country, came to power on a mandate to end the corruption within the clerical elite. During his first term as president, Ahmadinejad aligned with hardline clerics as well as Khamenei to undermine the position of Ayatollah Ali Akbar Hashemi Rafsanjani, who even after the rise of Ahmadinejad was considered the regime's second-most influential figure after the supreme leader. Having secured a second term in office, Ahmadinejad, playing on the popular sentiment that opposes elite corruption and the control of the clerics, turned against the same hardline clerics that brought him to power.

Until earlier this year, the struggle between Ahmadinejad and Khamenei remained largely behind the scenes. However, Khamenei's efforts to circumscribe Ahmadinejad's decision-making authority — both on the domestic and foreign policy fronts — have triggered growing resistance from the president. The clerical establishment is concerned that while Ahmadinejad and his faction may be a passing phenomenon, their goal of securing greater authority for elected officials over clerics is one that has great resonance within the country, especially within the reformist camp, which has been silenced but not eliminated.

Fragility of the Clerical Order

Most observers view the struggle between Ahmadinejad and Khamenei as one in which the supreme leader is trying to get all the various players within the system to align against the president. But while Ahmadinejad is only one individual, he represents a faction that would only be standing up to Khamenei and the clerics if it felt that it could do so. That Khamenei has had to intervene — and so publicly — underscores the fragility of the clerical order.

In this regard it was interesting to see both parliamentary speaker Ali Larijani and the commander of the country's elite Islamic Revolutionary Guard Corps (IRGC), Maj. Gen. Mohammad Ali Jaafari, both declare that reformists have a place within the political system provided they not challenge the position of the clerics. Larijani and Jaafari, both close allies of Khamenei, hoped to use the statements to garner broader support for the supreme leader, fearing that the moves of the Ahmadinejad faction could further undermine the foundation of the regime.

Considering the enmity between Ahmadinejad and the reformists over the 2009 election, it is difficult to see the two aligning with each other against the clerics. The reformists would, however, want to take advantage of the rift between Khamenei and Ahmadinejad to try to stage a comeback. To a great degree it was the Khamenei-Ahmadinejad alliance that cost the reformists the 2008 parliamentary elections and the 2009 presidential vote.

But reformists and assertive hard-liners like Ahmadinejad are not the only worries for the Khamenei-led clerical establishment. Their biggest concern is that the military, particularly the IRGC, will benefit from the intra-elite struggle. Iran has a unique form of civilian supremacy over the military because the security forces are religiously and constitutionally under the control of the supreme leader, a civilian. Due to concerns about the military, the head of the Guardians

Council (the six-member clerical body that oversees the legislature and has the authority to vet candidates for public office) criticized the IRGC chief's statements about reformists in the political system, saying the military had no say in political matters. Put simply, Khamenei's efforts to use Jaafari and the IRGC, the core of the security establishment, to contain Ahmadinejad has opened yet another fissure within the system — between the clerics and the military.

But at a time when the clergy has been significantly weakened due to infighting, the only other major institution is the IRGC. Over the decades the IRGC has developed into a major power center, but its leadership and rank-and-file members have remained loyal to Khamenei. The IRGC knows that its privileged position is due to its relationship with the clerics. But the IRGC is concerned about the future of the Islamic republic, especially as the clergy weakens.

Additionally, the IRGC already wields a disproportionate amount of influence and would like to build upon it. The IRGC has in fact benefited from the internal struggle — first between the hard-liners and the pragmatists and reformists and now between the conservative factions. Ahmadinejad's moves against Khamenei have been useful for the IRGC's efforts to enhance its clout, but it is rallying behind Khamenei in order to position itself to become kingmaker — both while the clergy still dominates the system and, more important, in the event that the republican part of the system gains more power.

Khamenei is aware of the IRGC's ambitions and has thus been trying to counter it by increasingly supporting the Artesh (the larger, regular armed forces). But the key issue is that Khamenei is the only supreme leader that the Islamic republic has seen since the death of its founder, Ayatollah Ruhollah Khomeini, in 1989. The turning point in the civil-military balance of power will come once the 73-year-old Khamenei dies and a third supreme leader is chosen — one who will likely be even more dependent upon the IRGC to maintain his position.

CHAPTER 3: CONVENTIONAL AND UNCONVENTIONAL CAPABILITIES

Hezbollah's Iranian Connection
July 21, 2006

Prior to the rise of the Shia in Iraq, Hezbollah — as a radical Shiite Islamist organization — was Iran's main asset in the Arab world. In fact, it likely will continue to be used by Tehran as a key tool for furthering Iranian geopolitical interests in the region, until Shiite power has been consolidated in Baghdad and Iran's interests there secured.

In its earliest days, Hezbollah was a classic militant organization — the creation of the Islamic Revolutionary Guard Corps (IRGC), the elite unit of the Iranian military. It was founded as a way to export the ideals of Ayatollah Ruholla Khomeini's Islamic revolution to the Shiite community of Lebanon, and served as a model for follow-on organizations (some even using the same name) in other Arab states. It did not take long, however, for Hezbollah to emerge in Lebanon as a guerrilla movement, whose fighters were trained in conventional military tactics.

In the mid-1980s, Iran's premier intelligence agency, the Ministry of Intelligence and Security (MOIS), assumed the task of managing Tehran's militant assets — not just in the Middle East but in other parts of the world as well. This allowed the Iranians, through a special

47

unit within MOIS, to strike at Israeli interests in places as diverse as Latin America and Southeast Asia.

The relationship between MOIS and Hezbollah remains a subject worthy of study in light of the current situation in Lebanon. Of course, Iran has been Hezbollah's chief source of funding and weapons over the years, and the Iranians continue to supply extensive training in weapons, tactics, communications, surveillance and other methods to the militant wing of Hezbollah in Lebanon. The relationship is sufficiently close that the Hezbollah branch within Iran recently declared it would unleash militant attacks against Israelis and Americans around the world if given the order by Supreme Leader Ayatollah Ali Khamenei. (Tehran insists that Hezbollah is not an arm of official policy.)

We have previously discussed the possibility that Hezbollah might be moved to seize hostages or engage in other militant acts, given the pressure the Israelis now are bringing to bear. There is some question, of course, as to whether Iran might be involved in future militant operations — and if so, what assets it might use and the modalities that would apply.

An Organizational Model

There is a division of labor of sorts in the way that Iran manages its foreign assets: The IRGC (which is led by a professional military officer with strong ideological credentials as an Islamist) oversees the Lebanese Hezbollah, while MOIS (which almost always is headed by a cleric) manages militant operatives and groups in other parts of the Muslim world — Afghanistan, Pakistan, Azerbaijan, India. Moreover, MOIS also maintains contacts among the Shiite immigrant populations in non-Muslim countries, including those in the West.

It also is important to note that radical Shiite Islamist ideology is only one factor that shapes Tehran's decisions. Ethnicity and nationalism also play an important role in Iran's dealings with Shiite allies of Arab, South Asian and other descent. The Persians claim a rich cultural heritage, which they view as superior to that of the Arabs.

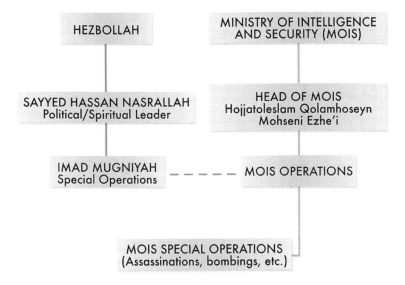

This attitude impacts the level of trust and cooperation between the Iranians and other Shiite groups — including Hezbollah — when it comes to sensitive international operations. It is little wonder, then, that the Lebanese organization's sphere of operations does not extend much beyond the Levant.

It follows that Hezbollah is a useful tool for Iran in its dealings with Israel, but in few other areas. However, Iranian intelligence has cultivated numerous groups that can serve its interests in other parts of the world, and it maintains contact with these groups through MOIS operatives placed in diplomatic posts.

A History of Cooperation

Though it has been many years since Hezbollah carried out significant attacks beyond the Middle East, the participation of MOIS agents in some of those attacks is worthy of note. Investigations into the 1988 hijacking of Kuwait Airways Flight 422 out of Bangkok and two bombings in Buenos Aires — in 1992 and 1994 — both revealed involvement by MOIS, coordinating with local Hezbollah operatives. However, to provide plausible deniability, the hijacking and bomb teams were deployed from outside the targeted country; the assets in place were used to conduct preoperational surveillance on potential targets.

Up close, what this would mean is that the MOIS officer at the Iranian embassy in the target country or city would maintain close contact with the Hezbollah cells in his area or responsibility. Given the rules of intelligence work, an "official asset" like a diplomat is usually under suspicion and surveillance as an intelligence officer (or IO); therefore, less-prominent Hezbollah members can be used to case potential targets. In a situation where a MOIS agent is believed to be under such tight surveillance that he cannot function effectively, the Iranians might call on the services of a clandestine MOIS agent instead. In the case of the 1992 bombing of the Israeli embassy in Buenos Aires, the MOIS officer was the Iranian cultural attache, who oversaw the operation from the safety of his embassy office. The Argentines eventually declared seven embassy employees as "persona non grata" due to suspected connections to the bombing.

Upon receiving a "go" order for an operation — such as assassinations of Iranian dissidents or the kidnappings of Western diplomatic and intelligence personnel (for instance, CIA station chief William F. Buckley in 1984 and U.S. Marine Lt. Col. William R. Higgins in 1988) — activity levels at the embassy spike. The role of MOIS frequently would be to provide the cash or supply weapons or materials needed for an attack carried out by its "militant assets." In some countries, such as Britain (where Hezbollah bombed a Jewish charity in 1994), it can be difficult to obtain items like blasting caps and explosives; these can be supplied with the protection of a diplomatic pouch.

Many MOIS intelligence operatives have been educated in the United States or in Britain, wear nice suits, are multilingual and move easily in Western social circles — unlike the IRGC operatives in Lebanon, who, socially speaking, are rougher around the edges. The combination of their brains and Hezbollah's willingness to pursue martyrdom can produce formidable capabilities.

With Hezbollah under attack in Lebanon and Iran unable to send significant reinforcements, there is some possibility that Hezbollah might resort to staging an attack abroad as a way of countering the Israeli assault. If so, it is highly likely that operatives already are on the move; the organization has been known to use "off the shelf" operational plans in the past, and its targeting information and surveillance would need to be updated — regardless of whether an order to strike is actually issued. It is reasonable to believe that Hezbollah would find it advantageous to coordinate with MOIS again, as in past operations. Whether the Iranians would see events through the same lens, however, is much less clear. Tehran might cooperate in an attack only if it is willing to seriously escalate the current conflict in the Middle East — which, given its many interests in the region, does not appear so far to be the case.

Iran: Entangled in the Web of Iraq's Shiite Factions
March 28, 2008

The chief of Iran's Guardian Council, Ayatollah Ahmad Jannati, called March 28 for negotiations between Iraq's central government and militias, while condemning the United States for the insecurity in Iraq. His comments come in the wake of intra-Shiite fighting due to the ongoing security operations in the southern oil-rich region of Basra.

Delivering the Friday prayer sermon at Tehran University, the ultraconservative Jannati spoke directly to Iraq's Shiite militias, saying "Oh brother, if you have something to say, come sit with the government. The government is popular and so are you." He also addressed "the esteemed and dear" Iraqi Prime Minister Nouri al-Maliki, who he said "is running the affairs of the people with wisdom and power," advising him to "listen to the voices of the popular forces and somehow compromise with one another." Jannati went on to say that negotiations are "in the interest of all" — which could have been an indirect offer of Iranian mediation.

The ayatollah's choice of language is very telling: it underscores the difficult balance Tehran is having to maintain in dealing with its various Iraqi proxies. It would appear that Iran's effort to advance its interests by exploiting intra-Shiite schisms in Iraq could finally be starting to backfire. Iran's own competing interests and those of its Iraqi proxies are now undermining Tehran's ability to corral the United States into a favorable deal — that is, one that ensures an Iranian-dominated Iraq — and Jannati's call for unity represents a desire by the Iranians to restore some order to the chaos before it is too late.

On one hand, the Iranians want to see the Iraqi government — now dominated by Tehran's main proxy and Iraq's most powerful Shiite group, the Islamic Supreme Council of Iraq (ISCI) — establish its writ over Basra and its energy resources. But on the other hand, Tehran also needs to preserve the militant al-Sadrite movement, with all its internal contradictions, as a tool for attempting to shape U.S. behavior. These parallel purposes can only be served if some kind of intra-communal balance can be maintained.

Complicating Iran's goals is the fact that both the ISCI and the al-Sadrites have their own agendas, which are beginning to collide with Tehran's. The Shia of Iraq have never before ruled Baghdad despite being in the majority, and part of the reason is their extreme factionalization. For that matter, the al-Sadrite Mehdi Army is itself splintered, with some militia members continuing to fight in the name of radical Shiite leader Muqtada al-Sadr, others acting as agents for

Iranian intelligence or for the United States, and still others exercising restraint in all the violence.

Already having a political proxy in the form of the ISCI, the Iranians do not wish to see the al-Sadrites (or others such as the al-Fadhila party) challenge the ISCI's hegemony. But Iran lacks the capability to control these sundry Shiite actors fully and manage them to achieve its objectives. For a long time, this was not a major problem for Tehran because negotiations with the United States were still in play. Now that Washington has demonstrated that it has other options, the Iranians are caught in the mire of Iraqi intra-Shiite rivalries.

The situation has deteriorated so much that Iranian influence over the various Iraqi Shiite actors is no longer a given, which explains Jannati's call for reconciliation. An intra-Shiite power-sharing agreement has become the need of the hour for the Iranians. Such a deal could allow Iran to bring some semblance of order to the chaos in the Iraqi Shiite community — and perhaps even jump-start Tehran's lapsed communications with the United States. But any future dealings that Iran will have with the United States will likely be from a position of relative weakness.

Iran and the Strait of Hormuz, Part 1:
A Strategy of Deterrence
October 5, 2009

It has often been said that Iran's "real nuclear option" is its ability to close — or at least try to close — the Strait of Hormuz, which facilitates the movement of 90 percent of the Persian Gulf's oil exports (40 percent of the global seaborne oil trade) as well as all of the gulf's liquefied natural gas exports. At a time when the world is crawling back from the worst economic crisis since the Great Depression, this is a serious threat and warrants close examination.

Iran actually has a broad range of military options for lashing out at energy exports in the strait, and this is not a new development. Almost since the founding days of the Islamic republic, Iran has been exercising military force in the Persian Gulf, starting with attacks against Iraqi tankers (and Kuwaiti tankers carrying Iraqi oil) during the Iran-Iraq War in the 1980s. But in all this time, Iran has never exercised the full measure of its capability to close the Strait of Hormuz to maritime commerce — if indeed it has that capability. Although Iran has an array of options for limited strikes, our interests here are the dynamics of an all-out effort.

While we look at Tehran's raw capability to close the strait, it is important to note that we are not delving into the equally important circumstances which would compel Iran to try to exercise that capability. And any discussion of Iran's military options in the Persian Gulf must begin with the caveat that there would be serious consequences for Tehran if it tried to prevent tanker traffic from transiting the strait. Indeed, the "nuclear option" analogy is quite apt not only because of its potentially devastating effect on Tehran's adversaries but also because of its potentially devastating effect on Iran itself.

Deterrence and the Potential for Conflict

Tehran has long been aware of the geostrategic significance of its proximity to the Strait of Hormuz. The threat of mining the strait or targeting tankers with anti-ship missiles is a central component of Iran's defensive strategy. By holding the strait at risk, Tehran expands the consequences of any military action against it to include playing havoc with global oil prices. Insofar as Iran has avoided military action to date, this strategy of deterrence to this point can be deemed a success.

Yet the strategy has several weaknesses. For one, it can only discourage an attack, not directly prevent one. By the time an attack against Iran begins, Tehran's military strategy has failed. Trying to close the strait after military strikes have begun cannot stop those strikes — it can only serve as a punitive measure. At best, an Iranian concession to stop its actions in the strait could serve as a card on the table in negotiating a cease-fire. But creating trouble in the strait is a hard sell internationally as a "defensive" measure. With the world just starting to recover from the global economic crisis, a move by Iran to close the strait could unite the world against Iran — perhaps more strongly than was the case against Iraq following Desert Storm in 1991.

Another weakness has to do with one of the classic problems of nuclear deterrence — the military incentive to strike first. In this case, the United States would very much want to leverage the element of surprise, catching and hitting as many targets as possible — not just the nuclear program but also Iran's offensive and defensive military capabilities — where it expects those targets to be. The flip side, of course, is that Iran also needs the element of surprise. Because high-priority targets in any U.S. airstrike would include Iran's capabilities to retaliate directly — its anti-ship missile sites, its mine warfare facilities, its ballistic missile arsenal — any retaliation by Iran after an American strike begins would be degraded, perhaps considerably, depending on the effectiveness of U.S. intelligence (Iran presents considerable intelligence problems for the United States).

As a result, while Iran's deterrence strategy has thus far delayed conflict, a line can be crossed that puts everything on its head. Instead of delaying matters further, each side will have more incentive to act aggressively in order to pre-empt the other. And the problem is not simply that this line exists. The line is defined for each side by its subjective, fallible perceptions of the other's intentions, leaving considerable room for miscalculation.

So, despite the considerable disincentives for Iran to try and close the strait, it can hardly be ruled out. Indeed, at the moment, with so much in motion politically, not just between Washington and Tehran but also between Washington and Moscow — and factoring in the Israeli wild card — the risks of miscalculation on all sides are very high.

The Strait of Hormuz

Connecting the Persian Gulf to the Gulf of Oman, the Arabian Sea and the world's oceans, the navigable waters of the Strait of Hormuz are roughly 20 miles wide at their narrowest point. Commercial and naval maritime traffic, which includes 16 or 17 million barrels of crude oil aboard some 15 tankers per day, transits two designated shipping lanes inside Omani waters. Each lane (one into the Gulf, one out) is two miles wide and is separated by a two mile-wide buffer. (Almost the entire strait south of Qeshm and Larak islands is deep enough to support tanker traffic, so there is certainly room to shift the traffic further from the Iranian coast.) The importance of this waterway to both American military and economic interests is difficult to overstate. Considering Washington's more general — and fundamental — interest in securing freedom of the seas, the U.S. Navy would almost be forced to respond aggressively to any attempt to close the Strait of Hormuz.

Tehran appreciates not only its strategic proximity to the strait but also the asymmetric military options related to it. A conventional interdiction in the strait by Iranian surface warships and submarines is perhaps the least likely scenario. Larger corvettes and frigates are few in number and would be easily targeted by U.S. naval and air power that is constantly within striking distance of the strait. While up to two of Iran's three Russian-built Kilo-class submarines could probably be sortied on short notice, the cramped and shallow waters of the strait make submarine operations there particularly challenging.

The challenges mean that the proficiency of Iranian submarine crews (questionable at best) would likely be severely tested in a genuine operational scenario. The United States also recognizes Iran's Kilos as an important Iranian asset and would make every effort to quickly neutralize them (whether at sea or in port) in any attack scenario. In any event, the Iranian navy does not have enough Kilos to have any confidence in its ability to sustain submarine operations for any meaningful period after hostilities began.

TOPOGRAPHY AND BATHYMETRY OF THE STRAIT OF HORMUZ

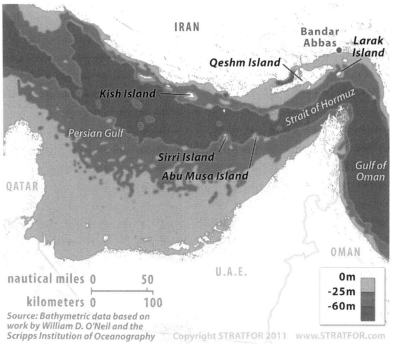

Source: Bathymetric data based on work by William D. O'Neil and the Scripps Institution of Oceanography   Copyright STRATFOR 2011   www.STRATFOR.com

Well aware of its qualitative weaknesses vis-a-vis the U.S. Navy, Iran has a number of more asymmetric options. The most "conventional" of these are its fast attack missile boats, particularly 10 French-built Kaman guided missile patrol craft (Iran has begun to build copies domestically, though the first three appear to have been built in the Caspian). Smaller than a corvette, each of these boats has a medium-caliber naval gun and two to four anti-ship missiles. These very vessels comprised some of the most active Iranian naval units in the Iran-Iraq War. Although the U.S.-built Harpoon anti-ship missiles with which they were originally equipped appear to have all been expended during that conflict, the missile boats have reportedly been equipped with Chinese-built C-802 anti-ship missiles, which are based on the U.S. Harpoon and French Exocet designs. Employed in a surprise strike, these missile boats could score some early hits on traffic in the strait.

Even with the fast missile boats, however, there is still the issue of port dependence and vulnerability. Iran's conventional navy, of which the fast attack missile boats are a part, would have to leave port immediately to avoid destruction alongside the pier — particularly challenging if the U.S. struck first. Of course, due to superior American naval and air power, Iran's ships and subs — including the fast missile boats — wouldn't be much safer at sea. Even if the missile boats succeeded in surviving long enough to expend their ordnance, they wouldn't have a port to return to capable of rearming them.

Iran, however, has other asymmetrical tricks up its sleeve.

Iran and the Strait of Hormuz, Part 2: Swarming Boats and Shore-Based Missiles
October 6, 2009

In addition to its fast attack missile boats, which are part of the conventional navy, Iran also has much smaller speedboats employed by the naval arm of the Islamic Revolutionary Guard Corps (IRGC). These vessels gained some notoriety in January 2008 when they were used to harass U.S. warships in the strait.

There are many ways these boats can be employed against tanker traffic in the strait, but most involve massing them in swarms to overwhelm any shipboard defenses. Scenarios include using these small, highly maneuverable vessels to launch rocket-propelled grenades (RPGs) and other ordnance at larger vessels or packing them with explosives for use in suicide attacks. Although an RPG peppering is unlikely to do more than irritate a conventional warship that displaces nearly 10,000 tons, U.S. war-gaming has suggested that suicide tactics could present a danger to warships as well as tankers trying to maneuver in the cramped waters of the strait.

The example that quickly comes to mind is the American guided missile destroyer USS Cole (DDG 67), which was struck by a small boat in a suicide attack in the Yemeni port of Aden in October 2000. At the time, however, the Cole was moored to a pier in the cramped waters of a port and its defenses were further hindered by restrictive rules of engagement. Underway in the Strait of Hormuz and engaged in a shooting war, U.S. warships would be subject to far less restrictive rules of engagement and would be keenly on guard against approaching vessels of any sort.

Moreover, modern warships — though hardly as agile or maneuverable as small boats — are heavily armed. U.S. surface combatants not only employ five-inch naval guns but also generally have multiple .50-caliber heavy machine guns arranged to cover all quadrants and often 25 mm Bushmaster cannons. Indeed, a potential attacker could well find a Bushmaster mounted amidships not far from where the USS Cole was struck on any Arleigh Burke-class destroyer it encounters in the strait. In addition, the U.S. Phalanx Close-In Weapon System, designed as a final line of defense against anti-ship missiles, is being upgraded to include optical and infrared sensors for use against surface targets.

In addition, the size of the small IRGC boats significantly limits the amount of explosives they can effectively deliver. A single strike could be managed by effective damage control on the targeted ship, as was the case with the Cole, where a small boat packed with explosives detonated against the warship's hull on the water line. Such a strike could well achieve a "mission kill" (scoring enough damage to prevent the ship from continuing to carry out its mission), but it would not likely sink the ship.

Also, the distance between the shoreline where such boats would lurk and the shipping lanes where ships transit the strait is considerable (on the order of 10 nautical miles), and even with suboptimal visibility, the armaments on a modern U.S. warship give it a substantial range advantage. Once hostilities commenced, swarms of small boats approaching alert warships would likely suffer considerable losses while closing the distance to the point where they could inflict damage themselves.

While a large tanker would lack the defensive and damage-control capabilities of a U.S. warship, its size would provide it with its own sort of protection. The bow wave alone would make it difficult for small craft to make contact with the hull. The flow of surface water along the hull of such a large, moving ship creates strong currents toward the ship's stern. This would not necessarily prevent a small boat from making contact with the hull, but it would certainly complicate the effort. Indeed, though these small boats are maneuverable, they are not designed to operate a dozen miles from shore; the sea state itself in the middle of the strait could present its own challenges.

In addition, crude oil does not easily ignite, so a supertanker's load can actually serve to absorb explosions if such contact does take place. Indeed, tankers' compartments for crude have long been segmented, limiting the damage from any one point of impact. Double hulls have been standard in new construction for nearly a decade now and will be required for all tankers by next year. This combination of design features and sheer size further limits the effectiveness of not only small boats but also anti-ship missiles and naval mines.

Though crude oil could certainly be spilled if both hulls were breached, even a series of impacts by small boats would have trouble doing more than bringing a large tanker to a slow halt. It is worth noting that when the French oil tanker Limburg was attacked by a small boat filled with explosives in 2002 in the more open waters of the Gulf of Aden, it burned for several days before being towed to port for expensive repairs.

Shore-Based Anti-Ship Missiles

Iran is also known to have a considerable arsenal of shore-based anti-ship missiles, although the exact composition of that arsenal is unclear (and has likely been distorted by the Iranians, in any case).

Indeed, the same intelligence problems that surround Iran's nuclear program extend to its arsenal of anti-ship missiles and naval mines.

Some of these missiles are U.S.-made, predating the Iranian revolution and fall of the Shah, and many were used in the Iran-Iraq War. Even in those days, Iran had begun to field Chinese missiles like Beijing's copy of the Soviet SS-N-2 "Styx," known as the "Silkworm." A number of improved variants have been spun off from this basic design, including one reportedly built in Iran. Although slower and "dumber" than more modern anti-ship missiles, this class of weapons carries a bigger punch: a warhead weighing about 1,000 pounds. Warheads on Iran's newer and smarter anti-ship missiles are one-half to one-third of that weight.

These newer weapons include a considerable quantity of Chinese C-801 and C-802 anti-ship missiles (including indigenously built copies). The C-801 is a derivative of the widely proliferated French Exocet and U.S. Harpoon, while the C-802 is an improved version of the C-801. It was one of these missiles — almost certainly provided by Tehran — that struck the Israeli warship INS Hanit off the Lebanese coast during the conflict in southern Lebanon in the summer of 2006. Iran is also thought to be building an indigenous copy of the C-801 and to be engaged in other domestic manufacturing efforts based on the various missiles in its arsenal. Iran's own production efforts not only cloud the size and composition of its arsenal but also allow it to work around limits to its industrial base and to tailor weapons for its own specific needs.

The C-801/802 missiles carry with them not only a warhead weighing some 300 pounds (similar to the amount of explosives a small boat might carry) but the kinetic energy of high-speed impact, which can lead to more extensive damage deeper inside the hull of the ship. It is worth recalling here that the recent history of anti-ship missiles vs. ship-board defenses — not only the Hanit but also the HMS Sheffield in the Falkland Islands campaign in 1982 and the USS Stark during the so-called "Tanker Wars" in 1987 — has come down consistently in favor of the anti-ship missile. (Of these three ships mentioned above, only the Sheffield sank — and then only after high seas took her down while under tow days after being struck.)

Missiles like the C-801/802 also have improved range and guidance systems. Even the shortest-range models (about 25 miles for the oldest Silkworms) have the reach to cover the strait's designated shipping lanes from the islands of Qeshm and Larak. Longer-range variants put much of the Persian Gulf and the Gulf of Oman at risk from Iranian shores.

This is not to say that a warship equipped with modern defenses does not have the ability to decoy or destroy a modern anti-ship missile; it does, and Iran's arsenal is hardly immune to modern countermeasures and defensive systems (they do not currently appear to field the most threatening classes of modern anti-ship missiles). But if Iran had the element of surprise, it could score some initial hits. And the situation could be further complicated once hostilities commenced, depending on whether Iran chose to expend its missile arsenal in single shots, hoping to survive and get lucky over time, or tried to score hits with larger salvos. The understanding of the performance of shipboard defenses at relatively close range against a large salvo is largely theoretical, since there is little operational experience in this area.

Iran has elements of its anti-ship missile arsenal deployed in batteries not only along its coast but also on key islands within the Persian Gulf near the Strait of Hormuz — with the islands of Qeshm, Sirri and Abu Musa most likely harboring significant quantities of anti-ship missiles. As a general rule, Iranian anti-ship missiles are launched from trucks and the batteries are mobile. Hence, they can be quickly repositioned as needed in a time of crisis. Fired from the coast, these missiles would emerge from the clutter of the shoreline and have very short flight times before impacting ships in the strait, leaving little time for defensive systems to react.

But the anti-ship missile option also presents fundamental challenges for Iran. Iran has only so many launch vehicles for its arsenal, so only a fraction of its anti-ship missile stockpile can be brought to bear at any given time. These batteries are not useful hidden in hills dozens of miles from shore. Most anti-ship missiles — including Iran's — do not have a terrain-following capability, so they must have a relatively straight, clear shot at the ocean, with no major obstructions. This limits the depth within Iran from which launchers can threaten the strait, and it increases their vulnerability to American naval and air power.

In addition, an anti-ship missile's maximum range generally exceeds — often greatly exceeds — the range at which it can acquire and guide itself to a target. This means that in addition to the actual launch vehicles, anti-ship missile batteries must be linked to search and fire-control radars. However, when these radars are activated and radiate, they are vulnerable to being pinpointed and jammed or hit with anti-radiation missiles. And without a battery's link to a search and fire-control radar, the effectiveness of its missiles is severely degraded. While some missiles can certainly be fired "blind" in the hope they can find targets on their own when their seekers activate, or against targets closer to shore, the effectiveness of Iran's anti-ship arsenal depends largely on its vulnerable search and fire-control radars.

Iran can also use air-launched anti-ship missiles of similar capability (and with similar payload limitations) in targeting vessels in the strait and the Persian Gulf. But fighter aircraft are much larger than anti-ship missiles and would provide additional warning when spotted by powerful American ship-borne radars. Moreover, Iran's air force would be subject to rapid attrition at the beginning of any air campaign, and the United States would be able to quickly establish air superiority. Iran's air force is in such a poor state of readiness that even in the early hours of a conflict it would not likely be able to sustain a high sortie rate for any significant length of time.

Thus, Iran must anticipate significant attrition of its anti-ship missiles once hostilities commenced, and it would certainly see an erosion of its ability to fully exploit the remaining missiles over time. So while Iran's anti-ship missile arsenal could play a role in interdicting commercial traffic in the strait — and it would probably be an effective tool for a limited or controlled escalation — it would not be able to sustain anything more than a short-term campaign to close the choke point.

To make it impassable for any length of time requires a different kind of weapon, one that is often far more primitive and difficult to counter — the naval mine.

Iran and the Strait of Hormuz, Part 3:
The Psychology of Naval Mines
October 7, 2009

Perhaps even less clear than the composition of Iran's anti-ship missile arsenal is its stockpile of naval mines. Over the years, Tehran has amassed thousands of mines, largely from Russia and China. Many are old free-floating and moored contact mines, which must physically make contact with a ship's hull in order to detonate. But Iran has also acquired more advanced naval mines that have complex and sensitive triggers — some can be detonated by acoustic noise, others by magnetic influence from the metal of a ship's hull. When deployed, many of these mines rest on the sea floor (for better concealment) and are designed to release what is essentially a small torpedo, either guided or unguided.

Iran also is thought to manufacture naval mines indigenously, and this is the real problem for mine-clearing operations in the Strait of Hormuz. Naval mines need not be particularly complex or difficult to build to be effective (though a long shelf life ashore and longevity in the maritime environment are important considerations and require a detailed understanding of naval mine design). Relatively cheap, cost effective and easy to deploy, mines are the improvised explosive devices of naval warfare, and the potential variations in the Iranian mine arsenal are practically limitless. The question is not how many modern mines Iran has acquired but what Iran has improvised and cobbled together within its own borders and manufactured in numbers. Although old, poorly maintained naval mines and poor storage conditions can be a recipe for disaster, many of Iran's mines may have been modified or purpose-built to suit Iran's needs and methods of deployment.

These methods of deployment extend far beyond Iran's small number of larger, purpose-built mine-warfare ships. Not only have fishing dhows and trawlers been modified for mine-warfare purposes, but the naval arm of the Islamic Revolutionary Guard Corps (IRGC) is known to have a fleet of small boats not just for swarming and suicide attacks but also to be employed to sow naval mines.

Because of the uncertainty surrounding Iran's mine-laying capability as well as its naval mine stockpile, it is as impossible to estimate the effort it would take to clear Iranian mines from the strait. It all depends on what plays out, and there are many scenarios. One envisions Iran surreptitiously sowing mines for several days before the U.S. military detects the effort. Another has Iran deploying mines after an initial American strike, in which case Iran's mine-laying capability would be severely degraded. The question of which side moves first is a critical one for almost any scenario.

But it is reasonably clear that Iran lacks both the arsenal and the capability for a "worst-case" scenario: sowing a full offensive field across the Strait of Hormuz composed of tens of thousands of mines that would effectively prevent any ship from entering the waterway. Though the IRGC and other forces that could be involved in mine-laying operations certainly practice their craft, their proficiency is not at all clear. And though the Iranians have a variety of mine-laying vessels at their disposal, their ability to perform the precise navigation and coordination required to lay a large-scale minefield with its hodgepodge of purpose-built minelayers, modified dhows and barges and small boats is questionable.

Most important — and most problematic for the Iranians — is the fact that the United States has a considerable presence near the strait and maintains close situational awareness in the region. Iran does not have the luxury of time when it comes to sowing mines. Some limited, covert mine laying cannot be ruled out, but Tehran cannot exclude the possibility of being caught — and the consequences of being caught would be significant, almost certainly involving a U.S. military strike. In any Iranian attempt to close the strait, it must balance the need to deploy as many mines as possible as quickly as possible with the need to do so surreptitiously. The former attempt could be quickly spotted, while the latter may fail to sow a sufficient number of mines to create the desired effect.

In addition, the damage that even a significant number of mines can physically do may be limited. Most naval mines — especially the older variety — can inflict only minor damage to a modern tanker or warship. During the "Tanker Wars," the Kuwaiti tanker MV Bridgeton and the guided missile frigate USS Samuel B Roberts (FFG 58) were struck by crude Iranian mines in 1987 and 1988, respectively. Though both were damaged, neither sank.

But in mine warfare, the ultimate objective is often psychological. The uncertainty of a threat can instill as much fear as the certainty of it, and Iran need not sow a particularly coherent field of mines to impede traffic through the strait. A single ship striking a naval mine (or even a serious Iranian move to sow mines) could quickly and dramatically drive up global oil prices and maritime insurance rates. This combination is bad enough in the best of times. But the Iranian threat to the Strait of Hormuz could not be more effective than at this moment, with the world just starting to show signs of economic recovery. The shock wave of a spike in energy prices — not to mention the wider threat of a conflagration in the Persian Gulf — could leave the global economy in even worse straits than it was a year ago.

We will not delve here into the calculations of maritime insurers other than to say that, when it comes to supertankers and their cargo, an immense amount of money is at stake — and this cuts both ways. Even damage to a supertanker can quickly run into the millions of dollars — not to mention the opportunity cost of having the ship out of commission. On the other hand, especially at a time when the strait is dangerous and oil prices are through the roof, there would be windfall profits to be made from a successful transit to open waters.

The initial shock to the global economy of a supertanker hitting a mine in the strait would be profound, but its severity and longevity would depend in large part on the extent of the mining, Iran's ability to continue laying mines and the speed of mine-clearing operations. And, as always, it would all hinge on the quality of intelligence. While some military targets — major naval installations, for example — are large, fixed and well known, Iran's mine-laying capability is more dispersed (like its nuclear program). That, along with Iran's armada of small boats along the Persian Gulf coast, suggests it may not be possible to bring Iran's mine-laying efforts to an immediate halt. Barring a cease-fire, limited, low-level mining operations could well continue.

Given the variables involved, it is difficult to describe exactly what a U.S. mine-clearing operation might look like in the strait, although enough is known about the U.S. naval presence in the region and other mine-clearing operations to suggest a rough scenario. The United States keeps four mine countermeasures ships forward deployed in the Persian Gulf. A handful of allied minesweepers are also generally on station, as well as MH-53E Sea Dragon helicopters, which are used in such operations. This available force in the region approaches the size of the mine-clearing squadron employed during Operation Iraqi Freedom to clear the waterway leading to the port of Umm Qasr, although it does not include a mine countermeasures command ship and represents a different clearing scenario.

The clearing of the Strait of Hormuz would begin with the clearing of a "Q-route," a lane calculated to entail less than a 10 percent chance of a mine strike. While there may be considerable uncertainty in this calculation, the route would be used for essential naval traffic and also would play a role in the ongoing clearing operation. The time it would take to clear such a route would vary considerably, based on a wide variety of factors, but it could be a week or more. And a Q-route suitable for large supertankers could take longer to clear than the initial route.

The sooner maritime commerce can resume transiting the strait (perhaps escorted at first by naval vessels), the shorter the crisis would be. The more time that passes without a mine strike, the faster confidence would return. But another mine strike could cause another shock to the global economy, even after clearing operations have been under way for some time.

The fact is, the United States and its allies have the capability to clear naval mines from the Strait of Hormuz, technically speaking. But mine countermeasures work is notoriously under-resourced — it is neither the sexiest nor the most career-enhancing job in the U.S. Navy. So while even a sizable mine-clearing operation in the strait would have historical precedent in other locations, it would be wrong to assume that such an operation would go smoothly and efficiently, even under the best of circumstances.

The efficiency of a mine-clearing effort in the strait would be subject to any number of variables. One thing is clear, however: Any Iranian mining effort could quickly have profound and far-reaching consequences — including an impact on the global economy far out of proportion to the actual threat. Naval mines laid by Iran would take a considerable amount of time — weeks or months — to clear from the strait, and their effect would be felt long after an American air campaign ended. Indeed, should hostilities continue for some time, having small boats continue to seed mines may be the most survivable of Iran's asymmetric naval capabilities.

Ultimately, Iran's military capabilities should not be understood as tools that can only be used independently. If it attempted to close the strait, Iran would draw on the full spectrum of its capabilities in order to be as disruptive as possible. For example, Iran could hold its anti-ship missiles in reserve and launch them at smaller mine countermeasures ships conducting clearing operations in the strait, since these vessels have nowhere near the defensive capabilities of surface combatants. It would also take a considerable amount of time for Washington to send more countermeasures ships to the area from the continental United States above what would likely be deployed ahead of a crisis (if Washington had the luxury of enough warning).

The bottom line is that there is considerable uncertainty and substantial risk for both sides. But while Iran's capability to actually "close" the strait is questionable, there is little doubt that it could quickly wreak havoc on the global economy by doing much less.

Iranian Proxies: An Intricate and Active Web
February 3, 2010

For the past few years, STRATFOR has been carefully following the imbroglio over the Iranian nuclear weapons program and efforts by the United States and others to scuttle the program. This situation has led to threats by both sides, with the United States and Israel discussing plans to destroy Iranian weapons sites with airstrikes and the Iranians holding well-publicized missile launches and military exercises in the Persian Gulf.

Much attention has been paid to the Iranian deterrents to an attack on its nuclear program, such as the ballistic missile threat and the potential to block the Strait of Hormuz, but these are not the only deterrents Iran possesses. Indeed, over the past several years, Iran has consistently reminded the world about the network of proxy groups that the country can call upon to cause trouble for any country that would attack its nuclear weapons program.

Over the past several weeks, interesting new threads of information about Iranian proxies have come to light, and when the individual strands are tied together they make for a very interesting story.

Iran's Proxies

From almost the very beginning of the Islamic republic, Iran's clerical regime has sought to export its Islamic revolution to other parts of the Muslim world. This was done not only for ideological purposes — to continue the revolution — but also for practical reasons, as a way to combat regional adversaries by means of proxy warfare. Among the first groups targeted for this expansion were the Shiite populations in Iraq, the Persian Gulf and, of course, Lebanon.

The withdrawal of the Palestine Liberation Organization (PLO) from Lebanon in 1982 left behind a cadre of trained Shiite militants who were quickly recruited by agents of Iran's Islamic Revolutionary Guard Corps (IRGC). These early Lebanese recruits included hardened PLO fighters from the slums of South Beirut such as Imad Mughniyah. These fighters formed the backbone of Iran's militant proxy force in Lebanon, Hezbollah, which, in the ensuing decades, would evolve from a shadowy terrorist group into a powerful political entity with a significant military capability.

One of the most impressive things about these early proxy efforts in Lebanon is that the IRGC and the Iranian Ministry of Intelligence and Security were both very young institutions at the time, and they were heavily pressured by the 1980 invasion of Iran by Saddam Hussein's Iraq, which was backed by the Gulf states and the United States. The Iranians also had to compete with the Amal movement, which was backed by Libya and Syria and which dominated the Lebanese Shiite landscape at the time. Projecting power into Lebanon under such conditions was quite an amazing feat, one that many more mature intelligence organizations have not been able to match.

Though these institutions were young, the Iranians were not without experience in intelligence tradecraft. The years of operating against the Shah's intelligence service, a brutal and efficient organization known as the SAVAK, taught the Iranian revolutionaries many hard-learned lessons about operational security and clandestine operations, and they incorporated many of these lessons into their handling of proxy operations. For example, it was very difficult for the U.S. government to prove that the Iranians, through their proxies, were behind the bombings of the U.S. Embassy (twice) and Marine barracks in Beirut or the kidnapping of Westerners in Lebanon. The use of different names in public statements such as the Islamic Jihad Organization, Revolutionary Justice Organization and the Organization of the Oppressed on Earth, when combined with very good Iranian operational security, served to further muddy the already murky waters of Lebanon's militant landscape. Iran has also done a fairly good job at hiding its hand in places like Kuwait and Bahrain.

While Iran has invested a lot of effort to build up Shiite proxy groups such as Hezbollah and assorted other groups in Iraq, Saudi Arabia and the Gulf states, the Iranians do not exclusively work with Shiite proxies. As we discussed last week, the Iranians also have a pragmatic streak and will work with Marxist groups like the Kurdistan Workers' Party, Sunni groups like Hamas in Gaza and various militant groups in Pakistan and Afghanistan (they sought to undermine the Taliban while that group was in power in Afghanistan but are currently aiding some Taliban groups in an effort to thwart the U.S. effort there). In an extremely complex game, the Iranians are also working with various Sunni and Kurdish groups in Iraq, in addition to their Shiite proxies, as they seek to shape their once-feared neighbor into something they can more-easily influence and control.

More than Foot Stomping

For several years now, every time there is talk of a possible attack on Iran there is a corresponding threat by Iran to use its proxy groups in response to such an attack. Iran has also been busy pushing intelligence reports to anybody who will listen (including STRATFOR) that it will activate its militant proxy groups if attacked and, to back that up, will periodically send operatives or proxies out to conduct not-so-subtle surveillance of potential targets. Hezbollah and Hamas have both stated publicly that they will attack Israel if Israel launches an attack against Iran's nuclear program, and such threats are far more than mere rhetorical devices. Iran has taken many concrete steps to prepare and arm its various proxy groups:

- On Dec. 11, 2009, authorities seized an Ilyushin-76 cargo plane in Bangkok that contained 35 tons of North Korean-produced military weapons that were destined for Iran (though Iran, naturally, denies the report). The weapons, which included man-portable air defense systems (MANPADS), were either equivalent to, or less advanced than, weapons Iran produces on its own. This fact raised the real possibility that the Iranians had purchased the North Korean weapons in order to distribute them to proxies and hide Iran's hand if those arms were recovered after an attack.

- In November 2009, Israeli naval commandos seized a ship off the coast of Cyprus that was loaded with hundreds of tons of weapons that were apparently being sent from Iran to Hezbollah. The seizure, which was the largest in Israel's history, included artillery shells, rockets, grenades and small-arms ammunition.

- In August 2009, authorities in the United Arab Emirates seized a ship carrying 10 containers of North Korean weapons disguised as oil equipment. The seized cache included weapons that Iran produces itself, like rockets and rocket-propelled grenade rounds, again raising the probability that the arms were intended for Iran's militant proxies.

- In April 2009, Egyptian authorities announced that they had arrested a large network of Hezbollah operatives who were planning attacks against Israeli targets inside Egypt. It is likely, however, that the network was involved in arms smuggling and the charges of planning attacks may have been leveled against the smugglers to up the ante and provide a warning message to anyone considering smuggling in the future.

- In January 2009, a convoy of suspected arms smugglers in northern Sudan near the Egyptian border was attacked by an apparent Israeli air strike. The arms were reportedly destined for Hamas and the Palestinian Islamic Jihad and were tied to an Iranian network that, according to STRATFOR sources in the region, had been purchasing arms in Sudan and shipping them across the Sinai to Gaza.

As illustrated by most of the above incidents (and several others we did not include for the sake of brevity), Israeli intelligence has been actively attempting to interdict the flow of weapons to Iran and Iranian proxy groups. Such Israeli efforts may explain the assassination of Mahmoud al-Mabhouh, whose body was discovered Jan. 20 in his room at a five-star hotel in Dubai. Al-Mabhouh, a senior commander of the Izz al-Din al-Qassam Brigades, Hamas' military wing, lived in exile in Damascus and was reportedly the Hamas official responsible for coordinating the transfer of weapons from Iran to Hamas forces in Gaza. A STRATFOR source advised us that, at the time of his death, al-Mabhouh was on his way to Tehran to meet with his IRGC handlers. The operation to kill al-Mabhouh also bears many similarities to past Israeli assassination operations. His status as an Izz al-Din al-Qassam Brigades commander involved in many past attacks against Israel would certainly make him an attractive target for the Israelis.

Of course, like anything involving the Iranians, there remains quite a bit of murkiness involving the totality of their meddling in the region. Hezbollah sources have told STRATFOR that they have troops actively engaged in combat in Yemen, with the al-Houthi rebels in the northern province of Saada along the Saudi border, and have lost several fighters there. Hezbollah also has claimed that its personnel have shot down several Yemeni aircraft using Iranian-manufactured Misagh-1 MANPADS.

The governments of Yemen and Saudi Arabia have very good reason to fear Iran's plans to expand its influence in the Gulf region, and the Yemenis in particular have been very vocal about blaming Iran for stirring up the al-Houthi rebels. Because of this, if there truly were Hezbollah fighters being killed in Saada and signs of Iranian ordnance (like MANPADS) being used by Hezbollah fighters or al-Houthi rebels, we believe the government of Yemen would have been documenting the evidence and providing the documentation to the world (especially in light of Yemen's long and unsuccessful attempt to gain U.S. assistance for its struggle against the al-Houthi insurgency). That said, while Hezbollah MANPADS teams are not likely to be running around Saada, there is evidence that the Iranians have been involved in smuggling weapons to the al-Houthi via Yemen's rugged

Red Sea coast. Indeed, such arms smuggling has resulted in a Saudi naval blockade of the Yemeni coast. Reports of al-Houthi militants being trained by the IRGC in Lebanon and Iran are also plausible.

Iran has long flirted with jihadist groups. This support has sporadically stretched from the early days of al Qaeda's stay in Sudan, where Hezbollah bomb makers instructed al Qaeda militants in how to make large vehicle bombs, to more recent times, when the IRGC has provided arms to Iraqi Sunni militants and Taliban factions in Afghanistan. Iran has also provided weapons to the now-defunct Supreme Islamic Courts Council in Somalia and one of its offshoots, al Shabaab.

Over the past several months we have also heard from a variety of sources in different parts of the Middle East that the Iranians are assisting al Qaeda in the Arabian Peninsula (AQAP). Some reports indicate that a jihadist training camp that had previously been operating in Syria to train and send international fighters to Iraq had been relocated to Iran, and that with Iranian assistance, the jihadists were funneling international militants from Iran to Yemen to fight with AQAP. Other reports say the Iranians are providing arms to the group. While some analysts downplay such reports, the fact that we have received similar information from a wide variety of sources in different countries and with varying ideological backgrounds suggests there is indeed something to these reports.

One last thing to consider while pondering Iran's militant proxies is that, while Iranian missiles will be launched (and mines laid) only in the case of open hostilities, Iranian militant proxies have been busily at work across the region for many years now. With a web of connections that reaches all the way from Lebanon to Somalia to Afghanistan, Iran can cast a wide net over the Middle East. If the United States has truly begun to assume a defensive posture in the Gulf, it will have to guard not only against Iranian missile strikes but also against Iran's sophisticated use of proxy militant groups.

Iranian Intelligence and Regime Preservation
June 22, 2010

Iran has two major and competing services that form the core of its intelligence community: the Ministry of Intelligence and Security (MOIS) and the intelligence office of the Islamic Revolutionary Guard Corps (IRGC). The bureaucratic battle between the two, as well as many examples of cooperation, may suggest the future makeup and character of Iranian intelligence and, by extension, the regime itself. Both services were purposefully designed so that no single organization in Iran could have a monopoly on intelligence. But over the past year, Iranian Supreme Leader Ayatollah Ali Khamenei has taken more direct control of both.

The operations of Iran's intelligence and military services are directed first and foremost at maintaining internal stability, particularly by minimizing the internal threat posed by minorities and their potential to be co-opted by external powers. While other countries such as North Korea must have strong internal security to preserve the regime, Iran has an even greater need because of the ethnic diversity of its population, which is spread throughout a mountainous country. Such an environment is ideal for the growth of separatist and other opposition groups, which must be contained by a strong intelligence and security apparatus.

The second focus of Iranian intelligence is maintaining awareness of foreign powers that could threaten Iran, and utilizing Iran's resources to distract those powers. This involves traditional espionage (obtaining secret information on an adversary's intentions or capabilities) and disinformation operations to obfuscate Iran's capabilities and redirect attention to militant and political proxy groups such as Hezbollah in Lebanon, the Badr Brigades in Iraq and even elements of the Taliban in Afghanistan. These non-state entities give Iran a threatening power-projection capability with a significant degree of plausible deniability.

The third focus is acquiring better capabilities for Iran's defense. This includes everything from Iran's nuclear program to missile and naval technology to spare parts for aging military equipment such as the F-14 jet fleet. The Iranians are also constantly recruiting and developing insurgent capabilities in case of war — both in and outside Iran. For example, Iran's paramilitary force has developed a guerrilla warfare strategy that requires acquiring or developing advanced speedboats and torpedoes to influence events in the Persian Gulf.

Iran is most successful at operating behind a veil of secrecy. The country's leadership structure is confusing enough to outside observers, but the parallel and overlapping structures of the intelligence and military services are even more effective in obscuring leadership at the top and links to proxies at the bottom. The prime example of this is the IRGC, which is a complex combination of institutions: military force, intelligence service, covert action/special operations force, police, paramilitary force and business conglomerate, with proxies worldwide. The MOIS is more traditional, a civilian internal and external intelligence service.

Both of these organizations have overlapping responsibilities, but one key difference is that the president has much more authority over the MOIS, which is a ministry of his government, than he has over the IRGC, which has become a national institution unto itself (the supreme leader has ultimate authority over both). The Supreme National Security Council (SNSC) and the Supreme Leader's Intelligence Unit are the semi-parallel organizations where overall intelligence authority lies. The SNSC is the official state body that makes broad political and military decisions that rely on intelligence collection and analysis as well as recommendations from advisers, but these decisions still must be approved by the supreme leader. His intelligence unit has the most power over Iranian intelligence activities and is designed to control the MOIS and the IRGC.

The secretive nature of Iranian institutions blends into operations as well. One of the first and most famous attacks instigated by an Iranian proxy was the 1983 U.S. Embassy bombing in Beirut, a case in which the identity of the bomber is still unknown, a notable exception to the culture of martyrdom within Islamist terrorist organizations (Hezbollah never claimed responsibility for the attack, which was likely perpetrated by one of its front groups). Through its intelligence services, Iran has connections with militant Islamist groups worldwide, but its influence is especially strong with those in the Middle East. And Iranian intelligence is careful to pad these relationships with layers of plausible deniability that help protect the Iranian state from any blowback.

The most pressing issue for Iranian intelligence is management of the complex parallel structures with overlapping responsibilities among intelligence, military and civil institutions. This structure guarantees that no single entity has a monopoly on intelligence or the political power that stems from it, but the safeguard can also be a source of conflict. Over the last year, Supreme Leader Ayatollah Ali Khamenei has gone to great lengths to bring the MOIS and IRGC under his direct control. This gives him even more direct power over the president and insulates him from political and security threats. And the parallel structures ensure duplication of activities and competitive intelligence analysis.

Eventually, however, centralization of power could insulate the supreme leader in an intelligence bubble, with officials telling him what he wants to hear rather than engaging in a rigorous reporting of the facts. This danger arises in all countries, but it could be a particularly serious problem for Iran as a kind of intelligence war continues across the Middle East. The regime of Mohammad Reza Shah Pahlavi, the last monarch of Iran, fell in large part because of a politicized intelligence service that ignored the reality on the ground. Today, as the supreme leader gains more direct control over Iranian intelligence services, such control could promote a better, more competitive process, but it could also make the supreme leader as disconnected from reality as the shah.

A Brief History

The modern history of Iranian intelligence begins with the infamous security services under the shah. In 1953, Prime Minister Mohammad Mossadegh was overthrown by a U.S.- and U.K.-sponsored coup, which began Pahlavi's gradual rise to power in Iran. His power was based on the strength of the National Intelligence and Security Organization, better known as SAVAK (a Farsi acronym for Sazeman-e Ettela'at va Amniyat-e Keshvar), which was formed in 1957, reportedly under the guidance of the CIA and the Israeli Mossad.

To enforce the rule of the shah, SAVAK created a police state through vast informant networks, surveillance operations and censorship. This was one of the first attempts in Iran's history to impose centralized control of the country, rather than rely on relationships between the government and local leaders. While SAVAK was instrumental in controlling dissent, it also exacerbated corruption and brutality, resulting in a disaffected Iranian populace. A 1974 article in Harper's magazine claimed that one in every 450 Iranian males was a paid SAVAK agent. Still in use today by the IRGC, Evin prison was infamous for torturing and indefinitely detaining anyone deemed threatening to the shah's regime.

The director of SAVAK was nominally under the authority of the prime minister, but he met with the shah every morning. The shah also created the Special Intelligence Bureau, which operated from his palace, and deployed his own Imperial Guard, a special security force that was the only Iranian military unit stationed in Tehran. Even with this extensive security apparatus — or perhaps because of it — the shah was ignorant of the Iranian public's hostility toward his regime until it was too late. He fled the country in January 1979 as the Islamic revolution reached its zenith.

Even before the revolution, the security forces for a new regime were already taking shape and establishing links in the Middle East. Ayatollah Ruhollah Khomeini, leader of the revolution and founder of the new Islamic republic, sent some of his loyalists for military training in Lebanon's Bekaa Valley, where they received instruction at Amal militia and Fatah training camps. By 1977, more than 700 Khomeini loyalists had graduated from these camps. They were founding members of what would become the IRGC (effectively the new Imperial Guard and Special Intelligence Bureau). During the revolution, the shah's forces were purged by Islamic revolutionaries and what was left of them were merged with the regular Iranian armed forces, or Artesh (Persian for "army"). The IRGC was formed on May 5, 1979, to protect the new Islamic regime in Iran against counterrevolutionary activity and monitor what was left of the shah's military.

In February 1979, the revolutionaries overran SAVAK headquarters, and its members were among the first targets of retribution. Internal security files were confiscated and high-ranking officers were arrested. By 1981, 61 senior intelligence officers had been executed. Even though SAVAK was dismantled, its legacy remained in the form of SAVAMA (Sazman-e Ettela'at va Amniat-e Melli-e Iran, or the National Intelligence and Security Apparatus of Iran). In 1984, in a reorganization by the Army Military Revolutionary Tribunal, SAVAMA became the current MOIS, and this was when Iran's parallel intelligence structure truly took form.

From Terrorists to Agents of Influence

In February 1982, about a month after Israeli forces invaded Lebanon to quash the Palestinian resistance, an unnamed IRGC officer met in Lebanon with Imad Mughniyah, a young and disaffected Lebanese man of Shiite faith. Mughniyah also was an experienced guerrilla fighter, a member of Fatah's Force 17 and a bodyguard to Yasser Arafat. For years there was no record of this meeting, even among the world's premier intelligence agencies, even though it would mark the inception of Iran's first militant proxy group, an organization that would later become known as Hezbollah.

Although the name of the IRGC officer is still unconfirmed, he was likely Hussein Moslehi, the IRGC's liaison with Hezbollah in the years afterward. The new Shiite militant group would conduct many terrorist attacks orchestrated by Mughniyah (and many different organizational names would be used, such as the Islamic Jihad Organization, or IJO, to create ambiguity and confusion). During that first meeting in Lebanon, and unbeknownst to many, Mughniyah received an officer's commission in the IRGC and would later be named commander of a secret IRGC proxy group, Amin Al-Haras, or Security of the Guards, for which he was told to recruit family members and friends from his time in Fatah to wage a new jihad under the IJO banner.

Mughniyah also became part of the security detail guarding Grand Ayatollah Mohammed Hussein Fadlallah, the spiritual leader of Hezbollah. In March 1983, he represented Fadlallah at a meeting in Damascus with the Iranian Ambassador to Syria, Ali Akhbar Mohtashemi. They decided to begin a terror campaign that would become the first to repel a "foreign occupier" in the modern era of Islamist militancy. Mughniyah orchestrated the truck-bomb attacks against the U.S. Embassy in Beirut on April 18, 1983, and against the U.S. Marine barracks and French paratrooper barracks on Oct. 23. By March 31, 1984, the multinational peacekeeping force had left Lebanon.

On behalf of Tehran, Mughniyah orchestrated many other bombings, kidnappings and plane hijackings that hid the hand of Iran (and sometimes even his own). When foreign governments wanted to negotiate the return of hostages held in Lebanon, however, they always went to Iran. The Iranians used their proxies' captives as playing cards for political concessions and arms deals (like the Iran-Contra affair in the mid-1980s).

By the 1990s, however, Iran had realized it could achieve its geopolitical goals more effectively not by engaging in provocative international terrorist activities but by promoting insurgencies and infiltrating political movements. So Hezbollah turned into a political group with an armed guerrilla wing to fight Israel and rival Lebanese forces while also gaining political power in Lebanon. Guerrilla warfare replaced terrorism as the primary tactic for Iran's proxies, which also came to include the Badr Brigades (then based in Iran); Hamas, the Popular Front for the Liberation of Palestine-General Command and Palestinian Islamic Jihad (PIJ) in the Palestinian territories; and various Afghan militant groups.

Tehran never wanted to lose the deterrent threat of Hezbollah's terrorist capabilities, however, and Hezbollah continued to develop plans and surveil targets, such as military installation and embassies, to threaten Iran's adversaries. (In 1994, Mughniyah was involved in planning attacks in Buenos Aires.) Hezbollah victories against Israel in 2000 and 2006 proved the group's effectiveness while Mughniyah became less active as a terrorist coordinator and more active as a military commander. By the time Mughniyah was assassinated in Damascus in February 2008, Iran had shifted its proxy tactics, for the most part, from international terrorism to regional insurgencies.

The secular Iraqi Shiite politician Ahmed Chalabi may have personified the next Iranian proxy shift, from guerrilla fighters to more careful agents of influence. Chalabi was one of three executives, and the de facto leader, of the Iraqi National Congress (INC), a supposedly broad-based Iraqi group opposed to Saddam Hussein's regime. It will never be clear who Chalabi really worked for, other than himself, since he played all sides, but Iran clearly had substantial involvement in his activities. STRATFOR laid out the case for Chalabi's relationship with Iran in 2004, noting that the false intelligence on Iraqi weapons of mass destruction provided by Iran through Chalabi did not inspire the U.S. government to go to war in Iraq, it only provided the means to convince the American public that it was the right thing to do. Chalabi was more influential in convincing the U.S. Defense Department's Office of Special Plans that the threat of Shiite groups in southern Iraq was minimal.

Chalabi's influence contributed to U.S. tactical failures in Iraq that allowed Iran's unseen hand to gain power through other Shiite proxies, most notably the Islamic Supreme Council of Iraq (ISCI), known at the time as the Supreme Council for Islamic Revolution in Iraq (SCIRI). The ISCI gained a substantial amount of power after the fall of Saddam Hussein, and its main militia group, the Badr Brigades, has since been integrated into the Iraqi security forces. In early 2004, Chalabi fell out of favor with the Bush administration, which continued to work with ISCI leader Abdel Aziz al-Hakim. For all practical purposes, the Dawa party of Iraqi Prime Minister Nouri al-Maliki, the al-Sadrite movement and assorted other political factions in Iraq are also, to varying degrees, proxies of the MOIS and of the IRGC's overseas operations arm, the Quds Force.

In May 2004, U.S. officials revealed that Chalabi gave sensitive intelligence to an Iranian official indicating that the United States had broken the MOIS communications code. And the fact that Chalabi was able to pass the intelligence revealed certain clandestine capabilities on the part of Iran, particularly the ability to use proxies for direct action and intelligence-gathering while keeping its involvement plausibly deniable. While there is much circumstantial evidence that Chalabi or Mughniyah were Iranian agents, the lack of direct evidence clouds the issue to this day.

Organizations and Operations

Ministry of Intelligence and Security

Iran's MOIS, also known by its Farsi acronym VEVAK (Vezarat-e Ettela'at va Amniat-e Keshvar), is the country's premier civilian external intelligence service, with approximately 15,000 employees as of 2006. The MOIS' internal organization is unclear, but its authority and operations are identifiable. The MOIS is a government ministry, which means its director is a minister in the Iranian Cabinet under the president. This gives Iran's president, who while popularly elected must also be approved by the clerics, considerable authority in MOIS intelligence activities. The minister of intelligence, currently Heidar Moslehi, also serves within the Supreme National Security Council, the highest decision-making body of the government. In addition, the MOIS chief is always a cleric, which means the supreme leader has considerable influence in his appointment and oversees his performance.

IRAN'S EXECUTIVE BRANCH AND INTELLIGENCE SERVICES

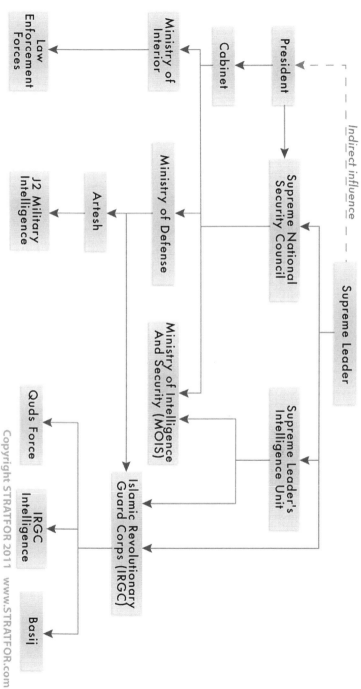

Training for MOIS officers begins with their recruitment in Iran. Like any employee of the Iranian government, intelligence officers must be strict "Twelver Shias" (those who expect the reappearance of the twelfth imam) and firm believers in the doctrine of velayat-e-faqih (a state ruled by jurists). Their loyalties to the Islamic republic are tested often during training at sites in northern Tehran and Qom, according to STRATFOR sources. Before training they also go through a careful clearance process, which almost certainly involves a lengthy background check by counterintelligence officers.

Intelligence officers are placed in many cover jobs, a standard practice among the world's intelligence services. As do most countries, Iran includes large intelligence sections in its embassies and missions, and official cover often includes positions in the Foreign Ministry abroad. This was the case when Iranian intelligence officers were caught surveilling targets in New York City in 2006 and when Iranian Embassy officials helped facilitate bombings in Argentina in 1994 by providing documentation, logistics and communications support to the bombers. The MOIS also employs non-official cover for its officers, including those of student, professor, journalist and employee of state-owned or state-connected companies (e.g., IranAir and Iranian banks). According to STRATFOR sources, some expatriate academics who often travel back to Iran from overseas positions because of family obligations or emergencies may be MOIS employees.

Recruitment of foreign agents, some of whom are given official positions within the MOIS or IRGC, occurs mostly in overseas Muslim communities. Many are also recruited while studying in Iran. Their first areas targeted for major recruitment outside of Iran were Lebanon and Iraq, and the scope eventually spread to other Shiite communities in the Middle East and in other parts of the world. The MOIS has individual departments for recruiting agents in the Persian Gulf, Yemen, Sudan, Lebanon and the Palestinian territories, Europe, South and East Asia, North America and South America. Its particular target in South America is the tri-state border region of Paraguay, Argentina and Brazil, where a large Lebanese Shiite population exists. Foreign agents may also be non-Shia, whether Sunni

Muslims or of other backgrounds. Shia, however, tend to be the only MOIS agents who are fully trusted.

On paper, the MOIS' domestic responsibilities remain a higher priority than its foreign responsibilities, but its primary duties no longer involve managing the domestic security environment. The IRGC has largely taken over domestic security, although the MOIS still maintains a few parallel responsibilities. One is to actively thwart reformists, preventing them, for example, from organizing demonstrations or secret meetings. MOIS officers also surveil and infiltrate Iran's ethnic minorities, especially the Baluchs, Kurds, Azeris and Arabs, in search of dissident elements. Another MOIS mission is monitoring the drug trade, and though the service is probably less involved in narcotics than the IRGC, its officers likely receive a percentage of the profits from the large quantities of Afghan heroin that transit Iran on their way to European consumers.

The service's intelligence-collection operations abroad follow traditional methodologies that its predecessor, SAVAK, learned from the CIA and Mossad, but the MOIS also is adept at conducting disinformation campaigns, which it learned how to do from the KGB after the Islamic revolution. In conducting its foreign intelligence operations, the MOIS focuses on the region but also extends its operations worldwide, where it faces growing competition from the IRGC and Quds Force (more on this below). As in its domestic efforts, the MOIS' first priority on foreign soil is to monitor, infiltrate and control Iranian dissident groups. Its second priority is to develop liaison and proxy networks for foreign influence and terrorist and military operations, an effort usually facilitated by pan-Islamism, Shiite sectarianism and Farsi ethno-linguistic connections. Currently, the MOIS is most involved with Shiite networks in Iraq and Farsi-speaking groups in Afghanistan. (The networks in Iraq and even in Afghanistan seem to be managed by IRGC, however, and this is explained in more detail below.)

The MOIS' third priority abroad is to identify any foreign threats, particularly surrounding Iran's nuclear program, and it is currently focusing primarily (and naturally) on Israel and the United States.

Its fourth foreign intelligence priority is to spread disinformation in order to protect Iran and further its interests, and in recent years this has mainly been an effort to convince the rest of the world that an attack on Iran not only would fail to stop its nuclear program but also would have disastrous consequences for the world economy by shutting down the flow of oil through the Strait of Hormuz. The MOIS' fifth and final foreign intelligence priority is to acquire technology for defensive purposes, including spare parts for aging military equipment such as F-14 jet fighters that the United States provided Iran during the reign of the shah.

The MOIS calls its disinformation operations nefaq, which is an Arabic word for discord. It learned the methodology from the KGB, which taught that 80 percent to 90 percent of information released to foreign media or intelligence agencies should be fact while only a small percentage should be fiction. In addition to its more recent use of disinformation to discourage an attack against Iran's nuclear program, the MOIS has used it to discredit reformist and opposition groups in foreign countries and to distract and confuse foreign powers regarding Iran's intelligence and military capabilities. Examples include Chalabi's deception of the United States and MOIS-operated websites claiming to represent Iranian dissident groups such as Tondar.

Throughout the 1980s and 1990s, Iranian intelligence operatives assassinated numerous dissidents abroad. Within the first year of the Islamic revolution, the monarchist Prince Shahriar Shafiq was assassinated in Paris and a former Iranian diplomat who was critical of the Islamic regime, Ali Akbar Tabatabai, was shot and killed in his home in a Washington suburb by an African-American operative who had converted to Islam and has lived in Iran since Tabatabai's murder. One of the most high-profile MOIS assassinations was the killing of the last prime minister under the shah, Shapour Bakhtiar, in Paris in 1991 (after at least two failed attempts). It is believed at least 80 people were assassinated by Iranian intelligence during the 1980s and 1990s across Europe, in Turkey and Pakistan and as far away as the Philippines. This was in addition to a series of murders of dissidents and scholars inside Iran between 1990 and 1998 (15 assassination were allegedly orchestrated by the MOIS).

Since the early years of the Islamic republic, assassinations of Iranian dissidents abroad have decreased as the intelligence services have evolved and as threats to the regime have diminished. This is largely because politically active Iranians living in other countries are involved in many different and competing opposition groups and are not united. This leads them to report on each other's activities to the local Iranian Embassy or consulate, and it has resulted in a shift in intelligence-service tactics, from assassination to harassment, intimidation and delegitimization. Representatives of Iranian missions have been known to monitor dissidents by infiltrating and observing their meetings and speeches, and MOIS officers often want dissidents to know they are being watched so that they will be intimidated. Some of these dissident groups are considered by the Iranian regime (and others internationally) to be terrorist groups, such as the Marxist-Islamist Mujahideen-e-Khalq, while others are royalists or democracy advocates. Often the reputation of a dissident group can be heavily influenced by the MOIS, which will work to get the group officially designated as a "terrorist organization" by foreign governments or otherwise discourage foreign governments from having anything to do with it.

The MOIS has its own section (reportedly called "Department 15") that is responsible for subversive activities abroad, or what the service calls "exporting revolution." It has done this by establishing liaisons with many types of resistance and terrorist movements throughout the world, not just Islamist groups (it shipped weapons, for example, to the Irish Republican Army). However, the MOIS concentrates on groups within or near Iran's borders. Although the Iranians will never fully trust a Sunni group, the MOIS has had a long-standing relationship with elements of al Qaeda, though it is as much an infiltration of the group for intelligence purposes as it is an alliance. As long as these elements share similar goals with Tehran, Iran will work with them.

The primary reason for Iran to have such non-ideological relationships is to collect intelligence on militant groups competing for the leadership of the worldwide radical Islamist movement. The secondary reason is to distract Iran's adversaries by forcing them to deal with militants in other countries. Reports differ on how close the MOIS and other Iranian services are with jihadists affiliated with al Qaeda, but the cooperation is definitely selective and tactical. In the early 1990s, Mughniyah and Hezbollah reportedly helped teach al Qaeda operatives how to make vehicle-borne improvised explosives devices in Sudan. After 9/11, Iran distanced itself from al Qaeda, going so far as to return al Qaeda suspects in Iran to their home countries. But in some cases the liaison between Iran and al Qaeda may be even stronger than before, in order to influence events in Iraq and Afghanistan.

The MOIS has relationships with many other non-Shiite groups around the world, particularly in the Palestinian territories. While the Iranian revolution was purely indigenous, it did receive some outside support, particularly from secular Fatah. Iran also has had long-term and close relationships with the more militant PIJ and Hamas, and its relationship with the latter has grown closer as Hamas leaders debate what country to choose as an ally. Iranian support played an important role in the most recent conflict in Gaza, when Israel attempted to eliminate Hamas. The relationships began in December 1992 when Israel expelled Hamas and PIJ operatives to Lebanon, where the MOIS developed contacts with them through Hezbollah. (These Sunni groups would go on to develop suicide terror tactics that until then had been used only by Shiite militants.) As Iranian largesse increased, Hamas transitioned from using homemade Qassam rockets in their attacks against Israel to using manufactured rockets supplied by Iran that have a much longer range.

Iran has expanded its links to groups as far away as Algeria and, in the other direction, to the Taliban in Afghanistan. These groups are ideologically different from Iran, but they all employ similar tactics and have the same broad goals in fighting non-Islamic influences in their respective countries. The MOIS is very good at covering up or obfuscating information on these links, so little is known but much is suspected.

The MOIS develops and organizes these contacts in many different ways. One common method is the use of embassy cover to meet and plan operations with its unofficial associates. For example, many of the Iranian-sponsored operations in Lebanon conducted by Hezbollah and associated groups are planned in the Iranian Embassy in Damascus, Syria. The MOIS also works with the IRGC in the operation of training camps for visiting jihadists and proxy groups along the Iranian border and in secure areas abroad like Lebanon's Bekaa Valley.

Iran's current minister of intelligence and MOIS head is Heidar Moslehi, a former IRGC officer who was appointed by President Mahmoud Ahmadinejad after the June 2009 election and protests. Moslehi's background working with the IRGC and Basij paramilitary forces, and being a close ally of Ahmadinejad's, furthers the IRGC's current advantage over the intelligence bureaucracy. With the support of Khamenei, the IRGC was able to accuse the MOIS of not fulfilling its domestic responsibilities and letting the election protests get out of hand.

Islamic Revolutionary Guard Corps

The full name of the IRGC is Sepah-e Pasdaran-e Enghelab-e Islami, literally "the Army of the Guardians of the Islamic Revolution." According to STRATFOR sources, its intelligence office is at least as powerful as the MOIS, if not more so. The IRGC was founded in May 1979 by decree of Ayatollah Khomeini as the ideological guard for the new regime and remains the main enforcer of velayat-e-faqih. Article 150 of Iran's Constitution gives the IRGC both the vague and expansive role of "guarding the Revolution and its achievements." To enforce its commitment to the cause, the supreme leader has placed political guides at every level of the organization.

The IRGC is as much a military force as an intelligence and security service, with an air force, navy and army. It is also a social, political and business organization that permeates Iranian society, producing a large number of political and business leaders and involved in many aspects of Iran's economy. The IRGC's intelligence office seems more active internally while its key operational group abroad is the Quds Force — possibly the most effective subversive-action group since the KGB's First Chief Directorate and its predecessor organizations, which were very adept in implementing what they referred to as "active measures." In its unique position as an elite military organization with major intelligence capabilities, the IRGC has essentially supplanted the Artesh as the military backbone of the state. Other countries, especially in the Middle East, have multiple military and security forces, but none with the expansive influence and control of the IRGC.

From the beginning of the revolution until the MOIS was completely established in 1984, the IRGC was Iran's most active domestic and foreign intelligence organization. After dismantling SAVAK, the IRGC worked with former SAVAK intelligence officers to disrupt and destroy many domestic dissident groups, including Forghan, the Mujahideen-e-Khalq and the Communist Tudeh Party. While the internal intelligence role was transferred to the MOIS in 1984, the IRGC remained a "shadow" intelligence organization, with its security division, Sazman-e Harassat, functioning more like a domestic intelligence unit, monitoring and arresting dissidents and separatists and putting them in IRGC-controlled prisons.

The IRGC's intelligence office, the Ettelaat-e-Pasdaran, had a staff of 2,000 in 2006 (though this number has very likely increased). It is difficult to separate its activities from the rest of the IRGC, but the office is known to be responsible for the security of Iran's nuclear program, which means that it monitors all scientists, manages the security force at nuclear installations, guards against sabotage and conducts counterintelligence to prevent the recruitment of Iran's nuclear scientists by other countries. Other activities of the intelligence office are unclear, but they likely include the coordination of intelligence gathered by the Basij for domestic security and overseas operations of the Quds Force. The 2009 post-election reshuffling also brought in Hassan Taeb, former head of the Basij and a conservative cleric who was instrumental in suppressing the 2009 protests, to lead the intelligence office and gave the office more power in Iran's intelligence community.

The IRGC intelligence office and the MOIS are, in fact, parallel intelligence and security organizations, and regime critics claim that the former currently includes the most conservative and violent elements of the latter. This may be an exaggeration, but it is clear that the members and missions of the two organizations do flow back and forth. When reformist President Mohammed Khatami appointed Hojjateleslam Ali Younessi minister of intelligence in 1997, conservative clerics were unhappy with the government's increased tolerance of political dissent reflected in a purge of the MOIS. The supreme leader then gave the IRGC control of the former MOIS intelligence officers and networks, which enabled operations like the assassination campaign in the 1980s and 1990s mentioned above. The momentum temporarily shifted back to MOIS when Ahmadinejad became president and appointed, as minister of intelligence, Gholam Hossein Mohseni-Ejei, who began to establish his bona fides by cracking down on internal dissent. He was later fired by Ahmadinejad in the intra-elite struggle sparked by the controversial 2009 presidential elections.

While Iran's two main intelligence organizations may oppose each other bureaucratically, in the end they both share the same goal: preservation of the clerical regime.

Quds Force

Originally, the IRGC's foreign covert-action and intelligence unit was known informally as Birun Marzi ("Outside the Borders"), or Department 9000. When the group was officially established in 1990, IRGC leaders settled on the name Quds Force (al-Quds is the Arabic name for Jerusalem and is intended to imply that the force will one day liberate the holy city). Such a unit is enabled by Article 154 of the Iranian Constitution, which states: "while scrupulously refraining from all forms of interference in the internal affairs of other nations, it supports the just struggles of the freedom fighters against the oppressors in every corner of the globe."

Since the IRGC took the lead in "exporting the revolution" by developing proxy forces, first in Lebanon in the early 1980s, its Quds Force would take on the responsibility after its formation in 1990. Proxy operations are directed by the Quds General Staff for the Export of the Revolution, a group that includes various directorates responsible for operations in Iraq, the Palestinian territories, Lebanon, Jordan, Turkey, the Indian subcontinent (including Afghanistan), North Africa, the Arabian Peninsula, former Soviet states and Western countries, including the United States, France, Germany and the Netherlands. The Quds Force also has liaison and advisory operations in Bosnia, Chechnya, Somalia and Ethiopia. The major Quds training centers are at Imam Ali University in Iran's holy city of Qom and at the Shahid, Kazemi, Beheshti and Vali-e-Asr garrisons. Foreign Muslim students who volunteer to work as intelligence agents or to become involved in covert activities receive their training at secret camps in western Iran and in Iranian universities. The IRGC/Quds also have established overseas training camps in Lebanon and Sudan.

One main responsibility of the IRGC/Quds is training the Hezbollah Special Security Apparatus, which is the most elite force within Hezbollah, Iran's principal proxy movement. Iranian military attaches in Damascus coordinate with the IRGC/Quds in the Bekaa Valley in its work with Hezbollah and other groups in the area. There also is an IRGC headquarters in the Syrian border village of Zabadani that coordinates operations and transfers funds and weapons.

In recent years, Quds operations have been most prevalent in Iraq and Afghanistan. Quds worked with multiple, often opposing, proxies throughout Iraq to destabilize the regime until an Iran-friendly government could be established, before and especially after the U.S. invasion. Quds operates out of a command center, the Fajr Base, in the city of Ahwaz near the Iraqi border and has an operational base in the Shiite holy city of Najaf in southern Iraq. Quds operatives worked with Abu Musab al-Zarqawi, the late leader of al Qaeda in Iraq, in addition to Iran's traditional Iraqi Shiite proxies like the al-Sadrite movement and its armed wing, the Mahdi Army, and the Badr Brigades, ISCI's military wing. IRGC operations in Iraq were highlighted in January 2007 when U.S. forces raided an Iranian consulate in Arbil and detained, among others, local Quds commander Hassan Abbasi, who was also a major strategic adviser to President Ahmadinejad.

Basij Force

Domestically, the IRGC enforces security mainly through the Basij, which also assists in intelligence-gathering. The Basij was founded in 1980 as the Niruyeh Moghavemat Basij, which literally means "Mobilization Resistance Force." At the beginning of the Iran-Iraq war, Ayatollah Khomeini issued a religious decree that boys older than 12 could serve on the front lines. Many of these youths were brought into the Basij for use in suicidal human-wave attacks and as human mine detectors. As many as 3 million Basij members served during the Iran-Iraq war and tens of thousands died. Of those who survived, many went on to become officers in the IRGC. President Ahmadinejad himself was a Basij member stationed in Kermanshah during the war and later became an IRGC officer.

The Basij formally came under the IRGC command structure in 2007, but the militia has long been affiliated with the guard, and membership in the former can lead to a commission in the latter. The Basij was founded for the same reasons and was based on similar principles as the IRGC — to quickly replace the shah's security forces and protect the regime of the ayatollahs. However, while the IRGC is considered (among other things) an elite military force of well-trained personnel, the Basij is more of an amateur paramilitary force whose members are largely untrained civilian volunteers which constitute a variety of units, ranging from neighborhood watch groups to a kind of national guard. In a speech in 2006, Basij commander Hussein Hamadani spoke proudly of the militia's vast informant pool, which is called the "36 million information network." The number was picked because it is half the population of Iran. While such an overwhelming number of informants is unlikely, the Basij serves as a pervasive internal vigilante force.

The Basij is organized almost as the Communist Party is in some authoritarian states, existing at many levels throughout civil society. Each Iranian city of a certain size is divided into "areas" and "zones," while smaller towns and villages have "cells." Units are organized at social, religious and government institutions, such as mosques and municipal offices. There are Basij units for students, workers and tribe members. The Basij has developed the Ashura Brigades for males and the al-Zahra Brigades for females. Basij members also are organized by their level of involvement and consist of "regular," "active" and "special" members. Special members are those who have been on the IRGC's payroll since 1991, 16 years before the Basij came under IRGC authority. Basij members are recruited through local mosques by informal selection committees of local leaders, though mosque leaders are the most influential committee members.

GlobalSecurity estimated the size of the militia in 2005 to be 90,000 active members and 300,000 reserve members, with a "potential strength" of 1 million or more, which would represent the lower-level volunteers. With such a large membership, the Basij claims to have been instrumental in preventing several coups and other threats to the Islamic republic. It is said to have stopped a Kurdish uprising in Paveh in July 1979 and to have infiltrated what is known as the Nojeh coup, organized by military and intelligence officers under the leadership of former Prime Minister Shapour Bakhtiar, in July 1980. In January 1982, the Union of Iranian Communists, a Maoist political and militant group, initiated an uprising near Amol that the Basij also claims to have suppressed.

All three of these incidents were considered substantial threats to a young regime without institutionalized security forces, and the Basij's success firmly established its role as the regime's de facto internal police force. The official Iranian police (Law Enforcement Forces, or LEF) have a mixed record, and during the Ashura protests in

December 2009, Ayatollah Khamenei considered the regular intelligence and security services unable to cope with the situation and thought the Basij was better suited to the task because of the revolutionary fervor of its members, who are usually hardcore Islamists recruited from mosques. Iran's conventional military forces are garrisoned away from population centers (which is not uncommon in the Middle East, where governments tend to maintain a second force to help prevent military coups). Other Iranian vigilante groups such as Ansar-e Hezbollah are more violent and less organized than the Basij and too undisciplined to effectively enforce security. And while the IRGC is being used more for internal security, it is a much smaller force, numbering less than 200,000. Hence, the IRGC must employ its sprawling Basij as the main force on which the regime relies for internal security, though the government also has been responding to the risk of this reliance.

Unlike the country's parallel intelligence apparatus, the Basij had become the last as well as main line of defense against internal unrest. In 2007, not confident that another organization could provide back up to the Basij, the regime refocused the IRGC inward, in part by merging the Basij into the IRGC command structure. The new IRGC commander, Maj. Gen. Mohammad Ali Jaafari, said at the time, "The main strategy of the IRGC [is different] now. Confrontation with internal threats is the main mission of the IRGC at present." The shift came about after Tehran saw a growing internal threat that it claimed was fueled by foreign governments. The 2007 shift and the more recent suppression of protests exemplify the intentional opacity and flexibility of the IRGC and its various components. The regime can use the force for any use it wants. As Maj. Gen. Jafari said in 2007, "We should adapt our structure to the surrounding conditions or existing threats in a bid to enter the scene promptly and with sufficient flexibility." Essentially, the IRGC, with its Basij and vast sea of informants, has become Iran's "911" security force capable of gathering intelligence and responding to any incident at any time to keep the Islamic regime in power.

Military Intelligence

Like all conventional military forces, Iran's regular armed forces (the Artesh) have their own joint military intelligence capability in the form of the J2 unit. This unit handles traditional tactical intelligence and is composed of officers and personnel from all branches of the armed forces, including the IRGC and some law enforcement entities. The organization also is responsible for all planning, intelligence and counterintelligence operations, security within the armed forces and coordinating the intelligence functions of all the regular services, combat units of the IRGC and police units that are assigned military duties.

Ministry of Interior and Law Enforcement Forces

The Ministry of Interior oversees Iran's police forces, but it has been all but pushed out of general security and intelligence functions even more so than the MOIS. The country's official LEF was established in 1991 when the country's urban police, rural gendarmerie and revolutionary committees were merged. According to Iranian law, the LEF, reportedly numbering some 40,000 personnel, remains officially responsible for internal and border security, but over time it has come to focus on day-to-day police work and serve as the first line of defense while the Basij has the ultimate responsibility for quelling civil unrest.

Oversight and Control

The government of Iran already has a convoluted organizational chart, and the structure of its intelligence services is even more complex. Understanding the internal workings of intelligence gathering, dissemination, command and control in the Islamic republic is most challenging, given their extreme secrecy, structural complexities, unclear legal mandate and shifting responsibilities.

In the end, the supreme leader, currently Ayatollah Khamenei, is both customer and commander of Iran's intelligence services.

Following the 2009 elections and the attendant unrest, the supreme leader expanded a special unit within his office to handle intelligence matters as part of his effort to keep a lid on unrest and better manage the bureaucratic competition between the MOIS and IRGC. Mohammad Mohammadi-Golpayegani, essentially Khamenei's chief of staff, manages the supreme leader's office, which was officially established as the "House of the Leader" by Ayatollah Khomeini, the Islamic republic's first supreme leader. Golpayegani was one of the founders of the MOIS and previously served as a deputy minister of intelligence. The new intelligence section within Khamenei's office, the Supreme Leader's Intelligence Unit (also known as "Section 101," according to STRATFOR sources), was established to manage the conflict between the country's two main intelligence services by clarifying their responsibilities, directing foreign intelligence gathering through the MOIS and covert action through the IRGC. These assignments fit more with the original responsibilities of the organizations as well as their cultures and specialties, though duplication still exists and serves an important purpose in keeping intelligence groups competitive.

Section 101 is reportedly headed by Asghar Mir Hejazi, another Khamenei loyalist who previously served in the MOIS. It is notable that two senior staffers in the House of the Leader have an MOIS rather than an IRGC background, since it is generally thought that the IRGC possesses the momentum in the rivalry. Regardless of where these people come from, as Khamenei appoints loyalists within his own office to control the intelligence flow, the intelligence officers closest to him are less likely to "speak truth to power." The reorganization is intended to create a more centralized intelligence apparatus in Iran, but it could also risk the kind of intelligence failures that contributed to the downfall of the shah. That is not to say the Islamic republic is at risk — indeed, its intelligence efforts have been quite successful at controlling dissent — only that that directing national intelligence functions from the House of the Leader can create a myopic view of reality. This will be an issue to watch as the country's intelligence capabilities continue to evolve.

The balance between the MOIS and the IRGC on any given day depends on how the ruling clerics feel about internal threats and the external powers supporting them. (Iranian leaders and the state-controlled media insist that the United States is waging a "soft war" on Iran and encouraging domestic revolution.) Recent as well as historic shifts in the intelligence balance can also be explained by the ongoing tension within Iran's intelligence and security apparatus. No one organization is allowed a monopoly over intelligence, so the equilibrium among competing agencies is constantly shifting. Today the IRGC appears to be gaining the advantage, in keeping with its growing involvement in so many aspects of Iranian life in addition to national intelligence. This, too, will be an evolution to watch.

CHAPTER 4: THE IRANIAN NUCLEAR DILEMMA

Decoupling the Nuclear and Iraq Issues
June 29, 2007

The United States and its Western allies are considering a British proposal that would commit the U.N. Security Council to holding off on new sanctions against Iran provided Tehran halts further development of its uranium enrichment program, The Associated Press reported June 29. Quoting unnamed diplomats, the wire service said that, while the United States is still publicly insisting on full suspension of enrichment, the proposal entails a potential compromise calling for accepting Iran's relatively advanced enrichment program — at least initially.

The idea is to resume multilateral negotiations with the ultimate aim of containing Iranian nuclear ambitions. The draft proposal is being circulated among the five permanent members of the U.N. Security Council and Germany. A diplomat was quoted as saying the Security Council is prepared to freeze work on new sanctions if Tehran agrees to maintain the status quo on enrichment and to resume negotiations, though the ultimate goal remains long-term suspension of the Iranian nuclear program. If Iran were to follow through on its promise to share sensitive information about its program with the International Atomic Energy Agency (IAEA), a compromise could emerge under which the Iranians could be allowed to retain some elements of their enrichment program.

The United States knows it cannot proceed with negotiations with Iran regarding the stabilization of Iraq while simultaneously imposing additional sanctions on Tehran because of Iranian defiance toward international calls to suspend enrichment. Such sanctions could have significant negative repercussions for U.S. efforts to reach an accommodation on Iraq with the Islamic republic — thus hampering U.S. efforts to bring stability and security to Iraq. But not maintaining the pressure on Iran regarding the nuclear issue is not an option.

Therefore, the way out is to seek a compromise allowing Washington to defer serious action on the nuclear issue, thus allowing the Iraq talks to continue unimpeded. In essence, Washington would be putting the nuclear issue on hold while the more pressing matter of Iraq is sorted out.

It remains unclear whether this particular proposal will see the light of the day, since the five permanent members of the U.N. Security Council and Germany are still deliberating on the measure. It appears Iran might be ready for such a compromise, since it too wants to remain firm on the nuclear issue but also needs to secure its interests in Iraq.

Iranian national security chief Ali Larijani recently held meetings with IAEA head Mohamed ElBaradei and EU foreign policy chief Javier Solana on the nuclear issue, and released statements to the effect that Tehran is ready for a compromise and is prepared to divulge critical information to the U.N. nuclear watchdog about the Iranian nuclear program. It is therefore likely Tehran's leadership has signed off on the matter.

Meanwhile, Washington and London are taking the lead in developing a new draft of harsher sanctions against Iran. The drafts currently circulating among the U.S. Congress and British Parliament aim to strangle Iran financially by freezing the assets of more Islamic Revolutionary Guard Corps commanders and other Iranian officials, cutting off arms exports to Iran and going after the clerical regime's Achilles' heel — its energy sector — by encouraging foreign governments to ban companies from investing in the Iranian energy sector and by cutting gasoline exports to Iran.

But the United States cannot afford to have the Iranian government collapse when Washington needs Tehran to press ahead with stabilizing Iraq. Therefore, the proposed sanctions could be aimed not at weakening the Iranian regime but at building leverage with which to counter Iranian moves by limiting Tehran's wiggle room and forcing it toward compromise.

Regardless of its actual shape, a compromise probably will be reached that allows both sides to get over the hurdle of the next U.N. Security Council resolution on the Iranian nuclear program and press ahead to the more immediate question of Iraq.

Misreading the Iranian Situation
September 15, 2009

The Iranians have now agreed to talks with the P-5+1, the five permanent members of the U.N. Security Council (the United States, the United Kingdom, France, Russia and China) plus Germany. These six countries decided in late April to enter into negotiations with Iran over the suspected Iranian nuclear weapons program by Sept. 24, the date of the next U.N. General Assembly meeting. If Iran refused to engage in negotiations by that date, the Western powers in the P-5+1 made clear that they would seriously consider imposing much tougher sanctions on Iran than those that were currently in place. The term "crippling" was mentioned several times.

Obviously, negotiations are not to begin prior to the U.N. General Assembly meeting as previously had been stipulated. The talks are now expected to begin Oct. 1, a week later. This gives the Iranians their first (symbolic) victory: They have defied the P-5+1 on the demand that talks be under way by the time the General Assembly meets. Inevitably, the Iranians would delay, and the P-5+1 would not make a big deal of it.

Talks About Talks and the Sanctions Challenge

Now, we get down to the heart of the matter: The Iranians have officially indicated that they are prepared to discuss a range of strategic and economic issues but are not prepared to discuss the nuclear program — which, of course, is the reason for the talks in the first place. On Sept. 14, they hinted that they might consider talking about the nuclear program if progress were made on other issues, but made no guarantees.

So far, the Iranians are playing their traditional hand. They are making the question of whether there would be talks about nuclear weapons the center of diplomacy. Where the West wanted a commitment to end uranium enrichment, the Iranians are trying to shift the discussions to whether they will talk at all. After spending many rounds of discussions on this subject, they expect everyone to go away exhausted. If pressure is coming down on them, they will agree to discussions, acting as if the mere act of talking represents a massive concession. The members of the P-5+1 that don't want a confrontation with Iran will use Tehran's agreement merely to talk (absent any guarantees of an outcome) to get themselves off the hook on which they found themselves back in April — namely, of having to impose sanctions if the Iranians don't change their position on their nuclear program.

Russia, one of the main members of the P-5+1, already has made clear it opposes sanctions under any circumstances. The Russians have no intention of helping solve the American problem with Iran while the United States maintains its stance on NATO expansion and bilateral relations with Ukraine and Georgia. Russia regards the latter two countries as falling within the Russian sphere of influence, a place where the United States has no business meddling.

To this end, Russia is pleased to do anything that keeps the United States bogged down in the Middle East, since this prevents

Washington from deploying forces in Poland, the Czech Republic, the Baltics, Georgia or Ukraine. A conflict with Iran not only would bog down the United States even further, it would divide Europe and drive the former Soviet Union and Central Europe into viewing Russia as a source of aid and stability. The Russians thus see Iran as a major thorn in Washington's side. Obtaining Moscow's cooperation on removing the thorn would require major U.S. concessions — beyond merely bringing a plastic "reset" button to Moscow. At this point, the Russians have no intention of helping remove the thorn. They like it right where it is.

In discussing crippling sanctions, the sole obvious move would be blocking gasoline exports to Iran. Iran must import 40 percent of its gasoline needs. The United States and others have discussed a plan for preventing major energy companies, shippers and insurers from supplying that gasoline. The subject, of course, becomes moot if Russia (and China) refuses to participate or blocks sanctions. Moscow and Beijing can deliver all the gasoline Tehran wants. The Russians could even deliver gasoline by rail in the event that Iranian ports are blocked. Therefore, if the Russians aren't participating, the impact of gasoline sanctions is severely diminished, something the Iranians know well.

Tehran and Moscow therefore are of the opinion that this round of threats will end where other rounds ended. The United States, the United Kingdom and France will be on one side; Russia and China will be on the other; and Germany will vacillate, not wanting to be caught on the wrong side of the Russians. In either case, whatever sanctions are announced would lose their punch, and life would go on as before.

There is, however, a dimension that indicates that this crisis might take a different course.

The Israeli Dimension

After the last round of meetings between Israeli Prime Minister Benjamin Netanyahu and U.S. President Barack Obama, the Israelis announced that the United States had agreed that in the event of a failure in negotiations, the United States would demand — and get — crippling sanctions against Iran, code for a gasoline cutoff. In return, the Israelis indicated that any plans for a unilateral Israeli strike on Iran's nuclear facilities would be put off. The Israelis specifically said that the Americans had agreed on the September U.N. talks as the hard deadline for a decision on — and implementation of — sanctions.

Our view always has been that the Iranians are far from acquiring nuclear weapons. This is, we believe, the Israeli point of view. But the Israeli point of view also is that, however distant, the Iranian acquisition of nuclear weapons represents a mortal danger to Israel — and that, therefore, Israel would have to use military force if diplomacy and sanctions don't work.

For Israel, the Obama guarantee on sanctions represented the best chance at a nonmilitary settlement. If it fails, it is not clear what could possibly work. Given that Supreme Leader Ayatollah Ali Khamenei has gotten his regime back in line, that Iranian President Mahmoud Ahmadinejad apparently has emerged from the recent Iranian election crisis with expanded clout over Iran's foreign policy, and that the Iranian nuclear program appears to be popular among Iranian nationalists (of whom there are many), there seems no internal impediment to the program. And given the current state of U.S.-Russian relations and that Washington is unlikely to yield Moscow hegemony in the former Soviet Union in return for help on Iran, a crippling sanctions regime is unlikely.

Obama's assurances notwithstanding, there accordingly is no evidence of any force or process that would cause the Iranians to change their minds about their nuclear program. With that, the advantage to Israel of delaying a military strike evaporates.

And the question of the quality of intelligence must always be taken into account: The Iranians may be closer to a weapon than is believed. The value of risking delays disappears if nothing is likely to happen in the intervening period that would make a strike unnecessary.

Moreover, the Israelis have Obama in a box. Obama promised them that if Israel did not take a military route, he would deliver them crippling sanctions against Iran. Why Obama made this promise — and he has never denied the Israeli claim that he did — is not fully clear. It did buy him some time, and perhaps he felt he could manage the Russians better than he has. Whatever Obama's motivations, having failed to deliver, the Israelis can say that they have cooperated with the United States fully, so now they are free by the terms of their understanding with Washington to carry out strikes — something that would necessarily involve the United States.

The calm assumptions in major capitals that this is merely another round in interminable talks with Iran on its weapons revolves around the belief that the Israelis are locked into place by the Americans. From where we sit, the Israelis have more room to maneuver now than they had in the past, or than they might have in the future. If that's true, then the current crisis is more dangerous than it appears.

Netanyahu appears to have made a secret trip to Moscow (though it didn't stay secret very long) to meet with the Russian leadership. Based on our own intelligence and this analysis, it is reasonable to assume that Netanyahu was trying to drive home to the Russians the seriousness of the situation and Israel's intent. Russian-Israeli relations have deteriorated on a number of issues, particularly over Israeli military and intelligence aid to Ukraine and Georgia. Undoubtedly, the Russians demanded that Israel abandon this aid.

As mentioned, the chances of the Russians imposing effective sanctions on Iran are nil. This would get them nothing. And if not cooperating on sanctions triggers an Israeli airstrike, so much the better. This would degrade and potentially even effectively eliminate Iran's nuclear capability, which in the final analysis is not in Russia's interest. It would further enrage the Islamic world at Israel. It would put the United States in the even more difficult position of having to support Israel in the face of this hostility. And from the Russian point of view, it would all come for free. (That said, in such a scenario the Russians would lose much of the leverage the Iran card offers Moscow in negotiations with the United States.)

Ramifications of an Israeli Strike

An Israeli airstrike would involve the United States in two ways. First, it would have to pass through Iraqi airspace controlled by the United States, at which point no one would believe that the Americans weren't complicit. Second, the likely Iranian response to an Israeli airstrike would be to mine the Strait of Hormuz and other key points in the Persian Gulf — something the Iranians have said they would do, and something they have the ability to do.

Some have pointed out that the Iranians would be hurting themselves as much as the West, as this would cripple their energy exports. And it must be remembered that 40 percent of globally traded oil exports pass through Hormuz. The effect of mining the Persian Gulf would be devastating to oil prices and to the global economy at a time when the global economy doesn't need more grief. But the economic pain Iran would experience from such a move could prove tolerable relative to the pain that would be experienced by the world's major energy importers. Meanwhile, the Russians would be free to export oil at extraordinarily high prices.

Given the foregoing, the United States would immediately get involved in such a conflict by engaging the Iranian navy, which in this case would consist of small boats with outboard motors dumping mines overboard. Such a conflict would be asymmetric warfare, naval style. Indeed, given that the Iranians would rapidly respond — and that the best way to stop them would be to destroy their vessels no matter how small before they have deployed — the only rational military process would be to strike Iranian boats and ships prior to an Israeli airstrike. Since Israel doesn't have the ability to do that, the United States would be involved in any such conflict from the beginning. Given that, the United States might as well do the attacking. This would increase the probability of success dramatically, and paradoxically would dampen the regional reaction compared to a unilateral Israeli strike.

When we speak to people in Tehran, Washington and Moscow, we get the sense that they are unaware that the current situation might spin out of control. In Moscow, the scenario is dismissed because the general view is that Obama is weak and inexperienced and is frightened of military confrontation; the assumption is that he will find a way to bring the Israelis under control.

It isn't clear that Obama can do that, however. The Israelis don't trust him, and Iran is a core issue for them. The more Obama presses them on settlements the more they are convinced that Washington no longer cares about Israeli interests. And that means they are on their own, but free to act.

It should also be remembered that Obama reads intelligence reports from Moscow, Tehran and Berlin. He knows the consensus about him among foreign leaders, who don't hold him in high regard. That consensus causes foreign leaders to take risks; it also causes Obama to have an interest in demonstrating that they have misread him.

We are reminded of the 1962 Cuban Missile Crisis only in this sense: We get the sense that everyone is misreading everyone else. In the run-up to the Cuban Missile Crisis, the Americans didn't believe the Soviets would take the risks they did and the Soviets didn't believe the Americans would react as they did. In this case, the Iranians believe the United States will play its old game and control the Israelis. Washington doesn't really understand that Netanyahu may see this as the decisive moment. And the Russians believe Netanyahu will be controlled by an Obama afraid of an even broader conflict than he already has on his hands.

The current situation is not as dangerous as the Cuban Missile Crisis was, but it has this in common: Everyone thinks we are on a known roadmap, when in reality, one of the players — Israel — has the ability and interest to redraw the roadmap. Netanyahu has been signaling in many ways that he intends to do just this. Everyone seems to believe he won't. We aren't so sure.

The Complications of Military Action Against Iran
September 28, 2009

U.S. Secretary of Defense Robert Gates insisted, in an interview broadcast by CNN on Sunday, that on the issue of Iran, "The reality is, there is no military option that does anything more than buy time." This statement encompasses a number of complications with the American military option against Iran.

The first is that Washington is attempting to balance the political positions of multiple countries. The White House is looking to ratchet up pressure on Tehran ahead of negotiations over its nuclear program, and to convince Iran that the United States is serious when it talks about considering the military option. But Washington is also moving to constrain Israel. Though the Jewish state is also looking to ratchet up pressure against Iran ahead of the negotiations, Israel's threshold for an attempt to strike at Iran's nuclear program is considerably lower than Washington's. Though it would be far less effective than a strike coordinated with or even conducted unilaterally by the United States, a unilateral Israeli strike against Iran quickly could implicate Washington in the conflict — especially if Tehran began targeting commercial maritime traffic in the Strait of Hormuz.

Thus, the United States is trying to hold the middle ground. There is a considerable divergence between U.S. President Barack Obama and Israeli Prime Minister Benjamin Netanyahu's positions, domestic political incentives and sense of urgency. Washington must convince Tehran that the final line has already been crossed (hence the warnings sparked by Iran's recent disclosure of a second enrichment facility near Qom) and that if Iran does not seriously negotiate now and make considerable concessions, air strikes are imminent. But it also must convince Israel to allow time for negotiations — and sanctions that appear increasingly likely — to work, even if such a prospect is limited in and of itself.

But aside from this delicate navigation of the middle ground, Gates also has a more objective point: Military efforts against Iran present profound difficulties. They begin with the costs of an Iranian reprisal following these strikes. Not only is there the threat of Tehran attempting to close the Strait of Hormuz (Iran's real "nuclear" option), but even a failed attempt to close the strait could short-circuit the economic recovery that now appears to be under way. Even before the current economic crisis emerged, the potential consequences for global oil prices due to an American strike on Iran were a real concern. Right now, this aspect of Iran's deterrent is perhaps at the height of its credibility.

In addition, Iran has proxies and influence from Beirut to Kabul. Whatever damage might be achieved in an air strike, Tehran still would be able to ignite or intensify conflicts across the Islamic world — and perhaps even carry out terrorist strikes beyond it. In addition to concerns about Israel, where Tehran's influence with Hezbollah and Hamas could create flare-ups, the U.S. position in both Iraq and Afghanistan could be considerably eroded. In short, even though the military imperative is to strike first once hostilities appear to be inevitable — so as to attempt to preempt any Iranian action in the Gulf and Strait of Hormuz — if there is a compelling way for Washington to avoid an air campaign against Tehran, the United States has considerable incentive to continue to hesitate.

The bottom line is that there is considerable uncertainty even with a full-scale U.S. air campaign. Though Iran's nuclear campaign inevitably will be degraded, the U.S. intelligence picture of Iran's program is at best incomplete; the facility at Qom is a case in point. Indeed, Tehran has done everything it can to create a very serious intelligence problem for Israel and the United States. With only limited situational awareness and understanding of Iran's undeclared nuclear efforts, any bombing campaign inevitably would miss some elements of the program. Though those elements might be insignificant (as they were with 1998's Operation Desert Fox against Iraq, which some now think effectively marked the end of Baghdad's nuclear, biological and chemical weapons programs), Washington cannot put much confidence in that prospect, since its intelligence capabilities in Iran now are more limited than those it had in Iraq in the late 1990s.

In addition, air strikes would only harden Iran's interest in establishing a nuclear deterrent, and likely would be used by the current regime to consolidate domestic support — which is currently divided (though not as divided as some Western governments might like to believe). So while the United States is absolutely capable of striking at Iran militarily and doing considerable damage to Iran's nuclear program, a military strike is not an option that the White House can or will pursue lightly.

Two Leaks and the Deepening Iran Crisis
October 5, 2009

Two major leaks occurred this weekend over the Iran matter.

In the first, The New York Times published an article reporting that staff at the International Atomic Energy Agency (IAEA), the U.N. nuclear oversight group, had produced an unreleased report saying that Iran was much more advanced in its nuclear program than the IAEA had thought previously. According to the report, Iran now has all the data needed to design a nuclear weapon. The New York Times article added that U.S. intelligence was re-examining the National Intelligence Estimate (NIE) of 2007, which had stated that Iran was not actively pursuing a nuclear weapon.

The second leak occurred in the British paper The Sunday Times, which reported that the purpose of Israeli Prime Minister Benjamin Netanyahu's highly publicized secret visit to Moscow on Sept. 7 was to provide the Russians with a list of Russian scientists and engineers working on Iran's nuclear weapons program.

The second revelation was directly tied to the first. There were many, including STRATFOR, who felt that Iran did not have the non-nuclear disciplines needed for rapid progress toward a nuclear device. Putting the two pieces together, the presence of Russian personnel in Iran would mean that the Iranians had obtained the needed expertise from the Russians. It would also mean that the Russians were not merely a factor in whether there would be effective sanctions but also in whether and when the Iranians would obtain a nuclear weapon.

We would guess that the leak to The New York Times came from U.S. government sources, because that seems to be a prime vector of leaks from the Obama administration and because the article contained information on the NIE review. Given that National Security Adviser James Jones tended to dismiss the report on Sunday television, we would guess the report leaked from elsewhere in the administration. The Sunday Times leak could have come from multiple sources, but we have noted a tendency of the Israelis to leak through the British daily on national security issues. (The article contained substantial details on the visit and appeared written from the Israeli point of view.) Neither leak can be taken at face value, of course. But it is clear that these were deliberate leaks — people rarely risk felony charges leaking such highly classified material — and even if they were not coordinated, they delivered the same message, true or not.

The Iranian Time Frame and the Russian Role

The message was twofold. First, previous assumptions on time frames on Iran are no longer valid, and worst-case assumptions must now be assumed. The Iranians are in fact moving rapidly toward a weapon; have been extremely effective at deceiving U.S. intelligence (read, they deceived the Bush administration, but the Obama administration has figured it out); and therefore, we are moving toward a decisive moment with Iran. Second, this situation is the direct responsibility of Russian nuclear expertise. Whether this expertise came from former employees of the Russian nuclear establishment now looking for work, Russian officials assigned to Iran or unemployed scientists sent to Iran by the Russians is immaterial. The Israelis — and the Obama administration — must hold the Russians responsible for the current state of Iran's weapons program, and by extension, Moscow bears responsibility for any actions that Israel or the United States might take to solve the problem.

We would suspect that the leaks were coordinated. From the Israeli point of view, having said publicly that they are prepared to follow the American lead and allow this phase of diplomacy to play out, there clearly had to be more going on than just last week's Geneva talks. From the American point of view, while the Russians have indicated that participating in sanctions on gasoline imports by Iran is not out of the question, Russian President Dmitri Medvedev did not clearly state that Russia would cooperate, nor has anything been heard from Russian Prime Minister Vladimir Putin on the subject. The Russian leadership appears to be playing "good cop, bad cop" on the matter, and the credibility of anything they say on Iran has little weight in Washington.

It would seem to us that the United States and Israel decided to up the ante fairly dramatically in the wake of the Oct. 1 meeting with Iran in Geneva. As IAEA head Mohamed ElBaradei visits Iran, massive new urgency has now been added to the issue. But we must remember that Iran knows whether it has had help from Russian scientists; that is something that can't be bluffed. Given that this specific charge has been made — and as of Monday not challenged by Iran or Russia — indicates to us more is going on than an attempt to bluff the Iranians into concessions. Unless the two leaks together are completely bogus, and we doubt that, the United States and Israel are leaking information already well known to the Iranians. They are telling Tehran that its deception campaign has been penetrated, and by extension are telling it that it faces military action — particularly if massive sanctions are impractical because of more Russian obstruction.

If Netanyahu went to Moscow to deliver this intelligence to the Russians, the only surprise would have been the degree to which the Israelis had penetrated the program, not that the Russians were there. The Russian intelligence services are superbly competent, and keep track of stray nuclear scientists carefully. They would not be surprised by the charge, only by Israel's knowledge of it.

This, of course leaves open an enormous question. Certainly, the Russians appear to have worked with the Iranians on some security issues and have played with the idea of providing the Iranians more substantial military equipment. But deliberately aiding Iran in building a nuclear device seems beyond Russia's interests in two ways. First, while Russia wants to goad the United States, it does not itself really want a nuclear Iran. Second, in goading the United States, the Russians know not to go too far; helping Iran build a nuclear weapon would clearly cross a redline, triggering reactions.

A number of possible explanations present themselves. The leak to The Sunday Times might be wrong. But The Sunday Times is not a careless newspaper: It accepts leaks only from certified sources. The Russian scientists might be private citizens accepting Iranian employment. But while this is possible, Moscow is very careful about what Russian nuclear engineers do with their time. Or the Russians might be providing enough help to goad the United States but not enough to ever complete the job. Whatever the explanation, the leaks paint the Russians as more reckless than they have appeared, assuming the leaks are true.

And whatever their veracity, the leaks — the content of which clearly was discussed in detail among the P-5+1 prior to and during the Geneva meetings, regardless of how long they have been known by Western intelligence — were made for two reasons. The first was to tell the Iranians that the nuclear situation is now about to get out of hand, and that attempting to manage the negotiations through endless delays will fail because the United Nations is aware of just how far Tehran has come with its weapons program. The second was to tell Moscow that the issue is no longer whether the Russians will cooperate on sanctions, but the consequence to Russia's relations with the United States and at least the United Kingdom, France and, most important, possibly Germany. If these leaks are true, they are game changers.

We have focused on the Iranian situation not because it is significant in itself, but because it touches on a great number of other crucial international issues. It is now entangled in the Iraqi, Afghan, Israeli, Palestinian, Syrian and Lebanese issues, all of them high-stakes matters. It is entangled in Russian relations with Europe and the United States. It is entangled in U.S.-European relationships and with relationships within Europe. It touches on the U.S.-Chinese relationship. It even touches on U.S. relations with Venezuela and some other Latin American countries. It is becoming the Gordian knot of international relations.

STRATFOR first focused on the Russian connection with Iran in the wake of the Iranian elections and resulting unrest, when a crowd of Rafsanjani supporters began chanting "Death to Russia," not one of the top-10 chants in Iran. That caused us to focus on the cooperation between Russia and Iranian President Mahmoud Ahmadinejad and Supreme Leader Ayatollah Ali Khamenei on security matters. We were aware of some degree of technical cooperation on military hardware, and of course on Russian involvement in Iran's civilian nuclear program. We were also of the view that the Iranians were unlikely to progress quickly with their nuclear program. We were not aware that Russian scientists were directly involved in Iran's military nuclear project, which is not surprising, given that such involvement would be Iran's single-most important state secret — and Russia's, too.

A Question of Timing

But there is a mystery here as well. To have any impact, the Russian involvement must have been under way for years. The United States has tried to track rogue nuclear scientists and engineers — anyone who could contribute to nuclear proliferation — since the 1990s. The Israelis must have had their own program on this, too. Both countries, as well as European intelligence services, were focused on Iran's program and the whereabouts of Russian scientists. It is hard to believe that they only just now found out. If we were to guess, we would say Russian involvement has been under way since just after the Orange Revolution in Ukraine, when the Russians decided that the United States was a direct threat to its national security.

Therefore, the decision suddenly to confront the Russians, and suddenly to leak U.N. reports — much more valuable than U.S. reports, which are easier for the Europeans to ignore — cannot simply be because the United States and Israel just obtained this information. The IAEA, hostile to the United States since the invasion of Iraq and very much under the influence of the Europeans, must have decided to shift its evaluation of Iran. But far more significant is the willingness of the Israelis first to confront the Russians and then leak about Russian involvement, something that obviously compromises Israeli sources and methods. And that means the Israelis no longer consider the preservation of their intelligence operation in Iran (or wherever it was carried out) as of the essence.

Two conclusions can be drawn. First, the Israelis no longer need to add to their knowledge of Russian involvement; they know what they need to know. And second, the Israelis do not expect Iranian development to continue much longer; otherwise, maintaining the intelligence capability would take precedence over anything else.

It follows from this that the use of this intelligence in diplomatic confrontations with Russians and in a British newspaper serves a greater purpose than the integrity of the source system. And that means that the Israelis expect a resolution in the very near future — the only reason they would have blown their penetration of the Russian-Iranian system.

Possible Outcomes

There are two possible outcomes here. The first is that having revealed the extent of the Iranian program and having revealed the Russian role in a credible British newspaper, the Israelis and the Americans (whose own leak in The New York Times underlined the growing urgency of action) are hoping that the Iranians realize that they are facing war and that the Russians realize that they are facing a massive crisis in their relations with the West. If that happens, then the Russians might pull their scientists and engineers, join in the sanctions and force the Iranians to abandon their program.

The second possibility is that the Russians will continue to play the spoiler on sanctions and will insist that they are not giving support to the Iranians. This leaves the military option, which would mean broad-based action, primarily by the United States, against Iran's nuclear facilities. Any military operation would involve keeping the Strait of Hormuz clear, meaning naval action, and we now know that there are more nuclear facilities than previously discussed. So while the war for the most part would be confined to the air and sea, it would be extensive nonetheless.

Sanctions or war remain the two options, and which one is chosen depends on Moscow's actions. The leaks this weekend have made clear that the United States and Israel have positioned themselves such that not much time remains. We have now moved from a view of Iran as a long-term threat to Iran as a much more immediate threat thanks to the Russians.

The least that can be said about this is that the Obama administration and Israel are trying to reshape the negotiations with the Iranians and Russians. The most that can be said is that the Americans and Israelis are preparing the public for war. Polls now indicate that more than 60 percent of the U.S. public now favors military action against Iran. From a political point of view, it has become easier for U.S. President Barack Obama to act than to not act. This, too, is being transmitted to the Iranians and Russians.

It is not clear to us that the Russians or Iranians are getting the message yet. They have convinced themselves that Obama is unlikely to act because he is weak at home and already has too many issues to juggle. This is a case where a reputation for being conciliatory actually increases the chances for war. But the leaks this weekend have strikingly limited the options and timelines of the United States and Israel. They also have put the spotlight on Obama at a time when he already is struggling with health care and Afghanistan. History is rarely considerate of presidential plans, and in this case, the leaks have started to force Obama's hand.

Iran: Sanctions and Smuggling
July 1, 2010

U.S. President Barack Obama is expected to sign into law a fresh sanctions bill against Iran the evening of July 1, according to White House officials. The legislation aims to strengthen U.N. Security Council sanctions on Iran by applying pressure on companies with investment interests in the United States to curtail their gasoline trade and financial exchanges with Iran. Meanwhile, nearly every statement emanating from Tehran in recent days has consisted of self-congratulatory announcements on how the country has achieved self-sufficiency in various industries in order to insulate the Islamic republic from sanctions.

Though such announcements are designed to reassure the Iranian public that current U.S. and European sanction efforts are futile, there is little hiding the fact that the Iranian economy is far from self-sufficient. While sitting on the world's second-largest natural gas reserves, Iran is the world's fourth-largest producer of crude oil at roughly 3.8 million barrels per day, with oil exports accounting for more than 24 percent of the country's gross domestic product and roughly 75 percent of government revenues. Decades of neglect, mismanagement and lack of foreign investment, however, have left the Iranian energy industry in severe disrepair. As a result, Iran needs to import roughly 30 percent of its gasoline and relies heavily on Western technology, capital and services to stay in business.

Iranian energy — in particular, its gasoline trade — is therefore at the top of the U.S. and European sanctions target list. Without the gasoline imports, technology and capital needed to keep Iran economically afloat, the country theoretically could be pressured enough to make concessions on its nuclear program in the interest of avoiding a social uprising that could unseat the clerical regime.

The key word is "theoretically." Policymakers in Washington and Brussels hope that after years of hollow war threats from the United States and Israel and loop-around negotiations with the Iranians, the so-called crippling sanctions that are finally coming to fruition will force Tehran to bend on its nuclear ambitions. Yet this all assumes that vessels carrying goods destined for Iran will actually be stopped. Unless the United States attempts to enforce a physical blockade of either Iranian fuel imports or crude oil exports — the former appears to be off the table for now, and the latter has yet to be formally discussed — the issue of trade with Iran very quickly falls out of the hands of the policymakers and lawyers and into the hands of organized criminals and shell companies that are looking for a profit and are not afraid of taking risks.

The 1996-2003 U.N. Oil-for-Food plan for Iraq is a perfect case in point. While the United Nations was supposed to monitor all oil sales by Saddam Hussein's regime, along with all goods bought with the oil proceeds, the member states were either unwilling or incapable of policing shipments to Iraq. As a result, a sanction-busting market took root in which even some of the most die-hard proponents of sanctions in the United Nations ended up making fortunes off blockade runs.

Sanctions without a blockade may be ineffective at influencing an adversary to undergo a behavioral change, but they can certainly make life more difficult for the adversary when it comes to conducting everyday business. The Iranian business community has spent years setting up various banking outlets, shell companies and circuitous business arrangements to keep the lines of trade open to the Islamic republic in countries such as Venezuela, Turkey, India, China, Malaysia and Indonesia. If Iran needs specific equipment or technology to refurbish its oil industry, for example, it could theoretically find an interested firm in Ecuador to order parts from a U.S. company. The equipment would then be assembled and sold as a finished product to Venezuela's state-owned PDVSA, which would then resell or lease the equipment to Iran. Monitoring for such activity is exceedingly difficult, and enforcement is nearly impossible in the vast majority of countries where customs officials are incompetent or can be bribed. Though setting up such elaborate smuggling and money-laundering schemes takes a great deal of time and effort and raises the cost of doing business with the target country, there is money to be made in every transaction along the way. And where there is money to be made, the politics of business — not government — take precedence.

The Status of Sanctions

There are three sets of sanctions in play against Iran:

U.N. Security Council Resolution 1929

Status: Passed June 9 with 12 in favor (notably including Russia and China), two against (Turkey and Brazil) and one abstention (Lebanon).

This resolution beefed up the three previous sets of U.N. sanctions against Iran by restricting shipments that would aid Iran's nuclear weapons and ballistic missile programs and by imposing visa bans and asset freezes on the Islamic Revolutionary Guard Corps (IRGC). The resolution lists 41 entities targeted in the sanctions, with the most critical designations being the Islamic Republic of Iran Shipping Lines (IRISL) and the Khatam al Anbiya construction company (Ghorb), which is controlled by the IRGC. The resolution calls on states to enforce compliance and empowers them to seize and destroy illicit Iranian cargo, to which Iran has responded by threatening vessels transiting the Strait of Hormuz. The resolution also contains significant loopholes that allow Russia to continue work on the Bushehr nuclear power plant and keep alive a threat to sell Iran the S-300 strategic air defense system. Though the sanctions resolution on its own is weak on enforcement, it has been effective in exposing the inherent weakness of Iran's relationship with Russia.

Comprehensive Iran Sanctions Accountability and Divestment Act

Status: Passed by the U.S. Senate and House of Representatives and expected to be signed into law by U.S. President Barack Obama on July 1. The precursor to this bill, the Iran Refined Petroleum Sanctions Act, passed the House and Senate in December and January.

The U.S. legislation attempts to exploit Iran's heavy reliance on gasoline imports by subjecting any company involved in the supply of gasoline to Iran, including producers, transportation companies and insurance providers, to sanctions. Two additional changes made in the conference committee are worth noting. One is the elimination of a sentence in the Iran Sanctions Act of 1996 that allowed companies to provide technology, goods and services to the Iranian oil and natural gas sectors without facing sanctions. The second is an additional clause that bars foreign companies that do business with the United States from entering into joint ventures, partnerships and investments with Iranian companies involved in energy projects outside Iran. Iran has been involved in energy joint ventures in countries such as Malaysia, Indonesia, Azerbaijan, the United Kingdom and Croatia in an attempt to gain the necessary technology and experience to develop its own fields and upgrade its refineries. Such sanctions, should the United States choose to impose them, could include denying companies access to the U.S. Export-Import Bank, restricting the ability of these companies to sell to the U.S. market and denying them U.S. government contracts.

EU Declaration on Iran

Status: Pending approval by EU foreign ministers. The EU Council of Ministers has unanimously approved the legislation and has passed the matter over to the Foreign Affairs Council to work out the details under its guidelines. Details of the legislation are expected to be released mid-July, and the Foreign Affairs Council is set to meet July 27. The EU foreign ministers will need to a pass the legislation with a two-thirds majority vote before they break for vacation in August.

The additional EU sanctions attempt to place restrictions on the Iranian financial, energy, shipping and air cargo sectors, something that is no small detail considering that European companies have long served as middlemen and tech providers in exactly the sort of sanctions-busting activities that are so prevalent (regardless of the sanctions target). Specifically, the European resolution calls for bar-ring "new investment, technical assistance and transfers of tech-nologies, equipment and services related to these areas, in particu-lar related to refining, liquefaction and LNG [liquefied natural gas] technology." Since Iran is believed to acquire the bulk of technology for its energy industry from Europe, most notably Germany, the EU sanctions address one of the bigger loopholes in the U.S. sanctions drive. Again, enforcement remains the key issue.

Enforcement and Intimidation

While the sanctions being pursued in the United States and European Union against Iran are the most comprehensive and tar-geted to date, they will probably do little to plug the enforcement hole. Even once the legislation is inked, it is extremely rare for the U.S. administration to actually follow through in sanctioning firms for noncompliance. Where the sanctions achieve greater success is in their ability to intimidate high-profile corporations into publicly withdrawing support for Iran. Many corporations concerned about safeguarding their reputation, avoiding the wrath of the anti-Iran lobbies in the United States and protecting their U.S. assets and investment interests have already announced that they have or will cut trade with Iran:

- Spain's Repsol announced June 28 that it has pulled out of a development contract with Royal Dutch Shell for Iran's South Pars gas field.

- France's Total announced June 28 that it has stopped gasoline sales to Iran.

- Italy's Eni SpA announced April 29 that it pulled out of a proj-ect to develop the Darkhovin oil field in Iran.

- Russia's LUKOIL announced April 7 that it would stop gaso-line sales to Iran.

- Malaysia's Petronas announced April 15 that it would stop gasoline sales to Iran.

- India's Reliance Industries announced April 1 that it would not renew a contract to import crude oil in 2010.

- Switzerland's Trafigura and Vitol stopped gasoline sales to Iran, according to March 8 reports.

- Royal Dutch Shell announced in March that it no longer supplies gasoline to Iran but reportedly resumed shipments in June.

- The United Kingdom's Lloyd's of London announced in February that it would comply with U.S. sanctions legislation against Iran.

- Germany's Munich Re announced in mid-February that it would not renew business or enter new deals with insurance companies in Iran.

- German reinsurer Hannover Re AG announced it would only do business with Iran if the Iranian government complies with EU and U.N. sanctions.

- European insurer Allianz said in February that it would cease its operations in Iran.

- Germany's Siemens announced in January that it would cease business with Iran.

- Swiss firm Glencore stopped supplying gasoline to Iran, according to November 2009 reports.

The list may be impressive at first glance, but underneath these public statements, a black market thrives. Many of the firms that have made the list of complaints are also known to sell refined product to third parties, which is then resold to Iran. In some cases, gasoline trade with Iran may not even be that direct. Gasoline refiners can sell to a host of clients on the spot market, where shell companies could then resell refined product to Iran without the producer's knowledge.

Companies such as Glencore, Vitol and Trafigura are well known in the industry for their sanction-busting expertise, and companies such as Reliance have been seen shipping gasoline to Iran through third parties like Malaysia's Petronas and Kuwait's Independent Petroleum Group. Though some companies like Repsol and Total recognized the warning signs with these sanctions and quickly decided to publicly bow out, others are waiting to see how serious the United States gets with these sanctions.

Announcing a cessation of gasoline shipments to Iran often entails finding more creative avenues to ship to Iran, rather than cutting off trade altogether. The simple fact is that without an expensive enforcement mechanism, such as a naval blockade, these sanctions efforts will likely end up having very little strategic impact on Iranian decision-making when it comes to the nuclear question. At the very least, they allow the U.S. administration and the Europeans to buy time and give the illusion that they are addressing the Iranian nuclear problem beyond the rhetoric while causing some political heartburn in Tehran. In the meantime, the smuggling arena in the energy industry will have undergone a massive expansion.

Attacks on Nuclear Scientists in Tehran
December 1, 2010

On the morning of Nov. 29, two Iranian scientists involved in Iran's nuclear development program were attacked. One was killed, and the other was injured. According to Iranian media, the deceased, Dr. Majid Shahriari, was heading the team responsible for developing the technology to design a nuclear reactor core, and Time magazine referred to him as the highest-ranking non-appointed individual working on the project.

Official reports indicate that Shahriari was killed when assailants on motorcycles attached a "sticky bomb" to his vehicle and detonated it seconds later. However, the Time magazine report says that an explosive device concealed inside the car detonated and killed him. Shahriari's driver and wife, both of whom were in the car at the time, were injured.

Meanwhile, on the opposite side of town, Dr. Fereidoon Abassi was injured in a sticky-bomb attack reportedly identical to the one officials said killed Shahriari. His wife was accompanying him and was also injured (some reports indicate that a driver was also in the car at the time of the attack). Abassi and his wife are said to be in stable condition. Abassi is perhaps even more closely linked to Iran's nuclear program than Shahriari was, since he was a member of the elite Iranian Revolutionary Guard Corps and was named in a 2007 U.N. resolution that sanctioned high-ranking members of Iran's defense and military agencies believed to be trying to obtain nuclear weapons.

Monday's incidents occurred at a time of uncertainty over how global powers and Iran's neighbors will handle an Iran apparently pursuing nuclear weapons despite its claims of developing only a civilian nuclear program and asserting itself as a regional power in the Middle East. Through economic sanctions that went into effect last year, the United States, United Kingdom, France, Russia, China and Germany (known as the "P-5+1") have been pressuring Iran to enter negotiations over its nuclear program and outsource the most sensitive aspects of the program, such as higher levels of uranium enrichment.

The Nov. 29 attacks came about a week before Saeed Jalili, Iran's national security chief, will be leading a delegation to meet with the P-5+1 from Dec. 6 to Dec. 7 in Vienna, the first such meeting in more than a year. The attacks also came within hours of the WikiLeaks release of classified U.S. State Department cables, which are filled with international concerns about Iran's controversial nuclear program.

Because of the international scrutiny and sanctions on just about any hardware required to develop a nuclear program, Iran has focused on developing domestic technologies that can fill the gaps. This has required a national initiative coordinated by the Atomic Energy Organization of Iran (AEOI) to build the country's nuclear program from scratch, an endeavor that requires thousands of experts from various fields of the physical sciences as well as the requisite technologies.

And it was the leader of the AEOI, Ali Akhbar Salehi, who told media Nov. 29 that Shahriari was "in charge of one of the great projects" at the agency. Salehi also issued a warning to Iran's enemies "not to play with fire." Iranian President Mahmoud Ahmadinejad elaborated on the warning, accusing "Zionist" and "Western regimes" of being behind the coordinated attacks against Shahriari and Abassi. The desire of the U.N. Security Council (along with Israel and Germany) to stop Iran's nuclear program and the apparent involvement of the targeted scientists in that program has led many Iranian officials to quickly blame the United States, United Kingdom and Israel for the attacks, since those countries have been the loudest in condemning Iran for its nuclear ambitions.

It seems that certain domestic rivals of the Iranian regime would also benefit from these attacks. Any one of numerous Iranian militant groups throughout the country may have been involved in one way or another, perhaps with the assistance of a foreign power. A look at the tactics used in the attacks could shed some light on the perpetrators.

Modus Operandi

According to official Iranian reports, Abassi was driving to work at Shahid Beheshti University in northern Tehran from his residence in southern Tehran. When the car in which he and his wife were traveling was on Artash Street, assailants on at least two motorcycles approached the vehicle and attached an improvised explosive device (IED) to the driver's side door. The device exploded shortly thereafter, injuring Abassi and his wife.

Images reportedly of Abassi's vehicle show that the driver's side door was destroyed, but the rest of the vehicle and the surrounding surfaces show very little damage. A few pockmarks can be seen on the vehicle behind Abassi's car but little else to indicate that a bomb had gone off in the vicinity. (Earlier reports indicating that this was Shahriari's vehicle proved erroneous.) This indicates that the IED was a shaped charge with a very specific target. Evidence of both the shaped charge and the utilization of projectiles in the device suggests that the device was put together by a competent and experienced bombmaker.

An eyewitness account of the attack offers one explanation why the device did not kill Abassi. According to the man who was driving immediately behind Abassi's car, the car abruptly stopped in traffic, then Abassi got out and went to the passenger side where his wife was sitting. The eyewitness said Abassi and his wife were about 2 meters from the car, on the opposite side when the IED exploded. Abassi appears to have been aware of the attack as it was under way, which apparently saved his life. The eyewitness did not mention whether he saw the motorcyclists attach the device to the car before it went off, but that could have been what tipped Abassi off. If this was the case, the bombmaker may have done his job well in building the device but the assailants gave themselves away when they planted it.

In the fatal attack against Shahriari, he also was on his way to work at Shahid Beheshti University in northern Tehran in his vehicle with his wife, according to official reports. These reports indicate that he definitely had a driver, which would suggest that Shahriari was considered a person of importance. Their car was traveling through a parking lot in northern Tehran when assailants on at least two motorcycles approached the vehicle and attached an IED to the car. Eyewitnesses say that the IED exploded seconds later and that the motorcyclists escaped. Shahriari was presumably killed in the explosion while his wife and driver were injured.

The official account of the attack is contradicted by the Time magazine report, which cites a "Western intelligence source with knowledge of the operation" as saying that the IED that killed Shahriari detonated from inside the vehicle. Images of what appears to be Shahriari's vehicle are much poorer quality than the images of Abassi's vehicle, but they do appear to show damage to the windshield and other car windows. The car is still very much intact, though, and the fact that Shahriari's driver and wife escaped with only injuries suggests that the device used against Shahriari was also a shaped charge, specifically targeting him.

Capabilities

Attacks like the two carried out against Abassi and Shahriari require a high level of tradecraft that is available only to well-trained operatives. There is much more going on below the surface in attacks like these that is not immediately obvious when reading media reports. First, the team of assailants that attacked Abassi and Shahriari had to identify their targets and confirm that the men they were attacking were indeed high-level scientists involved in Iran's nuclear program. The fact that Abassi and Shahriari held such high positions indicates they were specifically selected as targets and not the victims of a lucky, opportunistic attack.

Second, the team had to conduct surveillance of the two scientists. The team had to positively identify their vehicles and determine their schedules and routes in order to know when and how to launch their attacks. Both attacks targeted the scientists as they traveled to work, likely a time when they were most vulnerable, an MO commonly used by assassins worldwide.

Third, someone with sufficient expertise had to build IEDs that would kill their targets. Both devices appear to have been relatively small IEDs that were aimed precisely at the scientists, which may have been an attempt to limit collateral damage (their small size may also have been due to efforts to conceal the device). Both devices seem to have been adequate to kill their intended targets, and judging by the damage to his vehicle, it appears that Abassi would have received mortal wounds had he stayed in the driver's seat.

The deployment stage seems to be where things went wrong for the assailants, at least in the Abassi attack. It is unclear exactly what alerted him, but it appears that he was exercising some level of situational awareness and was able to determine that an attack was under way.

It is not at all surprising that someone like Abassi would have been practicing situational awareness. This is not the first time that scientists linked to Iran's nuclear program have been attacked, and Iranian agencies linked to the nuclear program have probably issued general security guidance to their employees (especially high-ranking ones like Abassi and Shahriari). In 2007, Ardeshir Hassanpour was killed in an alleged poisoning that STRATFOR sources attributed to an Israeli operation. Again, in January 2010, Massoud Ali-Mohammadi, another Iranian scientist who taught at Tehran University, was killed in an IED attack that also targeted him as he was driving to work in the morning. While some suspected that Ali-Mohammadi may have been targeted by the Iranian regime due to his connections with the opposition, Abassi and Shahriari appear much too close to the regime to be targets of their own government (however, nothing can be ruled out in politically volatile Tehran). The similarities between the Ali-Mohammadi assassination and the attacks against Abassi and Shahriari suggest that a covert campaign to attack Iranian scientists could well be under way.

There is little doubt that the Nov. 29 attacks struck a greater blow to the development of Iran's nuclear program than the previous two attacks. Shahriari appears to have had an integral role in the program. While he will likely be replaced and work will go on, his death could slow the program's progress (at least temporarily) and further stoke security fears in Iran's nuclear development community. The attacks come amid WikiLeaks revelations that Saudi King Abdullah and U.S. officials discussed assassinating Iranian leaders, accusations that the United States or Israel was behind the Stuxnet computer worm that allegedly targeted the computer systems running Iran's nuclear program and the return home of Shahram Amiri, an Iranian scientist who alleged that the United States held him against his will earlier in the summer.

The evidence suggests that foreign powers are actively trying to probe and sabotage Iran's nuclear program. However, doing so is not that simple. Tehran is not nearly as open a city as Dubai, where Israeli operatives are suspected of assassinating a high-level Hamas leader in January 2010. It is unlikely that the United States, Israel or any other foreign power could deploy its own team of assassins into Tehran to carry out a lengthy targeting, surveillance and attack operation without some on-the-ground help.

And there is certainly plenty of help on the ground in Iran. Kurdish militants like the Party of Free Life of Kurdistan have conducted numerous assassinations against Iranian clerics and officials in Iran's western province of Kordestan. Sunni separatist militants in the southeast province of Sistan-Balochistan, represented by the group Jundallah, have also targeted Iranian interests in eastern Iran in recent years. Other regional militant opposition groups like Mujahideen-e Khalq, which has offered intelligence on Iran's nuclear program to the United States, and Azeri separatists pose marginal threats to the Iranian regime. However, none of these groups has demonstrated the ability to strike such high-level officials in the heart of Tehran with such a degree of professionalism. While that is unlikely, they have the capability and a history of eliminating dissidents through assassinations. Furthermore, the spuriousness of many contradictory media reports makes the attacks suspicious.

It is unlikely that any foreign power was able to conduct this operation by itself and equally unlikely that any indigenous militant group was able to pull off an attack like this without some assistance. The combination of the two, however, could provide an explanation of how the attacks targeting Shariari and Abassi got so close to complete success.

CHAPTER 5: IRAN AND ITS ALLIES

————————

Red October: Russia, Iran and Iraq
September 17, 2007

The course of the war in Iraq appears to be set for the next year. Of the four options we laid out a few weeks ago, the Bush administration essentially has selected a course between the first and second options — maintaining the current mission and force level or retaining the mission but gradually reducing the force. The mission — creating a stable, pro-American government in Baghdad that can assume the role of ensuring security — remains intact. The strategy is to use the maximum available force to provide security until the Iraqis can assume the burden. The force will be reduced by the 30,000 troops who were surged into Iraq, though because that level of force will be unavailable by spring, the reduction is not really a matter of choice. The remaining force is the maximum available, and it will be reduced as circumstances permit.

Top U.S. commander in Iraq Gen. David Petraeus and others have made two broad arguments. First, while prior strategy indeed failed to make progress, a new strategy that combines aggressive security operations with recruiting political leaders on the subnational level — the Sunni sheikhs in Anbar province, for example — has had a positive impact, and could achieve the mission, given more time.

Therefore, having spent treasure and blood to this point, it would be foolish for the United States not to pursue it for another year or two.

The second argument addresses the consequence of withdrawal. U.S. Secretary of State Condoleezza Rice summed it up in an interview with NBC News. "And I would note that President [Mahmoud] Ahmadinejad said if the United States leaves Iraq, Iran is prepared to fill the vacuum. That is what is at stake here," she said. We had suggested that the best way to contain Iran would be to cede Iraq and defend the Arabian Peninsula. One reason is that it would release troops for operations elsewhere in the world, if needed. The administration has chosen to try to keep Iraq — any part of it — out of Iranian hands. If successful, this obviously benefits the United States. If it fails, the United States can always choose a different option.

Within the region, this seems a reasonable choice, assuming the political foundations in Washington can be maintained, foundations that so far appear to be holding. The Achilles heel of the strategy is the fact that it includes the window of vulnerability that we discussed a few weeks ago. The strategy and mission outlined by Petraeus commits virtually all U.S. ground forces to Iraq, with Afghanistan and South Korea soaking up the rest. It leaves air and naval power available, but it does not allow the United States to deal with any other crisis that involves the significant threat of ground intervention. This has consequences.

Iranian Foreign Minister Manouchehr Mottaki attended a meeting of the Iranian-Russian Joint Economic Commission in Moscow over the weekend. While in the Russian capital, Mottaki also met with Russian Atomic Energy Chief Sergei Kiriyenko to discuss Russian assistance in completing the Bushehr nuclear power plant. After the meeting, Mottaki said Russian officials had assured him of their commitment to complete the power plant. Iran's top nuclear negotiator, Ali Larijani, said, "With regards to the Bushehr power plant, we have reached good understanding with the Russians. In this understanding a timetable for providing nuclear fuel on time and inaugurating this power plant has been fixed." While the truth of Russian assurances is questionable — Moscow has been mere weeks away from making Bushehr operational for the better part of the last three years, and is about as excited about a nuclear-armed Iran as is Washington — the fact remains that Russian-Iranian cooperation continues to be substantial, and public.

Mottaki also confirmed — and this is significant — that Russian President Vladimir Putin would visit Tehran on Oct. 16. The occasion is a meeting of the Caspian Sea littoral nations, a group that comprises Russia, Iran, Azerbaijan, Kazakhstan and Turkmenistan. According to the Iranians, Putin agreed not only to attend the conference, but also to use the visit to confer with top Iranian leaders.

This is about the last thing the United States wanted the Russians to do — and therefore the first thing the Russians did. The Russians are quite pleased with the current situation in Iraq and Iran and do not want anything to upset it. From the Russian point of view, the Americans are tied down in an extended conflict that sucks up resources and strategic bandwidth in Washington. There is a similarity here with Vietnam. The more tied down U.S. forces were in Vietnam, the more opportunities the Soviets had. Nowadays, Russia's resources are much diminished compared with those of the Soviets — while Russia has a much smaller range of interest. Moscow's primary goal is to regain a sphere of influence within the former Soviet Union. Whatever ambitions it may dream of, this is the starting point. The Russians see the Americans as trying to thwart their ambitions throughout their periphery, through support for anti-Russian elements via U.S. intelligence.

If the United States plans to stay in Iraq until the end of the Bush presidency, then the United States badly needs something from the Russians — that they not provide arms, particularly air-defense systems, to the Syrians and especially the Iranians. The Americans need the Russians not to provide fighter aircraft, modern command-and-control systems or any of the other war-making systems that the Russians have been developing. Above all else, they want the Russians not to provide the Iranians any nuclear-linked technology.

Therefore, it is no accident that the Iranians claimed over the weekend that the Russians told them they would do precisely that.

Obviously, the discussion was of a purely civilian nature, but the United States is aware that the Russians have advanced military nuclear technology and that the distinction between civilian and military is subtle. In short, Russia has signaled the Americans that it could very easily trigger their worst nightmare.

The Iranians, fairly isolated in the world, are being warned even by the French that war is a real possibility. Obviously, then, they view the meetings with the Russians as being of enormous value. The Russians have no interest in seeing Iran devastated by the United States. They want Iran to do just what it is doing — tying down U.S. forces in Iraq and providing a strategic quagmire for the Americans. And they are aware that they have technologies that would make an extended air campaign against Iran much more costly than it would be otherwise. Indeed, without a U.S. ground force capable of exploiting an air attack anyway, the Russians might be able to create a situation in which suppression of enemy air defenses (SEAD, the first stage of a U.S. air campaign) would be costly, and in which the second phase — battle against infrastructure — could become a war of attrition. The United States might win, in the sense of ultimately having command of the air, but it could not force a regime change — and it would pay a high price.

It also should not be forgotten that the Russians have the second-largest nuclear arsenal in the world. The Russians very ostentatiously announced a few weeks ago that their Bear bombers were returning to constant patrol. This amused some in the U.S. military, who correctly regard the Bear as obsolete. They forget that the Russians never really had a bomber force designed for massive intercontinental delivery of nuclear devices. The announcement was a gesture — and reminder that Russian ICBMs could easily be pointed at the United States.

Russia obviously doesn't plan a nuclear exchange with the United States, although it likes forcing the Americans to consider the possibility. Nor do the Russians want the Iranians to gain nuclear weapons. What they do want is an extended conflict in Iraq, extended tension between Iran and the United States, and they wouldn't much mind if the United States went to war with Iran as well. The Russians would happily supply the Iranians with whatever weapons systems they could use in order to bleed the United States a bit more, as long as they are reasonably confident that those systems would not be pointed north any time soon.

The Russians are just as prepared to let the United States have a free hand against Iran and not pose any challenges while U.S. forces are tied down in Iraq. But there is a price and it will be high. The Russians are aware that the window of opportunity is now and that they could create nightmarish problems for the United States. Therefore, the Russians will want the following:

- In the Caucasus, they want the United States to withdraw support for Georgia and force the Georgian government to reach an accommodation with Moscow. Given Armenian hostility to Turkey and closeness to Russia, this would allow the Russians to reclaim a sphere of influence in the Caucasus, leaving Azerbaijan as a buffer with Iran.

- In Ukraine and Belarus, the Russians will expect an end to all U.S. support to nongovernmental organizations agitating for a pro-Western course.

- In the Baltics, the Russians will expect the United States to curb anti-Russian sentiment and to explicitly limit the Baltics' role in NATO, excluding the presence of foreign troops, particularly Polish.

- Regarding Serbia, they want an end to any discussion of an independent Kosovo.

- The Russians also will want plans abandoned for an anti-ballistic-missile system that deploys missiles in Poland.

In other words, the Russians will want the United States to get out of the former Soviet Union — and stay out. Alternatively, the Russians are prepared, on Oct. 16, to reach agreements on nuclear exchange and weapons transfers that will include weapons that the Iranians can easily send into Iraq to kill U.S. troops. Should the United States initiate an air campaign prior to any of this taking effect, the Russians will increase the supply of weapons to Iran dramatically, using means it used effectively in Vietnam: shipping them in. If the United States strikes against Russian ships, the Russians will then be free to strike directly against Georgia or the Baltic states, countries that cannot defend themselves without American support, and countries that the United States is in no position to support.

It is increasingly clear that Putin intends to reverse in practice, if not formally, the consequences of the fall of the Soviet Union. He does not expect at this point to move back into Central Europe or engage in a global competition with the United States. He knows that is impossible. But he also understands three things: First, his armed forces have improved dramatically since 2000. Second, the countries he is dealing with are no match for his forces as long as the United States stays out. Third, staying out or not really is not a choice for the United States. As long as it maintains this posture in Iraq, it is out.

This is Putin's moment and he can exploit it in one of two ways: He can reach a quiet accommodation with the Americans, and leave the Iranians hanging. Conversely, he can align with the Iranians and place the United States in a far more complex situation than it otherwise would be in. He could achieve this by supporting Syria, arming militias in Lebanon or even causing significant problems in Afghanistan, where Russia retains a degree of influence in the North.

The Russians are chess players and geopoliticians. In chess and geopolitics, the game is routine and then, suddenly, there is an opening. You seize the opening because you might never get another one. The United States is inherently more powerful than Russia, save at this particular moment. Because of a series of choices the United States has made, it is weaker in the places that matter to Russia. Russia will not be in this position in two or three years. It needs to act now.

Therefore, Putin will go to Iran on Oct. 16 and will work to complete Iran's civilian nuclear project. What agreements he might reach with Iran could given the United States nightmares. If the United States takes out Iran's nuclear weapons, the Russians will sympathize and arm the Iranians even more intensely. If the Americans launch an extended air campaign, the Russians will happily increase the supply of weapons even more. Talk about carpet-bombing Iran is silly. It is a big country and the United States doesn't have that much carpet. The supplies would get through.

Or the United States can quietly give Putin the sphere of influence he wants, letting down allies in the former Soviet Union, in return for which the Russians will let the Iranians stand alone against the Americans, not give arms to Middle Eastern countries, not ship Iran weapons that will wind up with militias in Iraq. In effect, Putin is giving the United States a month to let him know what it has in mind.

It should not be forgotten that Iran retains an option that could upset Russian plans. Iran has no great trust of Russia, nor does it have a desire to be trapped between American power and Russian willingness to hold Iran's coat while it slugs things out with the Americans. At a certain point, sooner rather than later, the Iranians must examine whether they want to play the role of the Russian cape to the American bull. The option for the Iranians remains the same — negotiate the future of Iraq with the Americans. If the United States is committed to remaining in Iraq, Iran can choose to undermine Washington, at the cost of increasing its own dependence on the Russians and the possibility of war with the Americans. Or it can choose to cut a deal with the Americans that gives it influence in Iraq without domination. Iran is delighted with Putin's visit. But that visit also gives it negotiating leverage with the Americans. This remains the wild card.

Petraeus' area of operations is Iraq. He may well have crafted a viable plan for stabilizing Iraq over the next few years. But the price to be paid for that is not in Iraq or even in Iran. It is in leaving the door wide open in other areas of the world. We believe the Russians are about to walk through one of those doors. The question in the White House, therefore, must be: How much is Iraq worth? Is it worth re-creating the geopolitical foundations of the Soviet Union?

Iran: Militant Proxies in the Shadows
April 15, 2008

Iran will be displaying fighter jets, ballistic missiles and marching soldiers April 17 when it commemorates the country's annual Army Day. While Iran is eager to flaunt its military might at a time when Israeli threats in the region are escalating, a key element of Iran's defense system will be lurking in the shadows: the militant proxy network.

Because of the country's widely dispersed population and intermingling of ethnic minorities in its mountainous periphery, Iran's military is designed primarily to maintain domestic control. The country's true offensive capability lies in its use of militant proxies — Shiite groups such as Hezbollah in Lebanon and the former Badr Brigade in Iraq.

With the fall of Saddam Hussein in Iraq, the Iranian government saw the need to step up its militant outsourcing to maintain leverage over Sunni Arab regimes that have long resisted Shiite rule in the region. This leverage involves establishing strong links with Shiite groups as well as select Sunni actors in key Arab states, thereby creating a fifth column to undermine Sunni governments and extend Iranian influence in the Arab world.

While Lebanon and Iraq remain Iran's Shiite militant strongholds, Iran has extended — to varying degrees — its reach to several other Islamic countries with sizable Shiite populations, including Bahrain (75 percent Shiite), Kuwait (30 percent Shiite), Saudi Arabia (15 percent Shiite), Afghanistan (19 percent Shiite) and Qatar (16 percent Shiite). Of course, Iran faces a number of constraints in solidifying connections in many of these heavily policed, predominantly Sunni states that are intent on keeping the Iranians at bay. But recent reports from numerous STRATFOR sources throughout the region suggest that Iran is throwing more effort behind its campaign to alter geopolitical reality on the Arab side of the Persian Gulf by empowering restless Shiite populations.

In Iraq, where Iran needs to consolidate its influence over the country's severely fractured Shiite community, a Hezbollah source said recently that Tehran is bolstering a force known as Kata'eb Hezbollah fil Iraq (Hezbollah Battalions in Iraq), using members of the now weakened Mehdi Army movement of Iraqi Shiite leader Muqtada al-Sadr. The Lebanese Hezbollah has reportedly been in charge of training these fighters. An Iranian source reported separately that the Iraqi Hezbollah would be composed of fighters from across the Shiite landscape (not only from the Mehdi Army) and would include trained militiamen who work regular jobs to disguise their connection to Hezbollah. Iran would rely on these forces to engage in an overt war with U.S. troops in Iraq should tensions between Washington and Tehran come to a head.

In Kuwait, a source reported that the Iranians are developing a Kuwaiti branch of Hezbollah in collaboration with the Lebanese Hezbollah. Several Kuwaiti Shiites reportedly arrived in Lebanon over the past two weeks to undergo military training in the northern Bekaa Valley. Kuwait's Shiite vulnerabilities were exposed most recently in the wake of the February assassination of top Hezbollah commander Imad Mughniyah. Following his death, scores of Kuwaiti Shia took to the streets in mourning — a sight that set off alarm bells within the Kuwaiti government. According to the source, Iran appears to be taking advantage of the weak pan-Arab orientation of Shiites in Kuwait and Bahrain and is working hard to recruit them to its side.

In the Palestinian Territories — where Iran lacks a Shiite community to draw from but has benefited from the anarchy in the area — a source in Fatah reported that Lebanese Hezbollah leader Hajj Ibrahim Aqil has taken on the task of buying off and training Palestinian activists, particularly top commanders in the al-Aqsa Martyrs Brigades, Fatah's militant offshoot. The idea reportedly is to create a Palestinian Hezbollah with fighters trained in camps in Lebanon's Bekaa Valley and in Iran who would rise above the divided Palestinian militant scene and serve as an effective fighting force against Israel. This would give Iran more direct leverage against the Jewish state from within the Palestinian Territories. The source reported that Hezbollah, which is as much a drug cartel as a militant organization, also has increased its smuggling of heroin into Israel, with an aim to provide a local source of much-needed financial assistance to pro-Hezbollah Palestinian militants.

STRATFOR acknowledges that many of these reports from sources could be exaggerated by Hezbollah to inflate Iran's militant capabilities in the Arab world. After all, the Iranians have quite a full plate managing politics in Iraq, negotiating with the United States, safeguarding a nuclear program and trying to stave off another military confrontation involving Hezbollah and Israel in Lebanon. There is a serious question as to how much the Iranians can afford to invest in more remote groups when the return on investment is uncertain.

At the same time, we cannot ignore the information trickling in that suggests — at least on some level — that Iran is putting more energy behind a long-standing campaign to advance its influence in the Arab world through militant proxies. With Sunni Arab regimes already on guard against Iranian expansionist desires, any uptick in Iranian activity on Sunni turf would further pressure Sunnis to ward off a U.S.-Israeli strike against Iran and work toward a modus vivendi with their Shiite rivals in Tehran.

Russia, Ahmadinejad and Iran Reconsidered
July 20, 2009

At Friday prayers July 17 at Tehran University, the influential cleric and former Iranian President Ali Akbar Hashemi Rafsanjani gave his first sermon since Iran's disputed presidential election and the subsequent demonstrations. The crowd listening to Rafsanjani inside the mosque was filled with Ahmadinejad supporters who chanted, among other things, "Death to America" and "Death to China." Outside the university common grounds, anti-Ahmadinejad elements — many of whom were blocked by Basij militiamen and police from entering the mosque — persistently chanted "Death to Russia."

Death to America is an old staple in Iran. Death to China had to do with the demonstrations in Xinjiang and the death of Uighurs at the hands of the Chinese. Death to Russia, however, stood out. Clearly, its use was planned before the protesters took to the streets. The meaning of this must be uncovered. To begin to do that, we must consider the political configuration in Iran at the moment.

The Iranian Political Configuration

There are two factions claiming to speak for the people. Rafsanjani represents the first faction. During his sermon, he spoke for the tradition of the founder of the Islamic republic, Ayatollah Ruhollah Khomeini, who took power during the 1979 Iranian Revolution. Rafjsanjani argued that Khomeini wanted an Islamic republic faithful to the will of the people, albeit within the confines of Islamic law. Rafsanjani argued that he was the true heir to the Islamic revolution. He added that Khomeini's successor — the current supreme leader, Ayatollah Ali Khamenei — had violated the principles of the revolution when he accepted that Rafsanjani's archenemy, Mahmoud Ahmadinejad, had won Iran's recent presidential election. (There is enormous irony in foreigners describing Rafsanjani as a moderate reformer who supports greater liberalization. Though he has long cultivated this image in the West, in 30 years of public political life it is hard to see a time when he has supported Western-style liberal democracy.)

The other faction is led by Ahmadinejad, who takes the position that Rafsanjani in particular — along with the generation of leaders who ascended to power during the first phase of the Islamic republic — has betrayed the Iranian people. Rather than serving the people, Ahmadinejad claims they have used their positions to become so wealthy that they dominate the Iranian economy and have made the reforms needed to revitalize the Iranian economy impossible. According to Ahmadinejad's charges, these elements now blame

Ahmadinejad for Iran's economic failings when the root of these failings is their own corruption. Ahmadinejad claims that the recent presidential election represents a national rejection of the status quo. He adds that claims of fraud represent attempts by Rafsanjani — who he portrays as defeated presidential candidate Mir Hossein Mousavi's sponsor — and his ilk to protect their positions from Ahmadinejad.

Iran is therefore experiencing a generational dispute, with each side claiming to speak both for the people and for the Khomeini tradition. There is the older generation — symbolized by Rafsanjani — that has prospered during the last 30 years. Having worked with Khomeini, this generation sees itself as his true heir. Then, there is the younger generation. Known as "students" during the revolution, this group did the demonstrating and bore the brunt of the shah's security force counterattacks. It argues that Khomeini would be appalled at what Rafsanjani and his generation have done to Iran.

This debate is, of course, more complex than this. Khamenei, a key associate of Khomeini, appears to support Ahmadinejad's position. And Ahmadinejad hardly speaks for all of the poor as he would like to claim. The lines of political disputes are never drawn as neatly as we would like. Ultimately, Rafsanjani's opposition to the recent election did not have as much to do with concerns (valid or not) over voter fraud. It had everything to do with the fact that the outcome threatened his personal position. Which brings us back to the question of why Rafsanjani's followers were chanting Death to Russia.

Examining the Anomalous Chant

For months prior to the election, Ahmadinejad's allies warned that the United States was planning a "color" revolution. Color revolutions, like the one in Ukraine, occurred widely in the former Soviet Union after its collapse, and these revolutions followed certain steps. An opposition political party was organized to mount an electoral challenge to the establishment. Then, an election occurred that was either fraudulent or claimed by the opposition as having been fraudulent. Next, widespread peaceful protests against the regime (all using a national color as the symbol of the revolution) took place, followed by the collapse of the government through a variety of paths. Ultimately, the opposition — which was invariably pro-Western and particularly pro-American — took power.

Moscow openly claimed that Western intelligence agencies, particularly the CIA, organized and funded the 2004-2005 Orange Revolution in Ukraine. These agencies allegedly used nongovernmental organizations (human rights groups, pro-democracy groups, etc.) to delegitimize the existing regime, repudiate the outcome of the election regardless of its validity and impose what the Russians regarded as a pro-American puppet regime. The Russians saw Ukraine's Orange Revolution as the break point in their relationship with the West, with the creation of a pro-American, pro-NATO regime in Ukraine representing a direct attack on Russian national security. The Americans argued that to the contrary, they had done nothing but facilitate a democratic movement that opposed the existing regime for its own reasons, demanding that rigged elections be repudiated.

In warning that the United States was planning a color revolution in Iran, Ahmadinejad took the Russian position. Namely, he was arguing that behind the cover of national self-determination, human rights and commitment to democratic institutions, the United States was funding an Iranian opposition movement on the order of those active in the former Soviet Union. Regardless of whether the opposition actually had more votes, this opposition movement would immediately regard an Ahmadinejad win as the result of fraud. Large demonstrations would ensue, and if they were left unopposed the Islamic republic would come under threat.

In doing this, Ahmadinejad's faction positioned itself against the actuality that such a rising would occur. If it did, Ahmadinejad could claim that the demonstrators were — wittingly or not — operating on behalf of the United States, thus delegitimizing the demonstrators. In so doing, he could discredit supporters of the demonstrators as not tough enough on the United States, a useful charge against Rafsanjani, whom the West long has held up as an Iranian moderate.

Interestingly, while demonstrations were at their height, Ahmadinejad chose to attend — albeit a day late — a multinational Shanghai Cooperation Organization conference in Moscow on the Tuesday after the election. It was very odd that he would leave Iran during the greatest postelection unrest; we assumed he had decided to demonstrate to Iranians that he didn't take the demonstrations seriously.

The charge that seems to be emerging on the Rafsanjani side is that Ahmadinejad's fears of a color revolution were not simply political, but were encouraged by the Russians. It was the Russians who had been talking to Ahmadinejad and his lieutenants on a host of issues, who warned him about the possibility of a color revolution. More important, the Russians helped prepare Ahmadinejad for the unrest that would come — and given the Russian experience, how to manage it. Though we speculate here, if this theory is correct, it could explain some of the efficiency with which Ahmadinejad shut down cell phone and other communications during the postelection unrest, as he may have had Russian advisers.

Rafsanjani's followers were not shouting Death to Russia without a reason, at least in their own minds. They are certainly charging that Ahmadinejad took advice from the Russians, and went to Russia in the midst of political unrest for consultations. Rafsanjani's charge may or may not be true. Either way, there is no question that Ahmadinejad did claim that the United States was planning a color revolution in Iran. If he believed that charge, it would have been irrational not to reach out to the Russians. But whether or not the CIA was involved, the Russians might well have provided Ahmadinejad with intelligence of such a plot and helped shape his response, and thereby may have created a closer relationship with him.

How Iran's internal struggle will work itself out remains unclear. But one dimension is shaping up: Ahmadinejad is trying to position Rafsanjani as leading a pro-American faction intent on a color revolution, while Rafsanjani is trying to position Ahmadinejad as part of a pro-Russian faction. In this argument, the claim that Ahmadinejad had some degree of advice or collaboration with the Russians is credible, just as the claim that Rafsanjani maintained some channels with the Americans is credible. And this makes an internal dispute geopolitically significant.

The Iranian Struggle in a Geopolitical Context

At the moment, Ahmadinejad appears to have the upper hand. Khamenei has certified his re-election. The crowds have dissipated; nothing even close to the numbers of the first few days has since materialized. For Ahmadinejad to lose, Rafsanjani would have to mobilize much of the clergy — many of whom are seemingly content to let Rafsanjani be the brunt of Ahmadinejad's attacks — in return for leaving their own interests and fortunes intact. There are things that could bring Ahmadinejad down and put Rafsanjani in control, but all of them would require Khamenei to endorse social and political instability, which he will not do.

If the Russians have in fact intervened in Iran to the extent of providing intelligence to Ahmadinejad and advice to him during his visit on how to handle the postelection unrest (as the chants suggest), then Russian influence in Iran is not surging — it has surged. In some measure, Ahmadinejad would owe his position to Russian warnings and advice. There is little gratitude in the world of international affairs, but Ahmadinejad has enemies, and the Russians would have proved their utility in helping contain those enemies.

From the Russian point of view, Ahmadinejad would be a superb asset — even if not truly under their control. His very existence focuses American attention on Iran, not on Russia. It follows, then, that Russia would have made a strategic decision to involve itself in the postelection unrest, and that for the purposes of its own negotiations with Washington, Moscow will follow through to protect the Iranian state to the extent possible. The Russians have already denied U.S. requests for assistance on Iran. But if Moscow has intervened in Iran to help safeguard Ahmadinejad's position, then the potential increases for Russia to provide Iran with the S-300 strategic air defense systems that it has been dangling in front of Tehran for more than a decade.

If the United States perceives an entente between Moscow and Tehran emerging, then the entire dynamic of the region shifts and the United States must change its game. The threat to Washington's interests becomes more intense as the potential of a Russian S-300 sale to Iran increases, and the need to disrupt the Russian-Iranian entente would become all the more important. U.S. influence in Iran already has declined substantially, and Ahmadinejad is more distrustful and hostile than ever of the United States after having to deal with the postelection unrest. If a Russian-Iranian entente emerges out of all this — which at the moment is merely a possibility, not an imminent reality — then the United States would have some serious strategic problems on its hands.

Revisiting Assumptions on Iran

For the past few years, STRATFOR has assumed that a U.S. or Israeli strike on Iran was unlikely. Iran was not as advanced in its nuclear program as some claimed, and the complexities of any attack were greater than assumed. The threat of an attack was thus a U.S. bargaining chip, much as Iran's nuclear program itself was an Iranian bargaining chip for use in achieving Tehran's objectives in Iraq and the wider region. To this point, our net assessment has been accurate.

At this point, however, we need to stop and reconsider. If Iran and Russia begin serious cooperation, Washington's existing dilemma with Iran's nuclear ambitions and its ongoing standoff with the Russians would fuse to become a single, integrated problem. This is something the United States would find difficult to manage. Washington's primary goal would become preventing this from happening.

Ahmadinejad has long argued that the United States was never about to attack Iran, and that charges by Rafsanjani and others that he has pursued a reckless foreign policy were groundless. But with the Death to Russia chants and signaling of increased Russian support for Iran, the United States may begin to reconsider its approach to the region.

Iran's clerical elite does not want to go to war. They therefore can only view with alarm the recent ostentatious transiting of the Suez Canal into the Red Sea by Israeli submarines and corvettes. This transiting did not happen without U.S. approval. Moreover, in spite of U.S. opposition to expanded Israeli settlements and Israeli refusals to comply with this opposition, U.S. Secretary of Defense Robert Gates will be visiting Israel in two weeks. The Israelis have said that there must be a deadline on negotiations with Iran over the nuclear program when the next G-8 meeting takes place in September; a deadline that the G-8 has already approved. The consequences if Iran ignores the deadline were left open-ended.

All of this can fit into our old model of psychological warfare, as representing a bid to manipulate Iranian politics by making Ahmadinejad's leadership look too risky. It could also be the United States signaling to the Russians that stakes in the region are rising. It is not clear that the United States has reconsidered its strategy on Iran in the wake of the postelection demonstrations. But if Rafsanjani's claim of Russian support for Ahmadinejad is true, a massive re-evaluation of U.S. policy could ensue, assuming one hasn't already started — prompting a reconsideration of the military option.

All of this assumes that there is substance behind a mob chanting "Death to Russia." There appears to be, but of course, Ahmadinejad's enemies would want to magnify that substance to its limits and beyond. This is why we are not ready to simply abandon our previous net assessment of Iran, even though it is definitely time to rethink it.

Hypothesizing on the Iran-Russia-U.S. Triangle
August 10, 2009

For the past several weeks, STRATFOR has focused on the relationship between Russia and Iran. As our readers will recall, a pro-Rafsanjani demonstration that saw chants of "Death to Russia," uncommon in Iran since the 1979 revolution, triggered our discussion. It caused us to rethink Iranian President Mahmoud Ahmadinejad's visit to Russia just four days after Iran's disputed June 12 presidential election, with large-scale demonstrations occurring in Tehran. At the time, we ascribed Ahmadinejad's trip as an attempt to signal his lack of concern at the postelection unrest. But why did a pro-Rafsanjani crowd chant "Death to Russia?" What had the Russians done to trigger the bitter reaction from the anti-Ahmadinejad faction? Was the Iranian president's trip as innocent as it first looked?

A Net Assessment Re-examined

At STRATFOR, we proceed with what we call a "net assessment," a broad model intended to explain the behavior of all players in a game. Our net assessment of Iran had the following three components:

1. Despite the rhetoric, the Iranian nuclear program was far from producing a deliverable weapon, although a test explosion within a few years was a distinct possibility.

2. Iran essentially was isolated in the international community, with major powers' feelings toward Tehran ranging from hostile to indifferent. Again, rhetoric aside, this led Iran to a cautious foreign policy designed to avoid triggering hostility.

3. Russia was the most likely supporter of Iran, but Moscow would avoid becoming overly involved out of fears of the U.S. reaction, of uniting a fractious Europe with the United States and of being drawn into a literally explosive situation. The

Russians, we felt, would fish in troubled waters, but would not change the regional calculus.

This view — in short, that Iran was contained — remained our view for about three years. It served us well in predicting, for example, that neither the United States nor Israel would strike Iran, and that the Russians would not transfer strategically significant weapons to Iran.

A net assessment is a hypothesis that must be continually tested against intelligence, however. The "Death to Russia" chant could not be ignored, nor could Ahmadinejad's trip to Moscow.

As we probed deeper, we found that Iran was swirling with rumors concerning Moscow's relationship with both Ahmadinejad and Ayatollah Ali Khamenei. Little could be drawn from the rumors. Iran today is a hothouse for growing rumors, and all our searches ended in dead ends. But then, if Ahmadinejad and Khamenei were engaging the Russians in this atmosphere, we would expect rumors and dead ends.

Interestingly, the rumors were consistent that Ahmadinejad and Khamenei wanted a closer relationship to Russia, but diverged on the Russian response. Some said the Russians already had assisted the Iranians by providing intelligence ranging from Israeli networks in Lebanon to details of U.S. and British plans to destabilize Iran through a "Green Revolution" like the color revolutions that had ripped through the former Soviet Union (FSU).

Equally interesting were our Russian sources' responses. Normally, they are happy to talk, if only to try to mislead us. (Our Russian sources are nothing if not voluble.) But when approached about Moscow's thinking on Iran, they went silent; this silence stood out. Normally, our sources would happily speculate — but on this subject, there was no speculation. And the disciplined silence was universal. This indicated that those who didn't know didn't want to touch the subject, and that those who did know were keeping secrets. None of this proved anything, but taken together, it caused us to put our net assessment for Iran on hold. We could no longer take any theory for granted.

All of the foregoing must be considered in the context of the current geopolitical system. And that is a matter of understanding what is in plain sight.

Potential Russian Responses to Washington

The U.S.-Russian summit that took place after the Iranian elections did not go well. U.S. President Barack Obama's attempt to divide Russian President Dmitri Medvedev and Russian Prime Minister Putin did not bear fruit. The Russians were far more interested in whether Obama would change the FSU policy of former U.S. President George W. Bush. At the very least, the Russians wanted the Americans to stop supporting Ukraine's and Georgia's pro-Western tendencies.

But not only did Obama stick with the Bush policy, he dispatched U.S. Vice President Joe Biden to visit Ukraine and Georgia to drive home the continuity. This was followed by Biden's interview with The Wall Street Journal, in which he essentially said the United States does not have to worry about Russia in the long run because Russia's economic and demographic problems will undermine its power. Biden's statements were completely consistent with the decision to send him to Georgia and Ukraine, so the Obama administration's attempts to back away from the statement were not convincing. Certainly, the Russians were not convinced. The only conclusion the Russians could draw was that the United States regards them as a geopolitical cripple of little consequence.

If the Russians allow the Americans to poach in what Moscow regards as its sphere of influence without responding, the Russian position throughout the FSU would begin to unravel — the precise outcome the Americans hope for. So Moscow took two steps. First, Moscow heated up the military situation near Georgia on the anniversary of the first war, shifting its posture and rhetoric and causing the Georgians to warn of impending conflict. Second,

Moscow increased its strategic assertiveness, escalating the tempo of Russian air operations near the United Kingdom and Alaska, and more important, deploying two Akula-class hunter-killer submarines along the East Coast of the United States. The latter is interesting, but ultimately unimportant. Increased tensions in Georgia are indeed significant, however, since the Russians have decisive power in that arena — and can act if they wish against the country, one Biden just visited to express American support.

But even a Russian move against Georgia would not be decisive. The Americans have stated that Russia is not a country to be taken seriously, and that Washington will therefore continue to disregard Russian interests in the FSU. In other words, the Americans were threatening fundamental Russian interests. The Russians must respond, or by default, they would be accepting the American analysis of the situation — and by extension, so would the rest of the world. Obama had backed the Russians into a corner.

When we look at the geopolitical chessboard, there are two places where the Russians could really hurt the Americans.

One is Germany. If Moscow could leverage Germany out of the Western alliance, this would be a geopolitical shift of the first order. Moscow has leverage with Berlin, as the Germans depend on Russian natural gas, and the two have recently been working on linking their economies even further. Moreover, the Germans are as uneasy with Obama as they were with Bush. German and American interests no longer mesh neatly. The Russians have been courting the Germans, but a strategic shift in Germany's position is simply not likely in any time frame that matters to the Russians at this juncture — though the leaders of the two countries are meeting once again this week in Sochi, Russia, their second meeting in as many months.

The second point where the Russians could hurt the Americans is in Iran. An isolated Iran is not a concern. An Iran with a strong relationship to Russia is a very different matter. Not only would sanctions be rendered completely meaningless, but Iran could pose profound strategic problems for the United States, potentially closing off airstrike options on Iranian nuclear facilities.

The Strait of Hormuz: Iran's Real Nuclear Option

The real nuclear option for Iran does not involve nuclear weapons. It would involve mining the Strait of Hormuz and the narrow navigational channels that make up the Persian Gulf. During the 1980s, when Iran and Iraq were at war, both sides attacked oil tankers in the Persian Gulf. This raised havoc on oil prices and insurance rates.

If the Iranians were to successfully mine these waters, the disruption to 40 percent of the world's oil flow would be immediate and dramatic. The nastiest part of the equation would be that in mine warfare, it is very hard to know when all the mines have been cleared. It is the risk, not the explosions, which causes insurance companies to withdraw insurance on vastly expensive tankers and their loads. It is insurance that allows the oil to flow.

Just how many mines Iran might lay before being detected and bringing an American military response could vary by a great deal, but there is certainly the chance that Iran could lay a significant number of mines, including more modern influence mines that can take longer to clear. The estimates and calculations of minesweepers — much less of the insurers — would depend on a number of factors not available to us here. But there is the possibility that the strait could be effectively closed to supertankers for a considerable period. The effect on oil prices would be severe; it is not difficult to imagine this aborting the global recovery.

Iran would not want this outcome. Tehran, too, would be greatly affected by the economic fallout (while Iran is a net exporter of crude, it is a net importer of gasoline), and the mining would drive the Europeans and Americans together. The economic and military consequences of this would be severe. But it is this threat that has given pause to American and Israeli military planners gaming out scenarios to bomb Iranian nuclear facilities. There are thousands of small watercraft along Iran's coast, and Iran's response to such raids might well be to use these vessels to strew mines in the Persian Gulf — or for swarming and perhaps even suicide attacks.

Notably, any decision to attack Iran's nuclear facilities would have to be preceded by (among other things) an attempt to neutralize Iran's mine-laying capability — along with its many anti-ship missile batteries — in the Persian Gulf. The sequence is fixed, since the moment the nuclear sites are bombed, it would have to be assumed that the minelayers would go to work, and they would work as quickly as they could. Were anything else attacked first, taking out the Iranian mine capability would be difficult, as Iran's naval assets would scatter and lay mines wherever and however they could — including by swarms of speedboats capable of carrying a mine or two apiece and almost impossible to engage with airpower. This, incidentally, is a leading reason why Israel cannot unilaterally attack Iran's nuclear facilities. They would be held responsible for a potentially disastrous oil shortage. Only the Americans have the resources to even consider dealing with the potential Iranian response, because only the Americans have the possibility of keeping Persian Gulf shipping open once the shooting starts. It also indicates that an attack on Iran's nuclear facilities would be much more complex than a sudden strike completed in one day.

The United States cannot permit the Iranians to lay the mines. The Iranians in turn cannot permit the United States to destroy their mine-laying capability. This is the balance of power that limits both sides. If Iran were to act, the U.S. response would be severe. If the United States moves to neutralize Iran, the Iranians would have to push the mines out fast. For both sides, the risks of threatening the fundamental interests of the other side are too high. Both Iran and the United States have worked to avoid this real "nuclear" option.

The Russian Existential Counter

The Russians see themselves facing an existential threat from the Americans. Whether Washington agrees with Biden or not, this is the stated American view of Russia, and by itself it poses an existential threat to Russia. The Russians need an existential counter-threat — and for the United States, that threat relates to oil. If the

Russians could seriously threaten the supply of oil through the Strait of Hormuz, the United States would lose its relatively risk-free position in the FSU.

It follows from this that strengthening Iran's ability to threaten the flow of oil, while retaining a degree of Russian control over Iran's ability to pull the trigger, would give Russia the counter it needs to American actions in the FSU. The transfer of more advanced mines and mining systems to Iran — such as mines that can be planted now and activated remotely (though most such mines can only lay, planted and unarmed, for a limited period) to more discriminating and difficult-to-sweep types of mines — would create a situation the Americans could neither suppress nor live with. As long as the Russians could maintain covert control of the trigger, Moscow could place the United States, and the West's economies, in check.

Significantly, while this would wreak havoc on Persian Gulf producers and global oil consumers at a time when they are highly vulnerable to economic fluctuations, a spike in the price of oil would not hurt Russia. On the contrary, Russia is an energy exporter, making it one of the few winners under this scenario. That means the Russians can afford much greater risks in this game.

We do not know that the Russians have all this in mind. This is speculation, not a net assessment. We note that if Russo-Iranian contacts are real, they would have begun well before the Iranian elections and the summit. But the American view on Russia is not new and was no secret. Therefore, the Russians could have been preparing their counter for a while.

We also do not know that the Iranians support this Russian move. Iranian distrust of Russia runs deep, and so far only the faction supporting Ahmadinejad appears to be playing this game. But the more the United States endorses what it calls Iranian reformists, and supports Rafsanjani's position, the more Ahmadinejad needs the Russian counter. And whatever hesitations the Russians might have had in moving closer to the Iranians, recent events have clearly created a sense in Moscow of being under attack. The Russians think politically.

The Russians play chess, and the U.S. move to create pressure in the FSU must be countered somewhere.

In intelligence, you must take bits and pieces and analyze them in the context of the pressures and constraints the various actors face. You know what you don't know, but you still must build a picture of the world based on incomplete data. At a certain point, you become confident in your intelligence and analysis and you lock it into what STRATFOR calls its net assessment. We have not arrived at a new net assessment by any means. Endless facts could overthrow our hypothesis. But at a certain point, on important matters we feel compelled to reveal our hypothesis not because we are convinced, but simply because it is sufficiently plausible to us — and the situation sufficiently important — that we feel we should share it with the appropriate caveats. In this case, the stakes are very high, and the hypothesis sufficiently plausible that it is worth sharing.

The geopolitical chessboard is shifting, though many of the pieces are invisible. The end may look very different than this, but if it winds up looking this way, it is certainly worth noting.

Et Tu, Moscow?
June 11, 2010

A day after Russia joined its fellow permanent U.N. Security Council members in passing a fresh round of sanctions against Iran, Ali Akbar Salehi, the head of Iran's Atomic Energy Organization, coolly told state-run Al Alam TV that "Iran has been under sanctions and economic, technological and political blockade for more than 30 years — we got used to it."

Iran may be used to a lot of things, but it is having an exceptionally difficult time getting used to the idea of Russia — long considered Iran's primary power patron — hanging Tehran out to dry. Iran made no secret of its displeasure with Moscow in the lead up to the sanctions vote, releasing statement after statement warning the Kremlin of the consequences of turning its back on Tehran. Now having received the sanctions slap in the face, Iranian President Mahmoud Ahmadinejad is showing his defiance by canceling his trip to the Russian and Chinese-led Shanghai Cooperation Organization summit in Tashkent on June 11, while Iran's oil minister has postponed a June 22 visit to Russia.

This is by no means the first time Iran has been betrayed by its Russian ally. After all, Russia voted in the affirmative the previous six times the Security Council passed sanctions resolutions against Iran. Those previous sanctions were a symbolic show of force against Iran, and everyone, including Iran, knew they lacked real bite and suffered from the enforceability dilemma. This latest round of sanctions will face the same enforcement challenges and were careful to avoid touching Iran's energy trade so as to get Russian and Chinese buy-in. That said, this did not end up being a fluff resolution.

The newest resolution expands travel and financial sanctions on Islamic Revolutionary Guard Corps entities — a preponderant force in the Iranian economy. The sanctions also go beyond inspections of Iranian air cargo to the seizure and disposal of Iranian contraband traveling by air or sea that could be used for military purposes. Instead of calling on states to exercise vigilance and restraint in the supply, transfer or sale of offensive weapons to Iran, the new resolution bans all of the above. Like previous resolutions, this one bars Iran from all enrichment-related activity, but now also emphasizes the construction of new nuclear sites. In short, this sanctions round expands the list of things Iran supposedly cannot do, while it allows action by interested states to interfere with a broader range of Iranian activities.

No sanctions resolution would be complete, however, without its caveats. With no real legal mechanism to enforce across international boundaries, the level of adherence to the sanctions will be left for individual states to decide. A closer look at the sanctions text also reveals a number of loopholes by Russian design. For example, Iran may be banned from nuclear and enrichment activities, and other countries may be banned from making nuclear investments in Iran, but Russia contends that in projects like the Bushehr nuclear power plant (and even future projects), it is not making such an "investment" if Iran is the one paying for the construction and training, and if the project and training are taking place on Iranian soil. Russia was also careful to include enough fine print in the clause banning arms sales to Iran to exempt a long-threatened Russian sale of the S-300 air defense system to Iran.

With more holes than Swiss cheese, the sanctions are by no means a call to war. But Iran's biggest fear goes beyond the actual text of the sanctions and into the meat of the negotiations currently taking place between Russia and the United States.

STRATFOR has been closely tracking a coming shift in Russia's foreign policy, one that would emphasize pragmatism over belligerence in dealing with the United States over thorny issues like Iran. Russia hopes to obtain much-needed Western technology and investment to modernize its economy and ensure Moscow's long-term competitiveness in the global system. While the United States and Russia have (for now) agreed to disagree on more contentious issues like U.S. military support for Poland and Georgia, the Russian decision to move against Iran with this sanctions resolution is quite telling of the progress made thus far in U.S.-Russia negotiations. And for those outstanding points of contention, Russia still has the S-300 and Bushehr levers to wave in Washington's face should its negotiations with the United States take a turn for the worse. Meanwhile, Washington has just acquired a very useful tool to bolster its negotiating position vis-a-vis Iran: the prospect of Russia abandoning its premier Mideast ally.

The Iranians have long known that their alliance with Russia stood on shaky ground, but they also worked fastidiously to try to keep U.S.-Russian relations as agonizing as possible to avoid being put in this very position. This is not to say Iran would be coming to the negotiating table empty-handed when it faced Washington. After all, Iran still has very strong levers against the United States in Iraq, Lebanon and Afghanistan that it can use at a time of its choosing.

The question, then, is whether that time may be approaching. As Iranian Foreign Minister Manouchehr Mottaki said Thursday, "It is now the Islamic republic's turn to make the next move."

Syria, Iran: Estranged Allies Collide in Lebanon
August 10, 2010

Iranian Foreign Minister Manouchehr Mottaki will leave Tehran for Damascus on Aug. 10 to meet with Syrian President Bashar al Assad and Syrian Foreign Minister Walid al-Moallem. Mottaki's trip immediately follows a visit to Beirut and then Damascus by Ali Akbar Velayati, the senior foreign policy adviser to Iranian Supreme Leader Ayatollah Ali Khamenei. It also follows a trip by Lebanese Foreign Minister Ali Shami to Tehran — a trip reportedly made without Cabinet approval — and comes ahead of a visit by Iranian President Mahmoud Ahmadinejad to Lebanon, which has been delayed until the conclusion of the Islamic holy month of Ramadan.

The flurry of diplomatic activity between the Levant and Iran stems primarily from the Islamic republic's concerns over Syria. The Syrians, while taking care to reassure Tehran that their alliance remains intact, have been working very closely with the Saudis lately in Lebanon to undermine Hezbollah, Iran's principal militant proxy. Saudi Arabia, the United States and Turkey are finally seeing progress in their attempts to pull Syria out of the Iran-Hezbollah nexus as a way to deprive Tehran of a key foothold in the Levant. Syria cannot be expected to sever ties with Iran and Hezbollah, especially since that alliance is precisely what gives it leverage with the Saudis, Americans and Turks in the first place. But Saudi Arabia is also taking the lead in giving Syria what it needs and wants: much-needed investment to revive the Syrian economy and, most important, valuable space for Damascus to fully reclaim its pre-eminent position in Lebanon. And as long as Syria gets what it wants in Lebanon, it will not be a reliable ally for Tehran there or in Iraq, another key battle-ground for regional influence.

Weakening Hezbollah's Hand in Lebanon

In Lebanon, Iran is trying to signal to Syria and Saudi Arabia that it still has more than enough clout to disrupt the Arab states' plans to undermine Hezbollah. The deadly Aug. 3 border clash between Lebanese and Israeli forces appears to fit with this Iranian agenda. According to STRATFOR sources, Iran instructed Hezbollah, which has substantial influence over the Lebanese Armed Forces, particularly those units in the south where the clash occurred, to instigate a low-level conflict. Iran's ability to influence this conflict was also made possible by Lebanese army chief Gen. Jean Qahwaji. Though it is unclear whether Qahwaji was in direct communication with Tehran or taking input from members within the military linked to Hezbollah, STRATFOR sources in the Lebanese government and military claim that Qahwaji gave the order to provoke Israel Defense Forces (IDF) into a contained conflict as a way to galvanize support against Israel and thus boost his own standing within the army. Qahwaji, who is known to have presidential ambitions, has since been reprimanded by former army commander and current Lebanese President Michel Suleiman, who does not want to provide Israel with another excuse to militarily intervene in Lebanon.

Hezbollah was able to distance itself a bit from the border clash by making the army directly responsible for the provocation, but is still extremely wary of provoking the Israelis into a more serious military confrontation — particularly one in which Hezbollah will be unable to count on Syrian support. Syria has already issued instructions to key proxies in Lebanon, such as the Syrian Social Nationalist Party (SSNP), to deny Hezbollah support in the event of a domestic crisis over the Special Tribunal on the assassination of Rafik al-Hariri that is expected to implicate Hezbollah members. STRATFOR has also received indications that Syria is working to shift some of its support to the Amal Movement, Lebanon's second-most significant

Shiite organization next to Hezbollah, demonstrated by the public attention it is giving to Amal leaders over Hezbollah officials. Amal remains far behind Hezbollah in terms of the influence it holds over the Lebanese Shiite community, but Syria is evidently diversifying its proxy options for steering Lebanese policy.

Most concerning to Hezbollah, however, is the vulnerability of the group's communication systems to Syrian intelligence operatives in Lebanon. Syria's intelligence apparatus has largely re-entrenched itself in Lebanon since the withdrawal of Syrian forces from the country in 2005. The recent discovery of another Israeli spy network that had tapped into the upper ranks of the Lebanese army and into Alpha, a major mobile communications provider for Lebanon, has given Syria yet another opening to lock down influence in Lebanon. According to a STRATFOR source, Lebanese Prime Minister Saad al-Hariri, who receives much of his political guidance from the Saudi government, has made a personal request to al Assad to have Syria restructure Lebanon's intelligence apparatus. Syria's former top intelligence official on Lebanon through April 2005, Rustom Ghazale, has reportedly paid several quiet visits to Lebanon to help in this effort and is expected to make additional visits in the near future. (Ghazale had earlier been accused of involvement in the Rafik al-Hariri assassination, but apparently has been cleared.)

Hezbollah's belligerent rhetoric may suggest otherwise, but Iran is exercising caution on how it uses the militant group. Having a Lebanese army contingent provoke a border skirmish with Israel in the south is far less risky than having Hezbollah directly provoke a larger military confrontation with the IDF. In fact, as a strong indication that U.S.-Iranian back-channel talks on Iraq may be gaining momentum, Velayati, Khamenei's senior aide, allegedly instructed Hezbollah to refrain from igniting a military conflict with rival Lebanese factions, as well as with Israel, while Iran tries to feel out U.S. flexibility in negotiations over the formation of the Iraqi government. But even if those talks go awry and Iran feels the need to spark a conflagration again in Lebanon, doubt is growing over how far Hezbollah would be willing to go for its Iranian patrons. The Shiite militant group is simply feeling too vulnerable to take big risks right now.

Colliding Interests in Iraq

The growing unreliability of Syria and Hezbollah comes at a crucial juncture in Iran's negotiations with the United States over Iraq. Tehran wants to demonstrate to Washington that it holds a powerful lever in the Levant, as well as in Afghanistan and Iraq, to turn the screws on the United States and its allies should its demands on the composition of the next Iraqi government go unfulfilled. Evidently, there are holes in that Iranian strategy. In addition to Hezbollah's increasingly risk-averse attitude, Syrian interests are not in sync with Iranian interests on Iraq. Syria, which is in the process of making a significant comeback in Arab politics, has an interest in going beyond its primary interests in Lebanon to earn an additional foothold in Baghdad. Despite the historic rivalry between the Syrian and Iraqi branches of the Baath party, Syria's link to Iraqi politics lies in Iraq's Sunni former Baathist community — the very faction that Iran is fighting to keep sidelined from the government and security apparatus. Though Syria has spent much of the Iraq war supporting former Baathists that formed the backbone of the insurgency, the U.S. withdrawal from Iraq and Syria's gains in Lebanon are likely to gradually shift Syria into a more cooperative role with the United States.

Syria, highly uncomfortable with having U.S. forces next door in Iraq, has an interest in facilitating the U.S. withdrawal as long as its demands are being met in Lebanon, which appears to be the case thus far. In addition, U.S. recognition of Syria's role as a key player in the region would provide an implicit security guarantee for the regime, something long sought by Damascus and which Washington has been reluctant to give. Iraq's coalition talks will intensify in the coming month as the U.S. drawdown to 50,000 troops continues, and as Syria attempts to edge itself into those coalition-forming negotiations, it will find itself competing once again with its estranged allies in Tehran.

Syria, Hezbollah and Iran: An Alliance in Flux
October 14, 2010

Iranian President Mahmoud Ahmadinejad arrived in Beirut on Oct. 13 for his first official visit to Lebanon since becoming president in 2005. He is reportedly returning to the country after a stint there in the 1980s as a young Islamic Revolutionary Guard Corps (IRGC) officer tasked with training Hezbollah in Lebanon's Bekaa Valley. A great deal of controversy is surrounding his return. Rumors are spreading of Sunni militants attempting to mar the visit by provoking Iran's allies in Hezbollah into a fight (already the car of a pro-Hezbollah imam who has been defending Ahmadinejad has been blown up), while elaborate security preparations are being made for Ahmadinejad to visit Lebanon's heavily militarized border with Israel.

Rather than getting caught up in the drama surrounding the Iranian president's visit, we want to take the opportunity provided by all the media coverage to probe into a deeper topic, one that has been occupying the minds of Iranian, Syrian and Hezbollah officials for some time. This topic is the durability of the Iran-Hezbollah-Syria alliance, which STRATFOR believes has been under great stress in recent months. More precisely, the question is: What are Syria's current intentions toward Hezbollah?

The Origins of the Alliance

To address this topic, we need to review the origins of the trilateral pact, starting with the formation of an alliance in 1979 between secular Alawite-Baathist Syria and the Islamic Republic of Iran. Ideologically speaking, the Syrian Alawite elite represent an offshoot of Shiite Islam that the Sunnis consider apostate. They found some commonality with the Shiite clerical elite in Tehran, but there were also broader strategic motivations in play. At the time, Syria was on a quest to establish the country's regional prowess, and it knew that the first steps toward this end had to be taken in Lebanon. From the Syrian point of view, Lebanon is not just a natural extension of Syria;

it is the heartland of the Greater Syria province that existed during Ottoman times. Since the days of Phoenicia, what is modern-day Lebanon has been a vibrant trading hub, connecting routes from the east and south to the Mediterranean basin. For Syria to feel like it has any real worth in the region, it must dominate Lebanon.

A civil war that had broken out in Lebanon in 1975 (and lasted through 1990) afforded Syria such an opportunity. The main obstruction to Syria's agenda at the time, besides Israel, was the Palestine Liberation Organization (PLO) under Yasser Arafat, whose vision for a unified Palestine and whose operations in Lebanon ran counter to Syria's bid for regional hegemony. The PLO, in fact, was one of the main reasons Syria intervened militarily in Lebanon in 1975 on behalf of its Maronite Christian allies. At the same time, Syria was looking for an ally to undermine the Baathist regime of Saddam Hussein in Iraq, with whom the Syrian Baathists had a deep-seated rivalry. An alliance with Iran would grant Syria some much-needed individuality in a region dominated by the Arab powers Saudi Arabia and Egypt.

Coming off the success of the 1979 Islamic Revolution in Iran and going into what would become a long and bloody war with Iraq, Iran was also looking for a venue to counter the Baathist regime in Baghdad. In addition, Iran was looking to undermine the Pan-Arab vision, establish a presence in the Levant and promote its own Islamic vision of government. In opposition to Israel, Hussein and Arafat, Iran and Syria thus uncovered the roots of an alliance, albeit one that was shifting uneasily between Syrian secularity and Iranian religiosity.

The adoption of Hezbollah by the two unlikely allies in 1982 was what helped bridge that gap. Hezbollah, an offshoot of Amal, the main Shiite political movement at the time, served multiple purposes for Damascus and Tehran. Syria found in Hezbollah a useful militant proxy to contain obstructions to Syrian influence in Lebanon and to compensate for its own military weakness in comparison to Israel. In the broader Syrian strategic vision, Hezbollah would develop into a bargaining chip for a future settlement with Israel once Syria could ensure that Lebanon was firmly within Syria's grasp and was there-fore unable to entertain a peace deal with Israel on its own.

The Iranians saw in Hezbollah the potential to export its Islamic Revolution into the Arab world, a strong binder for its still new and shaky alliance with Syria and a useful deterrent in dealing with adversaries like Israel, the United States and Saudi Arabia. So, Iran and Syria set out to divide their responsibilities in managing this militant proxy. Iran was primarily in charge of bankrolling, training and enforcing the group's ideological loyalty to Tehran with IRGC assistance. Syria was in charge of creating the conditions for Iran to nurture Hezbollah, mainly by permitting IRGC officers to set up training camps in the Bekaa Valley and by securing a line of supply for weapons to reach the group via Syria.

But the triumvirate did not get off to a very smooth start. In fact, Hezbollah and Syria clashed a number of times in the early 1980s, when Syria felt the group, under Iranian direction, went too far in provoking external intervention (and thus risked drawing Syria into conflict). If Hezbollah was to operate on Syrian territory (as Syria viewed it) in Lebanon, Syria wanted Hezbollah operating on its terms. It was not until 1987, when Syrian troops in Lebanon shot 23 Hezbollah members, that Hezbollah fully realized the importance of maintaining an entente with Syria. In the meantime, Hezbollah, caught between occasionally conflicting Syrian and Iranian agen-das, saw that the path to the group's survival lay in becoming a more autonomous political — as opposed to purely militant — actor in the Lebanese political arena.

A Syrian Setback

The Iran-Hezbollah-Syria alliance operated relatively smoothly through the 1990s as Hezbollah gradually built up its political arm and as Syria kept close watch on the group through its roughly 14,000 troops and thousands of intelligence agents who had remained in Lebanon since the end of the civil war. In 2000, with Iranian and Syrian help, Hezbollah succeeded in forcing Israel to withdraw from

Lebanon's southern Security Zone, an event that greatly boosted Hezbollah's credentials as a Lebanese nationalist actor.

But fresh challenges to the pact came with the turn of the century. The 2003 U.S. invasion of Iraq, in particular, was a defining moment for both Iran and Syria. The two allies felt enormously uncomfortable with having the world's most powerful military on their borders, but they were also presented with an immediate opportunity to unseat their mutual archrival, Saddam Hussein. Iran and Syria also had different endgames in mind for a post-Hussein Iraq. Iran used its political, militant and intelligence links to consolidate influence in Iraq through the country's Shiite majority. In contrast, Syria provided refuge to Iraq's Sunni Baathists with the aim of extending its sphere of influence in the region through a secularist former-Baathist presence in Baghdad. The Syrians also planned to use those Sunni links later to bargain with the United States for a seat at the negotiating table, thereby affirming Syrian influence in the region.

But before Syria could gain much traction in its plans for Iraq, its agenda in Lebanon suffered a serious setback. On Feb. 14, 2005, a massive car bomb in Beirut killed former Lebanese Prime Minister Rafik al-Hariri, a powerful and vocal opponent of Syrian authority in Lebanon. The bombing is strongly believed to have been orchestrated by elements within the Syrian regime and executed by members of Hezbollah. While a major opponent of the Syrian regime was thereby eliminated, Syria did not anticipate that the death of al-Hariri would spark a revolution in Lebanon (which attracted the support of countries like France and the United States) and end up driving Syrian troops out of Lebanon. The vacuum that Syria left in Lebanon was rapidly filled by Iran (via Hezbollah), which had a pressing need to fortify Hezbollah as a proxy force as war tensions steadily built up in the region over Iran's nuclear ambitions. Though Syria knew it would only be a matter of time before it would return to Lebanon, it also had a strategic interest in demonstrating to the Israelis and the Americans the costs of Syria's absence from Lebanon. The regime wanted to show that without a firm Syrian check on

Hezbollah, disastrous events like the 2006 summer confrontation between Hezbollah and Israel could occur.

The Syrian Comeback

It has now been more than five and a half years since the al-Hariri assassination, and there is little question that Syria, once again, has reclaimed its hegemonic position in Lebanon. The Syrian intelligence apparatus pervades the country, and Lebanese politicians who dared to speak out against the Syrian regime are now asking for forgiveness. In perhaps the most glaring demonstration of the political tide shifting back toward Damascus, Saad al-Hariri, the son of the slain al-Hariri and Lebanon's reluctant prime minister, announced in early June that Lebanon had "made a mistake" in making a "political accusation" against Syria for his father's murder. The message was clear: Syria was back.

That message did not necessarily sit well with Hezbollah and Iran. Syria wants to keep Hezbollah in check, returning to the 1990s model when Syrian military and intelligence could still tightly control the group's movements and supplies. Iran and Hezbollah have also watched as Syria has used its comeback in Lebanon to diversify its foreign policy portfolio over the past year. Saudi Arabia and Turkey, for example, have been cozying up to Damascus and have quietly bargained with the al Assad regime to place checks on Hezbollah as a way to undermine Iran's key proxy in the Levant. As long as these regional powers recognize Syria's authority in Lebanon, Syria is willing to use those relationships to exonerate itself from the al-Hariri assassination tribunal, rake much-needed investment into the Syrian economy and, most important, re-establish itself as a regional power. Syrian President Bashar al Assad's decision to visit Beirut alongside Saudi King Abdullah was a deliberate signal to Hezbollah and Iran that Syria had options and was not afraid to display them.

This does not mean Syria is ready and willing to sell out its Hezbollah and Iranian allies. On the contrary, Syria derives leverage from maintaining these relationships and acting as the bridge between the Shiite revivalists and the Sunni powers. Syria has illustrated as much in its current mediation efforts among the various Iraqi factions that are torn between Iran on one side and the United States, Saudi Arabia and Turkey on the other. But if we go back to reviewing the core reasons Syria agreed to an alliance with Iran and Hezbollah in the first place, it is easy to see why Hezbollah and Iran still have a lot of reason to be worried.

Syria's priority in the early 1980s was to achieve suzerainty in Lebanon (done), eliminate the threat posed by Saddam Hussein in Iraq (done) and remove any key obstacles in Lebanon that could challenge Syria's authority. In the 1970s, that obstacle was the PLO. Today, that obstacle is Hezbollah and its Iranian backers, who are competing for influence in Lebanon and no longer have a good read on Syrian intentions. Hezbollah relies heavily on Syria for its logistical support and knows that its communication systems, for example, are vulnerable to Syrian intelligence. Hezbollah has also grown nervous at the signs of Syria steadily ramping up support for competing militant groups — including the Amal Movement, the Syrian Social Nationalist Party, al-Ahbash, the Nasserites, the Baath Party and the Mirada of Suleiman Franjiyye — to counter Hezbollah's prowess.

Meanwhile, Iran is seeing one of the key prongs in its deterrent strategy — Hezbollah — grow increasingly vulnerable at a time when Iran is pressed to demonstrate to the United States and Israel that the costs of an attack on its nuclear installation are not worth incurring. The Iranian competition with Syria does not end in Lebanon, either. In Iraq, Syria is far more interested in establishing a secularist government with a former Baathist presence than it is in seeing Baghdad develop into a Shiite satellite for the Iranians.

For now, Syria is adroitly playing both sides of the geopolitical divide in the region, taking care to blend its reassurances toward the alliance and its primary negotiating partners in Saudi Arabia with threats of the destabilization that could erupt should Syria's demands go ignored. Syria, for example, has made clear that in return for recognition of its authority in Lebanon it will prevent Hezbollah from laying siege on Beirut, whether they are ordered to do so by Tehran as part of an Iranian negotiating ploy with the Americans or whether they act on their own in retaliation against the al-Hariri tribunal proceedings. At the same time, Syrian officials will shuttle regularly between Lebanon and Iran to reaffirm their standing in the triumvirate. Behind this thick veneer of unity, however, a great deal of apprehension and distrust is building among the allies.

The core fear residing in Hezbollah and Iran has to do with Syrian intentions moving forward. In particular, Hezbollah would like to know if, in Syria's eyes, the group is rapidly devolving from strategic patron to bargaining chip with every ounce of confidence that Syria gains in Lebanon. The answer to that question, however, lies not in Syria but in Israel and the United States. Israeli, U.S. and Saudi policymakers have grown weary of Syria's mercantilist negotiating style in which Syrian officials will extract as much as possible from their negotiating partners while delivering very little in return.

At the same time, Syria cannot afford to take any big steps toward militant proxies like Hezbollah unless it receives firm assurances from Israel in backchannel peace talks that continue to stagnate. But Syria is also sensing an opportunity at its door: The United States is desperate to complete its exit strategy from Iraq and, like Israel, is looking for useful levers to undermine Iranian clout in the region. One such lever is Syria, which is why the mere idea of Israel and Syria talking peace right now should give Iran and Hezbollah ample food for thought.

CHAPTER 6: HISTORIC OPPORTUNITIES IN THE MIDDLE EAST

Overdoing Chalabi
May 28, 2004

On Feb. 19, in a piece titled "Ahmed Chalabi and His Iranian Connection," STRATFOR laid out the close relationship Chalabi had with the Iranians, and the role that relationship played in the flow of intelligence to Washington prior to the war. This week, the story of Chalabi, accused of being an Iranian agent by U.S. intelligence, was all over the front pages of the newspapers. The media, having ignored Chalabi's Iranian connections for so long, went to the other extreme — substantially overstating its significance.

The thrust of many of the stories was that the United States was manipulated by Iran — using Chalabi as a conduit — into invading Iraq. The implication was that the United States would have chosen a different course, except for Chalabi's disinformation campaign. We doubt that very much. First, the United States had its own reasons for invading Iraq. Second, U.S. and Iranian interests were not all that far apart in this case. Chalabi was certainly, in our opinion, working actively on behalf of Iranian interests — as well as for himself

— but he was merely a go-between in some complex geopolitical maneuvering.

Iran wanted the United States to invade Iraq. The Iranians hated Saddam Hussein more than anyone did, and they feared him. Iran and Iraq had fought a war in the 1980s that devastated a generation of Iranians. More than Hussein, Iraq represented an historical threat to Iran going back millennia. The destruction of the Iraqi regime and army was at the heart of Iranian national interest. The collapse of the Soviet Union had for the first time in a century secured Iran's northern frontiers. The U.S. invasion of Afghanistan secured the Shiite regions of Afghanistan as a buffer. If the western frontier could be secured, Iran would achieve a level of national security it had not known in centuries.

What Iran Wanted

Iran knew it could not invade Iraq and win by itself. Another power had to do it. The failure of the United States to invade and occupy Iraq in 1991 was a tremendous disappointment to Iran. Indeed, the primary reason the United States did not invade Iraq was because it knew the destruction of the Iraqi army would leave Iran the dominant power native to the Persian Gulf. Invading Iraq would have destroyed the Iraq-Iran balance of power that was the only basis for what passed for stability in the region.

The destruction of the Iraqi regime not only would have made Iran secure, but also would have opened avenues for expansion. First, the Persian Gulf region is full of Shia, many of them oriented toward Iran for religious reasons. For example, the loading facilities for Saudi oil are in a region dominated by the Shia. Second, without the Iraqi army blocking Iran, there was no military force in the region that could stop the Iranians. They could have become the dominant power in the Persian Gulf, and only the permanent stationing of U.S. troops in the region would have counterbalanced Iran. The United States did not want that, so the conquest of Kuwait was followed by the invasion — but not the conquest — of Iraq. The United States kept Iraq in place to block Iran.

Iran countered this policy by carefully and systematically organizing the Shiite community of Iraq. After the United States allowed a Shiite rising to fail after Desert Storm, Iranian intelligence embarked on a massive program of covert organization of the Iraqi Shia, in preparation for the time when the Hussein regime would fall. Iranian intentions were to create a reality on the ground so the fall of Iraq would inevitably lead to the rise of a Shiite-dominated Iraq, allied with Iran.

What was not in place was the means of destroying Hussein. Obviously, the Iranians wanted the invasion and Chalabi did everything he could to make the case for invasion, not only because of his relationship with Iran, but also because of his ambitions to govern Iraq. Iran understood that an American invasion of Iraq would place a massive U.S. Army on its western frontier, but the Iranians also understood that the United States had limited ambitions in the area. If the Iranians cooperated with U.S. intelligence on al Qaeda and were not overly aggressive with their nuclear program, the two major concerns of the United States would be satisfied and the Americans would look elsewhere.

The United States would leave Iraq in the long run, and Iran would be waiting patiently to reap the rewards. In the short run, should the United States run into trouble in Iraq, it would become extremely dependent on the Iranians and their Shiite clients. If the Shiite south rose, the U.S. position would become untenable. Therefore if there was trouble — and Iranian intelligence was pretty sure there would be — Shiite influence would rise well before the Americans left.

Chalabi's job was to give the Americans a reason to invade, which he did with stories of weapons of mass destruction (WMD). But he had another job, which was to shield two critical pieces of information from the Americans: First, he was to shield the extent to which the Iranians had organized the Shiite south of Iraq. Second, he was to shield any information about Hussein's plans for a guerrilla campaign after the fall of Baghdad. These were the critical things — taken together, they would create the dependency the Iranians badly wanted.

What the United States Wanted

The Americans were focused on another issue. The balance of power in the Persian Gulf was not a trivial matter to them, but it had taken on a new cast after Sept. 11. For the United States, the central problem in the Persian Gulf — and a matter of urgent national security — was the unwillingness of Saudi intelligence and security services to move aggressively against al Qaeda inside the kingdom. From the U.S. viewpoint, forcing Saudi Arabia to change its behavior was the overriding consideration; without that, no progress against al Qaeda was possible.

The United States did not see itself as having many levers for manipulating the situation in Saudi Arabia. The Saudis were convinced that ultimately the United States would not be able to take decisive action against the Saudis, and the Saudi government was more concerned about the internal political consequences of a crackdown on al Qaeda than it was about the United States. It felt confident it could manage the United States as it had in the past.

The United States did not want to invade Saudi Arabia. The House of Saud was the foundation of Saudi stability, and the United States did not want it to fall. It wanted to change the Saudi strategy. Invading Saudi Arabia could have led to global economic disaster if oil shipments were disrupted. Finally, the invasion of Saudi Arabia, given its size, terrain and U.S. resources, was a difficult if not impossible task. The direct route would not work. The United States would take an indirect route.

If you wanted to frighten Saudi Arabia into changing its behavior without actually launching military operations against it, the way to do that would be: (a) demonstrate your will by staging an effective military campaign; and (b) wind up the campaign in a position to actually invade and take Saudi oil fields if they did not cooperate.

The Saudis doubted U.S. will and military capacity to do them harm (since Kuwait would never permit its territory to be used to invade Saudi Arabia). The solution: an invasion of Iraq.

The United States wanted to invade Iraq as an indirect route to influence Saudi Arabia. As in any military operation, there were also subsidiary political goals. The United States wanted to get rid of Hussein's regime, not because it was complicit with al Qaeda, but because it might later become complicit. Secondly, it wanted to use Iraqi territory as a base to pressure Syria and Iran as well.

Chalabi's claims about Iraqi WMD did not instigate the invasion, because the United States did not invade Iraq to get rid of WMD. An invasion would be the most dangerous route for doing that, because the other side might actually surprise you and use the weapons on your troops. You would use air strikes and special operations troops. What Chalabi did by providing his intelligence was, however, not insignificant. The administration had two goals: the destruction of al Qaeda and protection of the United States from WMD. By producing evidence of WMD in Iraq, Chalabi gave Donald Rumsfeld and Paul Wolfowitz the tool they needed. By introducing evidence of WMD, they triggered an automatic policy against Iraq having them, which closed off an argument — not really a raging argument — in the administration. It was important, but not earth-shattering.

There was a deeper dimension to this. The strategic planners in the administration were old enough to remember when Richard Nixon began the process that broke the back of the Soviet Union — his alliance with China against the Soviets. During World War II, the United States allied with Stalin against Hitler, preventing a potential peace agreement by Stalin. The United States had a known policy of using fault lines among potential enemies to split them apart, allying with the weaker against the stronger. If the United States allying with Stalin or Mao was not considered beyond the pale, then the Bush administration planners had another alliance in mind.

The fault line in the Islamic world is between Sunni and Shia. The Sunni are a much larger group than the Shia, but only if you include countries such as Indonesia. Within the Persian Gulf region, the two groups are highly competitive. Al Qaeda was a Sunni movement. Following U.S. grand strategy, logic held that the solution to the problem was entering into an alliance of sorts with the Shia. The key to the Shia was the major Shiite power — Iran.

The United States worked with Iranian intelligence during the invasion of Afghanistan, when the Iranians arranged relationships with Shiite warlords like Ahmed Khan. The United States and Iran had cooperated on a number of levels for years when it concerned Iraq. Therefore there were channels open for collaboration.

The United States was interested not only in frightening Saudi Arabia, but also in increasing its dependence on the United States. The United States needed a lever strong enough to break the gridlock in Riyadh. An invasion of Iraq would achieve the goal of fear. An alliance with Iran would create the dependency that was needed. The Saudis would do anything to keep the Iranians out of their oil fields and their country. After the invasion of Iraq, only the United States could stop them. The Saudis were trapped by the United States.

What Chalabi Didn't Say

What is important to see here is how the Iranians were using the Americans, and how the Americans were using the Iranians. Chalabi was an important channel, but hardly the only one. It is almost certain that his role was well known. Chalabi was probably left in place to convince the Iranians that the United States was naïve enough to believe them, or he was there simply as a token of good faith. But nothing he said triggered the invasion.

It was what he did not say that is significant. Chalabi had to know that the Iranians controlled the Iraqi Shia. It is possible that he even told the Pentagon that, since it wouldn't change fundamental strategy much. But there is one thing that Chalabi should have known that he certainly didn't tell the Americans: that Hussein was going to wage a guerrilla war. On that point, there is no question but that the Pentagon was surprised, and it mattered a lot.

Chalabi did not share intelligence that the Iranians almost certainly had because the Iranians wanted the Americans to get bogged down in a guerrilla war. That would increase U.S. dependence on the Shia and Iran, and would hasten the American departure.

Iranian intelligence had penetrated deep into Iraq. The preparations for the guerrilla war were extensive. Iran knew — and so did Chalabi. The United States would still have invaded, but would have been much better prepared, militarily and politically. Chalabi did not tell the Pentagon what he knew, and that has made a huge difference in the war.

We suspect that the Pentagon intelligence offices and the CIA both knew all about Chalabi's relation to Iranian intelligence. The argument was not over that, but over whether this disqualified his intelligence. The Pentagon had made up its mind for strategic reasons to invade Iraq. Chalabi's intelligence was of use in internal disputes in the administration, but decided nothing in terms of policy. The CIA, understanding that Chalabi was not really a source in the conventional sense but was a geopolitical pawn, did not like the game, but didn't call the Department of Defense on it until after DOD got into trouble in Iraq — and the CIA wanted to make certain that everyone knew it wasn't their mistake.

Chalabi was a minor player in a dance between Iran and the United States that began on Sept. 11 and is still under way. The United States wants a close relationship with Iran in order to split the Islamic world and force the Saudis to collaborate with the Americans. The Iranians want to use the United States in order to become the dominant power in the Persian Gulf. Each wants the other to be its hammer. In all of this, Chalabi was only an actor in a bit part.

The one place in which he was significant was negative — he kept the United States in the dark about the impending guerrilla war. That was where he really helped Iran, because it was the guerrilla war that locked the United States into a dependency on the Iraqi Shia that went much farther than the United States desired, and from which the United States is only now starting to extricate itself. That is a major act of duplicity, but it is a sin of omission, not commission.

In a way, the Americans and the Iranians used Chalabi for their own purposes. The Iranians used him to screen information from the Americans more than to give false information. The Americans used him to try to convince the Iranians that they had a sufficient degree of control over the situation and that it was in their interests to maintain stability in the Shiite regions. At this point, it is honestly impossible to tell who got the better of whom. But this much is certain. Chalabi, for all his cleverness, is just another used-up spook, trusted by no one, trusting even fewer. Geopolitics trumps conspiracy every time.

———————————

Iran and the Saudis' Countermove on Bahrain
March 14, 2011

Saudi Arabia is leading a coalition force into Bahrain to help the government calm the unrest there. This move puts Iran in a difficult position, as Tehran had hoped to use the uprising in Bahrain to promote instability in the Persian Gulf region. Iran could refrain from acting and lose an opportunity to destabilize the region, or it could choose from several other options that do not seem particularly effective.

The Bahrain uprising consists of two parts, as all revolutions do. The first is genuine grievances by the majority Shiite population — the local issues and divisions. The second is the interests of foreign powers in Bahrain. It is not one or the other. It is both.

The Iranians clearly benefit from an uprising in Bahrain. It places the U.S. 5th Fleet's basing in jeopardy, puts the United States in a difficult position and threatens the stability of other Persian Gulf Arab states. For the Iranians, the uprisings in North Africa and their spread to the Arabian Peninsula represent a golden opportunity for pursuing their long-standing interest (going back to the Shah and beyond) of dominating the Gulf.

The Iranians are accustomed to being able to use their covert capabilities to shape the political realities in countries. They did this effectively in Iraq and are doing it in Afghanistan. They regarded this as low risk and high reward. The Saudis, recognizing that this posed a fundamental risk to their regime and consulting with the Americans, have led a coalition force into Bahrain to halt the uprising and save the regime. Pressed by covert forces, they were forced into an overt action they were clearly reluctant to take.

We are now off the map, so to speak. The question is how the Iranians respond, and there is every reason to think that they do not know. They probably did not expect a direct military move by the Saudis, given that the Saudis prefer to act more quietly themselves. The Iranians wanted to destabilize without triggering a strong response, but they were sufficiently successful in using local issues that the Saudis felt they had no choice in the matter. It is Iran's move.

If Iran simply does nothing, then the wave that has been moving in its favor might be stopped and reversed. They could lose a historic opportunity. At the same time, the door remains open in Iraq, and that is the main prize here. They might simply accept the reversal and pursue their main line. But even there things are murky. There are rumors in Washington that U.S. President Barack Obama has decided to slow down, halt or even reverse the withdrawal from Iraq. Rumors are merely rumors, but these make sense. Completing the withdrawal now would tilt the balance in Iraq to Iran, a strategic disaster.

Therefore, the Iranians are facing a counter-offensive that threatens the project they have been pursuing for years just when it appeared to be coming to fruition. Of course, it is just before a project succeeds that opposition mobilizes, so they should not be surprised that resistance has grown so strong. But surprised or not, they now have a strategic decision to make and not very long to make it.

They can up the ante by increasing resistance in Bahrain and forcing fighting on the ground. It is not clear that the Bahraini opposition is prepared to take that risk on behalf of Iran, but it is a potential option. They have the option of trying to increase unrest elsewhere in order to spread the Saudi and Gulf Cooperation Council forces, weakening their impact. It is not clear how much leverage the Iranians have in other countries. The Iranians could try to create problems in Saudi Arabia, but given the Saudis' actions in Bahrain, this becomes more difficult.

Finally, they can attempt an overt intervention, either in Bahrain or elsewhere, such as Iraq or Afghanistan. A naval movement against Bahrain is not impossible, but if the U.S. Navy intervenes, which it likely would, it would be a disaster for the Iranians. Operations in Iraq or Afghanistan might be more fruitful. It is possible that Shiite insurgents will operate in Iraq, but that would guarantee a halt of the U.S. withdrawal without clearly increasing the Iranians' advantage there. They want U.S. forces to leave, not give them a reason to stay.

There is then the indirect option, which is to trigger a war with Israel. The killings in the West Bank and Israeli concerns about Hezbollah might be some of Iran's doing, with the emphasis on "might." But it is not clear how a Hezbollah confrontation with Israel would help Iran's position relative to Saudi Arabia in the Persian Gulf. It diverts attention, but the Saudis know the stakes and they will not be easily diverted.

The logic, therefore, is that Iran retreats and waits. But the Saudi move shifts the flow of events, and time is not on Iran's side.

There is also the domestic Iranian political situation to consider. Iranian President Mahmoud Ahmadinejad has been strong in part because of his successful handling of foreign policy. The massive failure of a destabilization plan would give his political opponents the ammunition needed to weaken him domestically. We do not mean a democratic revolution in Iran, but his enemies among the clergy who see him as a threat to their position, and hard-liners in the Islamic Revolutionary Guard Corps who want an even more aggressive stand.

Ahmadinejad finds himself in a difficult position. The Saudis have moved decisively. If he does nothing, his position can unravel and with it his domestic political strength. Yet none of the counters he might use seem effective or workable. In the end, his best option is to create a crisis in Iraq, forcing the United States to consider how deeply it wants to be drawn back into Iraq. He might find weakness there that he can translate into some sort of political deal.

At the moment we suspect the Iranians do not know how they will respond. The first issue will have to be determining whether they can create violent resistance to the Saudis in Bahrain, to both tie them down and increase the cost of occupation. It is simply unclear whether the Bahrainis are prepared to pay the price. The opposition does seem to want fundamental change in Bahrain, but it is not clear that they have reached the point where they are prepared to resist and die en masse.

That is undoubtedly what the Iranians are exploring now. If they find that this is not an option, then none of their other options are particularly good. All of them involve risk and difficulty. It also requires that Iran commit itself to confrontations that it has tried to avoid. It prefers covert action that is deniable to overt action that is not.

As we move into the evening, we expect the Iranians are in intense discussions of their next move. Domestic politics are affecting regional strategy, as would be the case in any country. But the clear roadmap the Iranians were working from has now collapsed. The Saudis have called their hand, and they are trying to find out if they have a real or a busted flush. They will have to act quickly before the Saudi action simply becomes a solid reality. But it is not clear what they can do quickly. For the moment, the Saudis have the upper hand. But the Iranians are clever and tenacious. There are no predictions possible. We doubt even the Iranians know what they will do.

Iraq, Iran and the Next Move
April 26, 2011

The United States told the Iraqi government last week that if it wants U.S. troops to remain in Iraq beyond the deadline of Dec. 31,

2011, as stipulated by the current Status of Forces Agreement between Washington and Baghdad, it would have to inform the United States quickly. Unless a new agreement is reached soon, the United States will be unable to remain. The implication in the U.S. position is that a complex planning process must be initiated to leave troops there and delays will not allow that process to take place.

What is actually going on is that the United States is urging the Iraqi government to change its mind on U.S. withdrawal, and it would like Iraq to change its mind right now in order to influence some of the events taking place in the Persian Gulf. The Shiite uprising in Bahrain and the Saudi intervention, along with events in Yemen, have created an extremely unstable situation in the region, and the United States is afraid that completing the withdrawal would increase the instability.

The Iranian Rise

The American concern, of course, has to do with Iran. The United States has been unable to block Iranian influence in Iraq's post-Baathist government. Indeed, the degree to which the Iraqi government is a coherent entity is questionable, and its military and security forces have limited logistical and planning ability and are not capable of territorial defense. The issue is not the intent of Prime Minister Nouri al-Maliki, who himself is enigmatic. The problem is that the coalition that governs Iraq is fragmented and still not yet finalized, dominated by Iranian proxies such Muqtada al-Sadr — and it only intermittently controls the operations of the ministries under it, or the military and security forces.

As such, Iraq is vulnerable to the influence of any substantial power, and the most important substantial power following the withdrawal of the United States will be Iran. There has been much discussion of the historic tension between Iraqi Shia and Iranian Shia, all of which is true. But Iran has been systematically building its influence in Iraq among all factions using money, blackmail and ideology delivered by a sophisticated intelligence service. More important, as the

United States withdraws, Iraqis, regardless of their feelings toward Iran (those Iraqis who haven't always felt this way), are clearly sensing that resisting Iran is dangerous and accommodation with Iran is the only solution. They see Iran as the rising power in the region, and that perception is neither unreasonable nor something to which the United States or Saudi Arabia has an easy counter.

The Iraqi government's response to the American offer has been predictable. While some quietly want the United States to remain, the general response has ranged from dismissal to threats if the United States did not leave. Given that the United States has reportedly offered to leave as many as 20,000 troops in a country that 170,000 American troops could not impose order on, the Iraqi perception is that this is merely a symbolic presence and that endorsing it would get Iraq into trouble with Iran, which has far more than 20,000 troops and ever-present intelligence services. It is not clear that the Iraqis were ever prepared to allow U.S. troops to remain, but 20,000 is enough to enrage Iran and not enough to deal with the consequences.

The American assumption in deciding to leave Iraq — and this goes back to George W. Bush as well as Barack Obama — was that over the course of four years, the United States would be able to leave because it would have created a coherent government and military. The United States underestimated the degree to which fragmentation in Iraq would prevent that outcome and the degree to which Iranian influence would undermine the effort. The United States made a pledge to the American public and a treaty with the Iraqi government to withdraw forces, but the conditions that were expected to develop simply did not.

Not coincidentally, the withdrawal of American forces has coincided with tremendous instability in the region, particularly on the Arabian Peninsula. All around the periphery of Saudi Arabia an arc of instability has emerged. It is not that the Iranians engineered it, but they have certainly taken advantage of it. As a result, Saudi Arabia is in a position where it has had to commit forces in Bahrain, is standing by in Yemen, and is even concerned about internal instability given the rise of both reform-minded and Shiite elements at a time of unprecedented transition given the geriatric state of the country's top four leaders. Iran has certainly done whatever it could to exacerbate this instability, which fits neatly into the Iraqi situation.

As the United States leaves Iraq, Iran expects to increase its influence there. Iran normally acts cautiously even while engaged in extreme rhetoric. Therefore, it is unlikely to send conventional forces into Iraq. Indeed, it might not be necessary to do so in order to gain a dominant political position. Nor is it inconceivable that the Iranians could decide to act more aggressively. With the United States gone, the risks decline.

Saudi Arabia's Problem

The country that could possibly counter Iran in Iraq is Saudi Arabia, which has been known to funnel money to Sunni groups there. Its military is no match for Iran's in a battle for Iraq, and its influence there has been less than Iran's among most groups. More important, as the Saudis face the crisis on their periphery they are diverted and preoccupied by events to the east and south. The unrest in the region, therefore, increases the sense of isolation of some Iraqis and increases their vulnerability to Iran. Thus, given that Iraq is Iran's primary national security concern, the events in the Persian Gulf work to Iran's advantage.

The United States previously had an Iraq question. That question is being answered, and not to the American advantage. Instead, what is emerging is a Saudi Arabia question. Saudi Arabia currently is clearly able to handle unrest within its borders. It has also been able to suppress the Shia in Bahrain — for now, at least. However, its ability to manage its southern periphery with Yemen is being tested, given that the regime in Sanaa was already weakened by multiple insurgencies and is now being forced from office after more than 30 years in power. If the combined pressure of internal unrest, turmoil throughout the region and Iranian manipulation continues, the stress on the Saudis could become substantial.

The basic problem the Saudis face is that they don't know the limits of their ability (which is not much beyond their financial muscle) to manage the situation. If they miscalculate and overextend, they could find themselves in an untenable position. Therefore, the Saudis must be conservative. They cannot afford miscalculation. From the Saudi point of view, the critical element is a clear sign of long-term American commitment to the regime. American support for the Saudis in Bahrain has been limited, and the United States has not been aggressively trying to manage the situation in Yemen, given its limited ability to shape an outcome there. Coupled with the American position on Iraq, which is that it will remain only if asked — and then only with limited forces — the Saudis are clearly not getting the signals they want from the United States. In fact, what further worsens the Saudi position is that they cannot overtly align with the United States for their security needs. Nevertheless, they also have no other option. Exploiting this Saudi dilemma is a key part of the Iranian strategy.

The smaller countries of the Arabian Peninsula, grouped with Saudi Arabia in the Gulf Cooperation Council, have played the role of mediator in Yemen, but ultimately they lack the force needed by a credible mediator — a potential military option to concentrate the minds of the negotiating parties. For that, they need the United States.

It is in this context that the crown prince of the United Arab Emirates (UAE), Sheikh Mohammed bin Zayed al-Nuhayyan, will be visiting Washington on April 26. The UAE is one of the few countries on the Arabian Peninsula that has not experienced significant unrest. As such, it has emerged as one of the politically powerful entities in the region. We obviously cannot know what the UAE is going to ask the United States for, but we would be surprised if it wasn't for a definitive sign that the United States was prepared to challenge the Iranian rise in the region.

The Saudis will be watching the American response very carefully. Their national strategy has been to uncomfortably rely on the United States. If the United States is seen as unreliable, the Saudis have only two options. One is to hold their position and hope for the best. The other is to reach out and see if some accommodation can be made with Iran. The tensions between Iran and Saudi Arabia — religious, cultural, economic and political — are profound. But in the end, the Iranians want to be the dominant power in the Persian Gulf, defining economic, political and military patterns.

On April 18, Iranian Supreme Leader Ayatollah Ali Khamenei's adviser for military affairs, Maj. Gen. Yahya Rahim Safavi, warned Saudi Arabia that it, too, could be invaded on the same pretext that the kingdom sent forces into Bahrain to suppress a largely Shiite rising there. Then, on April 23, the commander of Iran's elite Islamic Revolutionary Guard Corps, Maj. Gen. Mohammad Ali Jaafari, remarked that Iran's military might was stronger than that of Saudi Arabia and reminded the United States that its forces in the region were within range of Tehran's weapons. Again, the Iranians are not about to make any aggressive moves, and such statements are intended to shape perception and force the Saudis to capitulate on the negotiating table.

The Saudis want regime survival above all else. Deciding between facing Iran alone or reaching an unpleasant accommodation, the Saudis have little choice. We would guess that one of the reasons the UAE is reaching out to Obama is to try to convince him of the dire consequences of inaction and to move the United States into a more active role.

A Strategy of Neglect

The Obama administration appears to have adopted an increasingly obvious foreign policy. Rather than simply attempt to control events around the world, the administration appears to have selected a policy of careful neglect. This is not, in itself, a bad strategy. Neglect means that allies and regional powers directly affected by the problem will take responsibility for the problem. Most problems resolve themselves without the need of American intervention. If they don't, the United States can consider its posture later. Given that the world has become accustomed to the United States as first responder, other countries have simply waited for the American response. We have seen this in Libya, where the United States has tried to play a marginal role. Conceptually, this is not unsound.

The problem is that this will work only when regional powers have the weight to deal with the problem and where the outcome is not crucial to American interests. Again, Libya is an almost perfect example of this. However, the Persian Gulf is an area of enormous interest to the United States because of oil. Absent the United States, the regional forces will not be able to contain Iran. Therefore, applying this strategy to the Persian Gulf creates a situation of extreme risk for the United States.

Re-engagement in Iraq on a level that would deter Iran is not a likely option, not only because of the Iraqi position but also because the United States lacks the force needed to create a substantial deterrence that would not be attacked and worn down by guerrillas. Intruding in the Arabian Peninsula itself is dangerous for a number of reasons, ranging from the military challenge to the hostility an American presence could generate. A pure naval and air solution lacks the ability to threaten Iran's center of gravity, its large ground force.

Therefore, the United States is in a difficult position. It cannot simply decline engagement nor does it have the ability to engage at this moment — and it is this moment that matters. Nor does it have allies outside the region with the resources and appetite for involvement. That leaves the United States with the Saudi option — negotiate with Iran, a subject I've written on before. This is not an easy course, nor a recommended one, but when all other options are gone, you go with what you have.

The pressure from Iran is becoming palpable. All of the Arab countries feel it, and whatever their feelings about the Persians, the realities of power are what they are. The UAE has been sent to ask the United States for a solution. It is not clear the United States has one. When we ask why the price of oil is surging, the idea of geopolitical risk does come to mind. It is not a foolish speculation.

The U.S. Withdrawal and Limited Options in Iraq
August 17, 2010

It is August 2010, which is the month when the last U.S. combat troops are scheduled to leave Iraq. It is therefore time to take stock of the situation in Iraq, which has changed places with Afghanistan as the forgotten war. This is all the more important since 50,000 troops will remain in Iraq, and while they may not be considered combat troops, a great deal of combat power remains embedded with them. So we are far from the end of the war in Iraq. The question is whether the departure of the last combat units is a significant milestone and, if it is, what it signifies.

The United States invaded Iraq in 2003 with three goals: The first was the destruction of the Iraqi army, the second was the destruction of the Baathist regime and the third was the replacement of that regime with a stable, pro-American government in Baghdad. The first two goals were achieved within weeks. Seven years later, however, Iraq still does not yet have a stable government, let alone a pro-American government. The lack of that government is what puts the current strategy in jeopardy.

The fundamental flaw of the invasion of Iraq was not in its execution but in the political expectations that were put in place. As the Americans knew, the Shiite community was anti-Baathist but heavily influenced by Iranian intelligence. The decision to destroy the Baathists put the Sunnis, who were the backbone of Saddam's regime, in a desperate position. Facing a hostile American army and an equally hostile Shiite community backed by Iran, the Sunnis faced disaster. Taking support from where they could get it — from the foreign jihadists that were entering Iraq — they launched an insurgency against both the Americans and the Shia.

The Sunnis simply had nothing to lose. In their view, they faced permanent subjugation at best and annihilation at worst. The United States had the option of creating a Shiite-based government but realized that this government would ultimately be under Iranian control.

The political miscalculation placed the United States simultaneously into a war with the Sunnis and a near-war situation with many of the Shia, while the Shia and Sunnis waged a civil war among themselves and the Sunnis occasionally fought the Kurds as well. From late 2003 until 2007, the United States was not so much in a state of war in Iraq as it was in a state of chaos.

The new strategy of Gen. David Petraeus emerged from the realization that the United States could not pacify Iraq and be at war with everyone. After a 2006 defeat in the midterm elections, it was expected that U.S. President George W. Bush would order the withdrawal of forces from Iraq. Instead, he announced the surge. The surge was really not much of a surge, but it created psychological surprise — not only were the Americans not leaving, but more were on the way. Anyone who was calculating a position based on the assumption of a U.S. withdrawal had to recalculate.

The Americans understood that the key was reversing the position of the Sunni insurgents. So long as they remained at war with the Americans and Shia, there was no possibility of controlling the situation. Moreover, only the Sunnis could cut the legs out from under the foreign jihadists operating in the Sunni community. These jihadists were challenging the traditional leadership of the Sunni community, so turning this community against the jihadists was not difficult. The Sunnis also were terrified that the United States would withdraw, leaving them at the mercy of the Shia. These considerations, along with substantial sums of money given to Sunni tribal elders, caused the Sunnis to do an about-face. This put the Shia on the defensive, since the Sunni alignment with the Americans enabled the Americans to strike at the Shiite militias.

Petraeus stabilized the situation, but he did not win the war. The war could only be considered won when there was a stable government in Baghdad that actually had the ability to govern Iraq. A government could be formed with people sitting in meetings and talking, but that did not mean that their decisions would have any significance. For that there had to be an Iraqi army to enforce the will of the government and protect the country from its neighbors, particularly Iran (from the American point of view). There also had to be a police force to enforce whatever laws might be made. And from the American perspective, this government did not have to be pro-American (that had long ago disappeared as a viable goal), but it could not be dominated by Iran.

Iraq is not ready to deal with the enforcement of the will of the government because it has no government. Once it has a government, it will be a long time before its military and police forces will be able to enforce its will throughout the country. And it will be much longer before it can block Iranian power by itself. As it stands now, there is no government, so the rest doesn't much matter.

The geopolitical problem the Americans face is that, with the United States gone, Iran would be the most powerful conventional power in the Persian Gulf. The historical balance of power had been between Iraq and Iran. The American invasion destroyed the Iraqi army and government, and the United States was unable to recreate either. Part of this had to do with the fact that the Iranians did not want the Americans to succeed.

For Iran, a strong Iraq is the geopolitical nightmare. Iran once fought a war with Iraq that cost Iran a million casualties (imagine the United States having more than 4 million casualties), and the foundation of Iranian national strategy is to prevent a repeat of that war by making certain that Iraq becomes a puppet to Iran or, failing that, that it remains weak and divided. At this point, the Iranians do not have the ability to impose a government on Iraq. However, they do have the ability to prevent the formation of a government or to destabilize one that is formed. Iranian intelligence has sufficient allies and resources in Iraq to guarantee the failure of any stabilization attempt that doesn't please Tehran.

There are many who are baffled by Iranian confidence and defiance in the face of American pressure on the nuclear issue. This is the reason for that confidence: Should the United States attack Iran's nuclear facilities, or even if the United States does not attack, Iran holds the key to the success of the American strategy in Iraq. Everything done since 2006 fails if the United States must maintain tens of thousands of troops in Iraq in perpetuity. Should the United States leave, Iran has the capability of forcing a new order not only on Iraq but also on the rest of the Persian Gulf. Should the United States stay, Iran has the ability to prevent the stabilization of Iraq, or even to escalate violence to the point that the Americans are drawn back into combat. The Iranians understand the weakness of America's position in Iraq, and they are confident that they can use that to influence American policy elsewhere.

American and Iraqi officials have publicly said that the reason an Iraqi government has not been formed is Iranian interference. To put it more clearly, there are any number of Shiite politicians who are close to Tehran and, for a range of reasons, will take their orders from there. There are not enough of these politicians to create a government, but there are enough to block a government from being formed. Therefore, no government is being formed.

With 50,000 U.S. troops still in Iraq, the United States does not yet face a crisis. The current withdrawal milestone is not the measure of the success of the strategy. The threat of a crisis will arise if the United States continues its withdrawal to the point where the Shia feel free to launch a sustained and escalating attack on the Sunnis, possibly supported by Iranian forces, volunteers or covert advisers. At that point, the Iraqi government must be in place, be united and command sufficient forces to control the country and deter Iranian plans.

The problem is, as we have seen, that in order to achieve that government there must be Iranian concurrence, and Iran has no reason to want to allow that to happen. Iran has very little to lose by, and a great deal to gain from, continuing the stability the Petraeus strategy provided. The American problem is that a genuine withdrawal from Iraq requires a shift in Iranian policy, and the United States has little to offer Iran to change the policy.

From the Iranian point of view, they have the Americans in a difficult position. On the one hand, the Americans are trumpeting the success of the Petraeus plan in Iraq and trying to repeat the success in Afghanistan. On the other hand, the secret is that the Petraeus plan has not yet succeeded in Iraq. Certainly, it ended the major fighting involving the Americans and settled down Sunni-Shiite tensions. But it has not taken Iraq anywhere near the end state the original strategy envisioned. Iraq has neither a government nor a functional army — and what is blocking it is Tehran.

One impulse of the Americans is to settle with the Iranians militarily. However, Iran is a mountainous country of 70 million, and an invasion is simply not in the cards. Airstrikes are always possible, but as the United States learned over North Vietnam — or from the Battle of Britain or in the bombing of Germany and Japan before the use of nuclear weapons — air campaigns alone don't usually force nations to capitulate or change their policies. Serbia did give up Kosovo after a three-month air campaign, but we suspect Iran would be a tougher case. In any event, the United States has no appetite for another war while the wars in Iraq and Afghanistan are still under way, let alone a war against Iran in order to extricate itself from Iraq. The impulse to use force against Iran was resisted by President Bush and is now being resisted by President Barack Obama. And even if the Israelis attacked Iran's nuclear facilities, Iran could still wreak havoc in Iraq.

Two strategies follow from this. The first is that the United States will reduce U.S. forces in Iraq somewhat but will not complete the withdrawal until a more distant date (the current Status of Forces Agreement requires all American troops to be withdrawn by the end of 2011). The problems with this strategy are that Iran is not going anywhere, destabilizing Iraq is not costing it much and protecting itself from an Iraqi resurgence is Iran's highest foreign policy priority. That means that the decision really isn't whether the United States will delay its withdrawal but whether the United States will permanently base forces in Iraq — and how vulnerable those forces might be to an upsurge in violence, which is an option that Iran retains.

Another choice for the United States, as we have discussed previously, is to enter into negotiations with Iran. This is a distasteful choice from the American point of view, but surely not more distasteful than negotiating with Stalin or Mao. At the same time, the Iranians' price would be high. At the very least, they would want the

"Finlandization" of Iraq, similar to the situation where the Soviets had a degree of control over Finland's government. And it is far from clear that such a situation in Iraq would be sufficient for the Iranians.

The United States cannot withdraw completely without some arrangement, because that would leave Iran in an extremely powerful position in the region. The Iranian strategy seems to be to make the United States sufficiently uncomfortable to see withdrawal as attractive but not to be so threatening as to deter the withdrawal. As clever as that strategy is, however, it does not hide the fact that Iran would dominate the Persian Gulf region after the withdrawal. Thus, the United States has nothing but unpleasant choices in Iraq. It can stay in perpetuity and remain vulnerable to violence. It can withdraw and hand the region over to Iran. It can go to war with yet another Islamic country. Or it can negotiate with a government that it despises — and which despises it right back.

Given all that has been said about the success of the Petraeus strategy, it must be observed that while it broke the cycle of violence and carved out a fragile stability in Iraq, it has not achieved, nor can it alone achieve, the political solution that would end the war. Nor has it precluded a return of violence at some point. The Petraeus strategy has not solved the fundamental reality that has always been the shadow over Iraq: Iran. But that was beyond Petraeus' task and, for now, beyond American capabilities. That is why the Iranians can afford to be so confident.

Iran Sees an Opportunity in the Persian Gulf
March 3, 2011

For many observers, the instability in North Africa bodes ill for the oil-rich Persian Gulf states, which constitute the world's primary oil-producing region — and what bodes ill for the Persian Gulf would also be a grave concern for the global economy. But it is important to keep in mind that North African states are quite poor as a rule, while the Arab states of the Persian Gulf are among the richest locations on the planet, largely due to their petroleum wealth. Moreover, while Arab leaders in the Persian Gulf certainly take a large slice of the national wealth for themselves, they do not hoard all of the wealth as the regimes of Egypt and Libya traditionally have done.

In many of the Persian Gulf states, the elite realize full well that the groups they represent do not form a plurality, much less a majority, of the populations of their states. The ruling family of Saudi Arabia is only 100,000 (at the most) out of a population of roughly 20 million. More than 80 percent of the inhabitants of the United Arab

PERSIAN GULF ENERGY

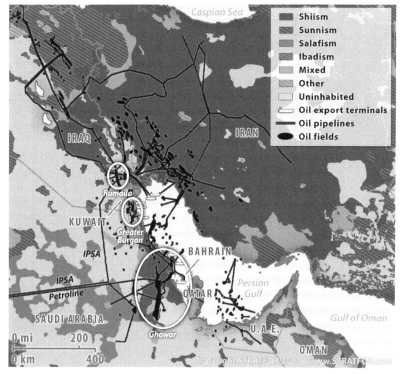

Emirates are imported labor without citizenship. At least two-thirds of Bahraini citizens are Shiite while the ruling family is Sunni.

The Arab elite's solution to this demographic mismatch is to mix an authoritarian political setup with an aggressive sharing of the petroleum largess. Subsidy rates — whether for food, electricity, housing or gasoline — are lavish. The rulers of the Arab states of the Persian Gulf essentially purchase political quietude.

The real reason STRATFOR sees the Persian Gulf's Arab states as being threatened has less to do with spontaneous protests and more to do with foreign-instigated unrest — and this would-be instigator is Iran. Iran has struggled to increase its sway on the western shores of the Gulf since long before the mullahs rose to power in 1979, and in this new viral-protest age, Tehran sees an opportunity.

In recent days, the Iranians have encouraged unrest in the Persian Gulf state that has the highest proportion of Shia: Bahrain. Luckily for the energy markets, Bahrain is practically a non-player. The real game is in the energy heavyweights of Iraq, Kuwait and Saudi Arabia. In these states, we see three specific regions as being in potential danger because they are large sources of oil, they are immediately adjacent to Shiite population centers, and the oil-export routes pass through these to Shiite-populated ports:

- Southern Iraq's Rumaila region is the country's most productive. The cluster of fields around the Rumaila super-field generates roughly 2 million barrels per day (bpd) of crude, nearly all of which is funneled into pipes that run just south of Shiite-dominated Basra, Iraq's second largest city, to loading platforms in the Persian Gulf.

- The Burgan region of southern Kuwait is home to the Greater Burgan field, by far Kuwait's largest. It also is just inland from all of Kuwait's population centers, which wrap from the capital, Kuwait City, down to the Saudi border. Here the population is more of a Sunni-Shiite mix than it is in southern Iraq, but all of Kuwait's exports ship out from predominantly Shiite regions on the southern coast rather than Sunni-dominated Kuwait

City itself. Greater Burgan produces slightly less than 1.7 million bpd and serves as the gathering point for all of Kuwait's 2.5 million bpd of output.

- Saudi Arabia's Ghawar super-field is the most important of these areas of concern. With about 5 million bpd of output, Ghawar is the largest oil field in the world, and it lies right alongside the city of Al Hofuf, which has a mostly Shiite population of 650,000. Oil produced from Ghawar travels via pipes to the northeast across and parallel to major Saudi highways to reach a trio of tanker ports on the Persian Gulf — all of which are within Shiite-dominated areas.

There are only two possible routes for oil from these locations to be shipped should problems erupt within the Shiite populations. Iraq has the Iraq Petroleum Saudi Arabia (IPSA) pipeline, which could transfer 1.7 million bpd of oil from southern Iraq to the Saudi Red Sea port of Yanbu — in theory, at least. The problem is that IPSA has been closed since the earliest days of Operation Desert Shield, and it is not clear how soon it could be rehabilitated, if at all. The second alternative is Saudi Arabia's Petroline, which links Ghawar to Yanbu. It can handle 5 million bpd, which is roughly half of Saudi Arabia's entire production capacity.

Such disruptions could take three forms. The first are outright attacks by angry citizens or disgruntled guest workers. By far the most vulnerable assets would be pipelines, the routes of which are obvious since they travel along transportation corridors or near population centers. To date, this has happened only once in recent weeks, against Egypt's natural gas export line to Jordan and Israel. The second would be disruptions caused by citizens — or guest workers — either not showing up for work or placing physical restrictions on the ability of energy workers to reach their jobs. Such disruptions have taken roughly two-thirds of Libya's energy output offline. In the Persian Gulf, the vulnerability varies greatly from location to location, based on how close to the fields the workers live.

The final possible form of disruption is the most worrisome: foreign sabotage. Unlike the North Africa protests, which were by people rallying to improve their own countries — who thus had no interest in burning their countries to the ground — in the Persian Gulf any serious protests would receive significant foreign encouragement from a state wanting to change the regional power balance. Iran has a strong interest in limiting the power of Iraq, Kuwait and Saudi Arabia, even if it means taking Arab oil offline.

Bahrain and the Battle Between Iran and Saudi Arabia
March 8, 2011

The world's attention is focused on Libya, which is now in a state of civil war with the winner far from clear. While crucial for the Libyan people and of some significance to the world's oil markets, in our view, Libya is not the most important event in the Arab world at the moment. The demonstrations in Bahrain are, in my view, far more significant in their implications for the region and potentially for the world. To understand this, we must place it in a strategic context.

As STRATFOR has been saying for quite a while, a decisive moment is approaching, with the United States currently slated to withdraw the last of its forces from Iraq by the end of the year. Indeed, we are already at a point where the composition of the 50,000 troops remaining in Iraq has shifted from combat troops to training and support personnel. As it stands now, even these will all be gone by Dec. 31, 2011, provided the United States does not negotiate an extended stay. Iraq still does not have a stable government. It also does not have a military and security apparatus able to enforce the will of the government (which is hardly of one mind on anything) on the country, much less defend the country from outside forces.

Filling the Vacuum in Iraq

The decision to withdraw creates a vacuum in Iraq, and the question of the wisdom of the original invasion is at this point moot. The Iranians previously have made clear that they intend to fill this vacuum with their own influence; doing so makes perfect sense from their point of view. Iran and Iraq fought a long and brutal war in the 1980s. With the collapse of the Soviet Union, Iran is now secure on all fronts save the western. Tehran's primary national security imperative now is to prevent a strong government from emerging in Baghdad, and more important, a significant military force from emerging there. Iran never wants to fight another war with Iraq, making keeping Iraq permanently weak and fragmented in Tehran's interest. The U.S. withdrawal from Iraq sets the stage for Iran to pursue this goal, profoundly changing the regional dynamic.

Iran has another, more challenging strategic interest, one it has had since Biblical times. That goal is to be the dominant power in the Persian Gulf.

For Tehran, this is both reasonable and attainable. Iran has the largest and most ideologically committed military of any state in the Persian Gulf region. Despite the apparent technological sophistication of the Gulf states' militaries, they are shells. Iran's is not. In addition to being the leading military force in the Persian Gulf, Iran has 75 million people, giving it a larger population than all other Persian Gulf states combined.

Outside powers have prevented Iran from dominating the region since the fall of the Ottoman Empire, first the United Kingdom and then the United States, which consistently have supported the countries of the Arabian Peninsula. It was in the outsiders' interests to maintain a divided region, and therefore in their interests to block the most powerful country in the region from dominating even when the outsiders were allied with Iran.

With the U.S. withdrawal from Iraq, this strategy is being abandoned in the sense that the force needed to contain Iran is being withdrawn. The forces left in Kuwait and U.S air power might be able to limit a conventional Iranian attack. Still, the U.S. withdrawal leaves the Iranians with the most powerful military force in the region regardless of whether they acquire nuclear weapons. Indeed, in my view, the nuclear issue largely has been an Iranian diversion from the more fundamental issue, namely, the regional balance after the departure of the United States. By focusing on the nuclear issue, these other issues appeared subsidiary and have been largely ignored.

The U.S. withdrawal does not mean that the United States is powerless against Iran. It has been reconstituting a pre-positioned heavy brigade combat team set in Kuwait and has substantial air and naval assets in the region. It also can bring more forces back to the region if Iran is aggressive. But it takes at least several months for the United States to bring multidivisional forces into a theater and requires the kind of political will that will be severely lacking in the United States in the years ahead. It is not clear that the forces available on the ground could stop a determined Iranian thrust. In any case, Iraq will be free of American troops, allowing Iran to operate much more freely there.

And Iran does not need to change the balance of power in the region through the overt exercise of military force. Its covert capability, unchecked by American force, is significant. It can covertly support pro-Iranian forces in the region, destabilizing existing regimes. With the psychology of the Arab masses changing, as they are no longer afraid to challenge their rulers, Iran will enjoy an enhanced capacity to cause instability.

As important, the U.S. withdrawal will cause a profound shift in psychological perceptions of power in the region. Recognition of Iran's relative power based on ground realities will force a very different political perception of Iran, and a desire to accommodate Tehran. The Iranians, who understand the weakness of their military's logistics and air power, are pursuing a strategy of indirect approach. They are laying the foundation for power based on a perception of greater Iranian power and declining American and Saudi power.

Bahrain, the Test Case

Bahrain is the perfect example and test case. An island off the coast of Saudi Arabia, Bahrain and Saudi Arabia are linked by a causeway. For most purposes, Bahrain is part of Saudi Arabia. Unlike Saudi Arabia, it is not a major oil producer, but it is a banking center. It is also the home of the U.S. 5th Fleet, and has close ties to the United States. The majority of its population is Shia, but its government is Sunni and heavily linked to Saudi Arabia. The Shiite population has not fared as well economically as Shia in other countries in the region, and tensions between the government and the public have long existed.

The toppling of the government of Bahrain by a Shiite movement would potentially embolden Shia in Saudi Arabia, who live primarily in the oil-rich northeast near Bahrain. It also would weaken the U.S. military posture in the region. And it would demonstrate Iranian power.

If the Saudis intervened in Bahrain, the Iranians would have grounds to justify their own intervention, covert or overt. Iran might also use any violent Bahraini government suppression of demonstrators to justify more open intervention. In the meantime, the United States, which has about 1,500 military personnel plus embassy staff on the ground in Bahrain, would face the choice of reinforcing or pulling its troops out.

Certainly, there are internal processes under way in Bahrain that have nothing to do with Iran or foreign issues. But just as the internal dynamic of revolutions affects the international scene, the international scene affects the internal dynamic; observing just one of the two is not sufficient to understand what is going on.

The Iranians clearly have an interest in overthrowing the Bahraini regime. While the degree to which the Iranians are involved in the Bahraini unrest is unclear, they clearly have a great deal of influence over a cleric, Hassan Mushaima, who recently returned to Bahrain from London to participate in the protests. That said, the Bahraini government itself could be using the unrest to achieve its own political goals, much as the Egyptian military used the Egyptian uprising. Like all revolutions, events in Bahrain are enormously complex — and in Bahrain's case, the stakes are extremely high.

Unlike Libya, where the effects are primarily internal, the events in Bahrain clearly involve Saudi, Iranian and U.S. interests. Bahrain is also the point where the Iranians have their best chance, since it is both the most heavily Shiite nation and one where the Shiites have the most grievances. But the Iranians have other targets, which might be defined as any area adjoining Saudi Arabia with a substantial Shiite population and with American bases. This would include Oman, which the United States uses as a support facility; Qatar, headquarters of U.S. Central Command and home to Al Udeid Air Base; and Kuwait, the key logistical hub for Iraqi operations and with major army support, storage and port facilities. All three have experienced or are experiencing demonstrations. Logically, these are Iran's first targets.

The largest target of all is, of course, Saudi Arabia. That is the heart of the Arabian Peninsula, and its destabilization would change the regional balance of power and the way the world works. Iran has never made a secret of its animosity toward Saudi Arabia, nor vice versa. Saudi Arabia could now be in a vise. There is massive instability in Yemen with potential to spill over into Saudi Arabia's southern Ismaili-concentrated areas. The situation in Iraq is moving in the Iranians' favor. Successful regime changes in even one or two of the countries on the littoral of the Persian Gulf could generate massive internal fears regardless of what the Saudi Shia did and could lead to dissension in the royal family. It is not surprising, therefore, that the Saudis are moving aggressively against any sign of unrest among the Shia, arresting dozens who have indicated dissent. The Saudis clearly are uneasy in the extreme.

Iran's Powerful Position

The Iranians would be delighted to cause regime change throughout the region, but that is not likely to occur, at least not everywhere in the region. They would be equally happy simply to cause massive instability in the region, however. With the United States withdrawing from Iraq, the Saudis represent the major supporter of Iraq's Sunnis. With the Saudis diverted, this would ease the way for Iranian influence in Iraq. At that point, there would be three options: Turkey intervening broadly, something it is not eager to do; the United States reversing course and surging troops into the region to support tottering regimes, something for which there is no political appetite in the United States; and the United States accepting the changed regional balance of power.

Two processes are under way. The first is that Iran will be the single outside power with the most influence in Iraq, not unlimited and not unchallenged, but certainly the greatest. The second is that as the United States withdraws, Iran will be in a position to pursue its interests more decisively. Those interests divide into three parts:

1. eliminating foreign powers from the region to maximize Iranian power,

2. convincing Saudi Arabia and other countries in the region that they must reach an accommodation with Iran or face potentially dangerous consequences, and

3. a redefinition of the economics of oil in the Persian Gulf in favor of Iran, including Iranian participation in oil projects in other Persian Gulf countries and regional investment in Iranian energy development.

The events in the Persian Gulf are quite different from the events in North Africa, with much broader implications. Bahrain is the focal point of a struggle between Saudi Arabia and Iran for control of the western littoral of the Persian Gulf. If Iran is unable to capitalize on events in Bahrain, the place most favorable to it, the moment will pass. If Bahrain's government falls, the door is opened to further actions. Whether Iran caused the rising in the first place is unclear and unimportant; it is certainly involved now, as are the Saudis.

The Iranians are in a powerful position whatever happens given the U.S. withdrawal from Iraq. Combine this with a series of regime changes, or simply destabilization on the border of Saudi Arabia, and two things happen. First, the Saudi regime would be in trouble and would have to negotiate some agreement with the Iranians — and not an agreement the Saudis would like. Second, the U.S. basing position in the Persian Gulf would massively destabilize, making U.S. intervention in the region even more difficult.

The problem created by the U.S. leaving Iraq without having been able to install a strong, pro-American government remains the core issue. The instability in the Persian Gulf allows the Iranians a low-risk, high-reward parallel strategy that, if it works, could unhinge the balance of power in the entire region. The threat of an uprising in Iran appears minimal, with the Iranian government having no real difficulty crushing resistance. The resistance on the western shore of the Persian Gulf may be crushed or dissolved as well, in which case Iran would still retain its advantageous position in Iraq. But if the perfect storm presents itself, with Iran increasing its influence in Iraq and massive destabilization on the Arabian Peninsula, then the United States will face some extraordinarily difficult and dangerous choices, beginning with the question of how to resist Iran while keeping the price of oil manageable.

History Repeats Itself in Eastern Arabia
March 15, 2011

For the second time in less than two years, Saudi Arabia deployed troops beyond its borders to contain Shiite unrest in its immediate neighborhood. In late 2009, Saudi forces fought to suppress Houthi rebels in the country's Shiite borderland to the south in Yemen. This time around, a Saudi-led force, operating under the umbrella of the Gulf Cooperation Council's (GCC) Peninsula Shield Force, deployed forces to the Sunni-ruled island kingdom of Bahrain to suppress Shiite unrest.

The Saudi royals, highly dependent on the United States for the security of their regime, do not deploy their forces without good reason — especially when they already have their own simmering Shiite unrest to deal with in the country's oil-rich eastern region and are looking at the potential for instability in Yemen to spill into the kingdom from the south.

From the Saudi perspective, the threat of an Iranian-backed destabilization campaign to reshape the balance of power in favor of the Shia is more than enough reason to justify a deployment of forces to Bahrain. The United States, Saudi Arabia and its GCC allies have been carefully monitoring Iran's heavy involvement in fueling Shiite protests in their Sunni sheikhdoms and understand the historic opportunity that Iran is pursuing.

The historical attraction of Bahrain lies in its geography. Bahrain is a tiny island nestled between the Arabian and Qatar peninsulas. It is vulnerable to external interference and valuable to whomever can lay claim to its lands, whether that be the Shia, the Sunni or any outside power capable of projecting authority to the Persian Gulf. Control of the island together with the Strait of Hormuz allowed for domination of the Indian Ocean trade along the Silk Road and the Arabian trade route from Mecca to the Red Sea.

The isles of Bahrain, along with the oases of al Qatif and al Hasa (both located in the modern-day Eastern province of Saudi Arabia), have been the three key economic hubs of the eastern Arabia region since antiquity. Bahrain sat atop a wealth of natural pearls while all three of these areas traded dates and spices and later on, oil, with buyers abroad. Critically, Bahrain, al Qatif and al Hasa have also been heavily populated with Shiite peoples throughout their history.

As a result, Bahrain, al Qatif and al Hasa have vacillated between Sunni and Shiite domination for hundreds of years. The Bahraini island can never exist comfortably in either domain. As a natural extension of the Arabian Peninsula, it would often fall under the influence of roaming Sunni Bedouin tribes, which found it difficult to subjugate the majority Shiite inhabitants. When under Shiite domination, as it was during the century-and-a-half-reign of the Banu Jarwan in the 14th century and during the 17th century with the rise of the Persian Safavid empire in Iran, the Shia in Bahrain struggled to fend off Sunni incursions without significant foreign backing. The Persians, sitting some 125 miles across the Persian Gulf, would often find it difficult to project power to the island, relying instead on the local religious elite, traders, judges and politicians to assert their will, but frequently finding themselves outmatched against outside powers vying for control and/or influence over eastern Arabia. From the Portuguese to the Ottomans to the British (and now) to the United States, each of these outside forces exercised a classic balance of power politics in playing Sunni and Shiite rivalries off each other, all with an eye on controlling, or at least influencing, eastern Arabia.

History repeated itself Monday.

A Saudi-led contingent of Arab forces crossed into Bahraini territory in defense against an Iranian-led attempt to reorient eastern Arabia toward the Shia. And yet again, the Persians are facing a strategic dilemma in projecting power to aid its Shiite proxies living in Sunni shadows. At the same time, the predominant naval power of the Persian Gulf, the United States, is pursuing its own strategic aim of shoring up the Sunni forces to counterbalance a resurgent Iran. It remains to be seen how this latest chapter unfolds, but if history is to serve as a guide, the question of whether Bahrain remains in Sunni hands or flips to the Shiite majority (currently the less likely option) will serve as the pivot to the broader Sunni-Shiite balance of power in the Persian Gulf.

CHAPTER 7: THE U.S.-IRANIAN STRUGGLE

The Region After Iraq
February 4, 2003

Last week, the focus was on Europe — where heavy U.S. pressure, coupled with the internal dynamics, generated a deep division. From the U.S. point of view, regardless of what France and Germany ultimately say about the war, these two countries no longer can claim to speak for Europe. Ultimately, for the Americans, that is sufficient.

This week, U.S. attention must shift to a much more difficult target — the Islamic world. More precisely, it must shift to the countries bordering Iraq and others in the region as well. In many ways, this is a far more important issue than Europe. The Europeans, via multinational organizations, can provide diplomatic sanction for the invasion of Iraq. The countries around Iraq constitute an essential part of the theater of operations, potentially influencing the course of the war and even more certainly, the course of history after the war. What they have to say and, more important, what they will do, is of direct significance to the war.

As it stands at this moment, the U.S. position in the region, at the most obvious level, is tenuous at best. Six nations border Iraq: Kuwait, Saudi Arabia, Jordan, Syria, Turkey and Iran. Of the six, only one — Kuwait — is unambiguously allied with the United States.

205

The rest continue to behave ambiguously. All have flirted with the United States and provided varying degrees of overt and covert cooperation, but they have not made peace with the idea of invasion and U.S. occupation.

Of the remaining five, Turkey is by far the most cooperative. It will permit U.S. forces to continue to fly combat missions against Iraq from bases in Turkey as well as allow them to pass through Turkey and maintain some bases there. However, there is a split between the relatively new Islamist government of Turkey, which continues to be uneasy about the war, and the secular Turkish military, which is committed to extensive cooperation. And apart from Kuwait, Turkey is the best case. Each of the other countries is even more conflicted and negative toward an invasion.

Saudi Arabia, Jordan, Syria and Iran are very different countries and have different reasons for arriving at their positions. They each have had very different experiences with Hussein's Iraq.

Iran fought a brutal war with Iraq during the 1980s — a war initiated by the Iraqis and ruinous to Iran. Hussein is despised by Iranians, who continue to support anti-Hussein exiles. Tehran certainly is tempted by the idea of a defeated Iraq. It also is tempted by the idea of a dismembered Iraq that never again could threaten Iran, and where Iran could gain dominance over its Shiite regions. Tehran certainly has flirted with Washington and particularly with London on various levels of cooperation, and clearly has provided some covert intelligence cooperation to the United States and Britain. In the end, though — however attractive the collapse of Iraq might be — internal politics and strategic calculations have caused Iranian leaders to refuse to sanction the war or to fully participate. Iran might be prepared to pick up some of the spoils, but only after the war is fought.

Syria stands in a similar relation to Iraq. The Assad family despises the Husseins, ideologically, politically and personally. Syria sided openly with the United States in 1991. Hussein's demise would cause no grief in Damascus. Yet, in spite of a flirtation with Britain in particular — including a visit with both Queen Elizabeth II and Prince

Charles for Syrian President Bashar Assad — Syria has not opted in for the war.

Nor have the Jordanians — at least not publicly. There are constant reports of U.S. (and Israeli) special operations troops operating out of Jordan. U.S. Marines have trained during the past month in Jordan, but the government remains officially opposed to the war — and what support it will give, it will give only covertly.

Finally, there is Saudi Arabia, which has been one of the pillars of U.S. power in the region since the 1950s and which has, in turn, depended on Washington for survival against both Arab radicals and Iraq itself. The Saudis have been playing the most complex game of all, cooperating on some levels openly, cooperating on other levels covertly, while opposing the war publicly.

For all of the diversity in the region, there is a common geopolitical theme. If the U.S. invasion is successful, Washington intends to occupy Iraq militarily, and it officially expects to remain there for at least 18 months — or to be more honest, indefinitely. The United States will build air bases and deploy substantial ground forces — and, rather than permit the disintegration of Iraq, will create a puppet government underwritten by U.S. power.

On the day the war ends, and if the United States is victorious, then the entire geopolitics of the region will be redefined. Every country bordering Iraq will find not the weakest formations of the Iraqi army along their frontiers, but U.S. and British troops. The United States will be able to reach into any country in the region with covert forces based in Iraq, and Washington could threaten overt interventions as well. It would need no permission from regional hosts for the use of facilities, so long as either Turkey or Kuwait will permit transshipment into Iraq. In short, a U.S. victory will change the entire balance of power in the region, from a situation in which the United States must negotiate its way to war, to a situation where the United States is free to act as it will.

Consider the condition of Syria. It might not have good relations with Hussein's Iraq, but a U.S.-occupied Iraq would be Syria's worst nightmare. It would be surrounded on all sides by real or potential enemies — Israel, Turkey, Jordan and the United States — and, in the Mediterranean, by the U.S. Sixth Fleet. Syria — which traditionally has played a subtle, complex balancing game between various powers — would find itself in a vise, no longer able to guarantee its national security except through accommodating the United States.

A similar situation is shaping up for Saudi Arabia. The United States is operating extensively in Yemen; it also has air force facilities in Qatar and naval facilities in Bahrain. U.S. B-1 bombers and some personnel are going to be based in Oman. The United States has established itself along the littoral of the Arabian peninsula. With U.S. forces deployed along the Saudi-Iraqi border, and with U.S. domination of the Red Sea and Persian Gulf, the Saudis will be in essence surrounded.

The same basic problem exists for Iran, although on a less threatening scale. Iran is larger, more populated and more difficult to intimidate. Nevertheless, with at least some U.S. forces in Afghanistan — and the option for introducing more always open — and U.S. forces in Iraq and the Persian Gulf, the Iranians too find themselves surrounded, albeit far less overwhelmingly than would be the case for Syria or Saudi Arabia.

The only probable winners would be Turkey, which would lay claim to the oil fields around Mosul and Kirkuk; Jordan, whose security would be enhanced by U.S. forces to the east; and Kuwait, which is betting heavily on a quick U.S. victory and a prolonged presence in the region.

If we consider the post-Iraq war world, it is no surprise that the regional response ranges from publicly opposed and privately not displeased to absolute opposition. Certainly, Syria, Saudi Arabia and Iran have nothing to gain from a war that will be shaped entirely by the United States. Each understands that the pressure from the United States to cooperate in the war against al Qaeda will be overwhelming, potentially irresistible and politically destabilizing. This is not the world in which they want to live.

Add to this the obvious fact of oil, and the dilemma becomes clear. The United States is not invading Iraq for oil: If oil was on

Washington's mind, it would invade Venezuela, whose crisis has posed a more serious oil problem for the United States than Iraq could. Nevertheless, Washington expects to pay for the reconstruction of Iraq from oil revenues, and there will be no reason to limit Iraqi production. This cannot make either Riyadh or Tehran happy, since it will drive prices down and increase competition for market share.

Saudi Arabia, Iran and Syria have every reason to oppose a war in Iraq. The consequences of such a war will undermine their national interests. They were depending on Europe's ability to block the war, but that strategy has failed. The Saudis and Syrians then launched into an attempt to find a political solution that would prevent a U.S. occupation of Iraq. That centered around either Hussein's voluntary resignation and exile, or a coup in Baghdad that would produce a new government — one that would cooperate fully with weapons inspectors, and remove the U.S. justification for occupation.

This attempt, in collaboration with other regional powers and countries like Germany and Russia, is still under way. The problem is that Hussein has little motivation to resign, and his security forces remain effective. Hussein apparently still is not convinced that the United States will invade, or that he will be defeated. His seems to assume that, if his troops can inflict some casualties on U.S. forces, then the United States will accept a cease-fire without toppling him. He will not abdicate, nor will his followers overthrow him, until those two assumptions are falsified. What that means is that the United States still would occupy Iraq militarily, even if there was a coup or resignation as the campaign unfolded.

If you can't beat them, join them. The European split — and the real possibility that France and Germany ultimately will endorse war in some way — mean that war cannot be prevented. Hussein will not abdicate or be overthrown until the war is well under way. Therefore, it is highly likely that the war will take place, the United States will occupy Iraq and that the map of the Middle East will change profoundly.

Continued opposition to the war, particularly from Riyadh's standpoint, makes little sense. The issue until now has been to cope with the internal political challenges that have arisen in the kingdom since Sept. 11, 2001. After the Iraq war, this issue will be supplemented by the question of how the United States regards the kingdom. It is not prudent for a nation surrounded by a much more powerful nation to allow itself to be regarded as an enemy. Therefore, we are witnessing a shift in the Saudi position that might evolve to reluctant, public support for the war by the time an attack is launched.

Iranian leaders do not feel themselves to be quite in such desperate straits — since they are not. However, the presence of U.S. power on Iran's borders will create an urgent need to settle the internal disputes that divide the country. The need to do so, however, does not guarantee a successful outcome. The division between those who feel that an opening to the United States is essential and those who feel that protecting Iran against the United States is paramount might become exacerbated and destabilize the country. However, there is no immediate, overt threat to Iran, although the possibilities for covert operations increase dramatically.

Jordan will do well, but Syria's future is cloudier. Washington has concerns about Syria's long-term commitment to U.S. interests, and Damascus might find itself squeezed unbearably. Turkey will fatten on oil and manage the Kurds as it has done in the past. But nothing will be the same after this war. Unlike Desert Storm, which was about restoring the status quo ante, this war is about establishing an entirely new reality.

The United States is, of course, well-aware that its increased presence in the region will result in greater hostility and increased paramilitary activity against U.S. forces there. However, the U.S. view is that this rising cost is acceptable so long as Washington is able to redefine the behavior of countries neighboring Iraq. In the long run, the Bush administration believes, geopolitical power will improve U.S. security interests in spite of growing threats. To be more precise, the United States sees Islamic hostility at a certain level as a given, and does not regard an increase in that hostility as materially affecting its interests.

The conquest of Iraq will not be a minor event in history: It will represent the introduction of a new imperial power to the Middle East and a redefinition of regional geopolitics based on that power. The United States will move from being an outside power influencing events through coalitions, to a regional power that is able to operate effectively on its own. Most significant, countries like Saudi Arabia and Syria will be living in a new and quite unpleasant world.

Therefore, it is not difficult to understand why the regional powers are behaving as they are. The disintegration of the European bloc has, however, left them in an untenable position. The United States will occupy Iraq, and each regional power is now facing that reality. Unable to block the process, they are reluctantly and unhappily finding ways to accustom themselves to it.

A Positive Iranian Influence in Iraq?
September 26, 2003

Iranian Foreign Minister Kamal Kharrazi was in New York on Sept. 25, attending the United Nations General Assembly session. It wasn't clear if he would meet with any U.S. officials, secretly or officially, but he was doing the next best thing — meeting with Ahmed Chalabi, president of the Iraqi Governing Council and as close to a U.S. official as possible without being one. Chalabi would not be meeting with Kharrazi without U.S. approval and guidance. Therefore, Chalabi's statement before the dinner was noteworthy. He said, "The Iranians are a positive influence." Given the official position of the United States, that's quite a statement for Chalabi to make.

International Atomic Energy Agency inspectors found traces of enriched uranium at a second site in Iran on Sept. 25. We don't like being suspicious, but the timing was superb for Tehran — it wants the United States to know it has a nuclear program. In Iran's view, the United States will never take it seriously if it doesn't have one. Moreover, a nuclear program gives Tehran a bargaining chip. As Kharrazi put it in an interview in the Washington Post, "We want to make sure the additional protocol would be enough and would solve the problem. We don't have anything to hide because we do not have a program for producing nuclear weapons. Therefore, we are ready to be quite transparent. But we cannot let others deny our rights."

In other words, Iran is prepared to bargain on nuclear weapons, but the United States has to make an offer. Kharrazi's view, as noted in the Post article, is that Iran and the United States have common interests in Iraq, including stabilizing the country and ensuring that Saddam Hussein and his followers never return to power. In discussing the last round of talks in Geneva, Kharrazi said, "At those talks, we advised it is better to leave Iraq in the hands of the Iraqis. They were reluctant at first, but later on they understood. They know much less than us about Iraq, but we tried to educate them about the psychology of the Iraqis, the way to deal with them." That translates to: "We told the United States not to set up a military government, but it wouldn't listen. We know a lot more about Iraq than the Americans and they had better listen to us."

The United States is certainly listening now. Washington's problem is the difficulty of publicly acknowledging the growing accommodation with Tehran. As we move into the presidential election year, what was hard before has become impossible. Labeling Iran as a point on the "axis of evil" made entering into formal, or even informal, public agreements with it extremely difficult for U.S. President George W. Bush.

Washington wants an unacknowledged alignment with Iran. The conditions for a Shiite-dominated constitutional assembly already have been established. The assembly will declare an Islamic republic in Iraq. The United States is transferring security responsibilities to Shiite-dominated institutions in southern Iraq. The United States wants to appear to be hostile to the Iranians, while actually accommodating them. That's one reason the nuclear issue is so important to the United States — it allows Washington to publicly attack and even threaten Iran while privately working with it. But even here, Kharrazi is trying to trap the United States by offering reasonable compromises.

Washington's goal is deniable accommodation with Tehran. This is driven by U.S. political needs, not strategic reality. From a strategic standpoint, whether overt or covert, the U.S.-Iranian deal will result in an Iran-dominated Iraq. There are strategic problems with that from the U.S. point of view, but they have nothing to do with secrecy.

The secrecy has to do with electoral politics, as well as with an internal split in the Bush administration. Some view the Iraq situation as requiring rapid, radical solution. If that means working with Iran, so be it. This faction includes the president's political advisers as well as the State Department. In contrast, Defense Department leaders regard an accommodation with Iran as an instance of the cure being worse than the disease.

Leaving aside the interesting question of which side is right, the whole issue points to a very strange policymaking style. We have reached a point where policy disputes do not result in clear-cut decisions. Rather, policies are implemented in such complex and creeping ways that no one wants to acknowledge that policies actually are being implemented — no one seems to own them. Not only does the administration, as a whole, want deniability — individual factions want it, too.

So there are hundreds of little facts on the ground indicating accommodation between the United States and Iran. The Iranians are positively jovial these days when speaking of the Americans. The Americans send Chalabi to speak to the Iranians and senior commanders to work with the Shiites. All of this is going on without any clear acknowledgment of the obvious by anyone.

It is a fascinating style for foreign policymakers. We wonder if it can possibly work.

Iran's View of the Surge
January 12, 2007

U.S. forces raided an Iranian nondiplomatic office on Thursday in the Iraqi city of Arbil and captured several people. This is the second operation of this kind in a month against Iranians in Iraq, but this one took place shortly after the end of U.S. President George W. Bush's speech announcing a new "surge" of troops into the country. The Iranians, obviously, objected strenuously to the raid, which they argued was carried out without the approval of the Iraqi government — diplomatically important since it was an office of the Iranian Consulate. The United States did not comment directly, but clearly couldn't care less.

We have been talking about the psychological and political dimension of Washington's new strategy. Obviously, the increase in troops, rather than the drawdown expected after the Democratic victory and the Iraq Study Group report, was a surprise to the Iranians. It seems that the Bush administration is now trying to increase the pressure. The Israeli discussion of using nuclear weapons against Iran, the report that the CIA has been authorized to act against Hezbollah (which is Iran's asset in Lebanon), attacks on Iranian offices in Iraq, and statements by various Bush administration officials warning Tehran, taken together, point to a concerted effort to intimidate Iran.

The question, of course, is whether Iran finds itself intimidated. Certainly, the world has changed since November 2006, when the Iranians reasonably felt they were on the verge of the strategic triumph of dominating Iraq. Washington has now taken the game to extra innings. But extra innings do not mean victory. From the Iranian point of view, it would seem, the fundamentals have not changed much. The United States is still in the game with too little, and too late; Israeli nuclear strikes would create an interesting political dynamic for Iran, even more interesting than having nukes; Hezbollah can take care of itself against the CIA; and the U.S. raids in Iraq are pinpricks.

At the same time, the Iranians are also aware of American resiliency and American deviousness. They recall how the Iraqi invasion of Iran bogged down the revolution for a decade and how the United States quietly manipulated the situation. They watched the Soviet Union collapse after the United States seemed to be a declining power in the 1970s. There are leaders in Iran who remember that the Americans have enormous reserves of power and resources and a very unpredictable political process.

Things always look better on the other side of the hill. From the Iranian point of view — as opposed to the gloomy American view — the United States is resourceful and treacherous. As events diverge from the expected path, the Iranians, at least some of them, have to be wondering whether they have made another major miscalculation. So, just as the Americans are gloomily trying one last gambit, the Iranians are wondering if their strategic hopes are going to fade.

There are interesting developments in Iranian politics that have been discussed here before. With Supreme Leader Ayatollah Ali Khamenei apparently ill, and impeachment moves in the works against President Mahmoud Ahmadinejad, one wonders how much of this apparent instability is due to unease over the possibility that the Iranians are more vulnerable than they might appear. Iranian politics are opaque, and it is not clear whether any of this is serious; but still, it is there and has arisen at the same time that the United States has shifted policy and defied expectations.

Obviously, this is Bush's hope. He hopes that he can force Iran to re-evaluate its position in light of his unexpected moves. That might seem unlikely from an American point of view, but we have to wonder whether the Iranians see things as Americans do. Pessimism and exaggerated fears could well be endemic in this situation.

The NIE Report: Solving a Geopolitical Problem with Iran
December 3, 2007

The United States released a new National Intelligence Estimate (NIE) on Dec. 3. It said, "We judge with high confidence that in the fall of 2003, Tehran halted its nuclear weapons program." It went on to say, "Tehran's decision to halt its nuclear weapons program suggests it is less determined to develop nuclear weapons than we have been judging since 2005." It further said, "Our assessment that Iran halted the program in 2003 primarily in response to international pressure indicates Tehran's decisions are guided by a cost-benefit approach rather than a rush to a weapon irrespective of the political, economic and military costs."

With this announcement, the dynamics of the Middle Eastern region, Iraq and U.S.-Iranian relations shift dramatically. For one thing, the probability of a unilateral strike against Iranian nuclear targets is gone. Since there is no Iranian nuclear weapons program, there is no rationale for a strike. Moreover, if Iran is not engaged in weapons production, then a broader air campaign designed to destabilize the Iranian regime has no foundation either.

The NIE release represents a transformation of U.S. policy toward Iran. The Bush administration made Iran's nuclear weapons program the main reason for its attempt to create an international coalition against Iran, on the premise that a nuclear-armed Iran was unacceptable. If there is no Iranian nuclear program, then what is the rationale for the coalition? Moreover, what is the logic of resisting Iran's efforts in Iraq, rather than cooperating?

In looking at the report, a number of obvious questions come up. First, how did the intelligence community reach the wrong conclusion in the spring of 2005, when it last released an NIE on Iran, and what changed by 2007? Also, why did the United States reach the wrong conclusions on Iran three years after its program was halted?

There are two possible answers. One is intelligence failure and the other is political redefinition. Both must be explored.

Let's begin with intelligence failure. Intelligence is not an easy task. Knowing what is going on inside of a building is harder than it might seem. Regardless of all the technical capabilities — from imagery in all spectra to sensing radiation leakage at a distance — huge uncertainties always remain. Failing to get a positive reading does not mean the facility is not up and running. It might just have been obscured, or the technical means to discover it are insufficient. The default setting in technical intelligence is that, while things can be ruled in, they cannot simply be ruled out by lack of evidence.

You need to go into the building. Indeed, you need to go into many buildings, look around, see what is happening and report back. Getting into highly secure buildings may be easy in the movies. It is not easy in real life. Getting someone into the building who knows what he is seeing is even harder. Getting him out alive to report back, and then repeating the process in other buildings, is even harder. It can be done — though not easily or repeatedly.

Recruiting someone who works in the building is an option, but at the end of the day you have to rely on his word as to what he saw. That too, is a risk. He might well be a double agent who is inventing information to make money, or he could just be wrong. There is an endless number of ways that recruiting on-site sources can lead you to the wrong conclusion.

Source-based intelligence would appear to be the only way to go. Obviously, it is better to glean information from someone who knows what is going on, rather than to guess. But the problem with source-based intelligence is that, when all is said and done, you can still be just as confused — or more confused — than you were at the beginning. You could wind up with a mass of intelligence that can be read either way. It is altogether possible to have so many sources, human and technical, that you have no idea what the truth is. That is when an intelligence organization is most subject to political pressure. When the intelligence could go either way, politics can tilt the system. We do not know what caused the NIE to change its analysis. It could be the result of new, definitive intelligence, or existing intelligence could have been reread from a new political standpoint.

Consider the politics. The assumption was that Iran wanted to develop nuclear weapons — though its motivations for wanting to do so were never clear to us. First, the Iranians had to assume that, well before they had an operational system, the United States or Israel would destroy it. In other words, it would be a huge effort for little profit. Second, assume that it developed one or two weapons and attacked Israel, for example. Israel might well have been destroyed, but Iran would probably be devastated by an Israeli or U.S. counter-strike. What would be the point?

For Iran to be developing nuclear weapons, it would have to have been prepared to take extraordinary risks. A madman theory, cen-tered around the behavior of President Mahmoud Ahmadinejad, was essential. But as the NIE points out, Iran was "guided by a cost-ben-efit approach." In simple terms, the Iranians weren't nuts. That is why they didn't build a nuclear program.

That is not to say Iran did not benefit from having the world believe it was building nuclear weapons. The United States is obsessed with nuclear weapons in the hands of states it regards as irrational. By appearing to be irrational and developing nuclear weap-ons, the Iranians created a valuable asset to use in negotiating with the Americans. The notion of a nuclear weapon in Iranian hands appeared so threatening that the United States might well negotiate away other things — particularly in Iraq — in exchange for a halt of the program. Or so the Iranians hoped. Therefore, while they halted development on their weapons program, they were not eager to let the Americans relax. They swung back and forth between asserting their right to operate the program and denying they had one. Moreover, they pushed hard for a civilian power program, which theoretically worried the world less. It drove the Americans up a wall — precisely where the Iranians wanted them.

As we have argued, the central issue for Iran is not nuclear weap-ons. It is the future of Iraq. The Iran-Iraq war of 1980-1988 was the defining moment in modern Iranian history. It not only devastated

Iran, but also weakened the revolution internally. Above all, Tehran never wants to face another Iraqi regime that has the means and motivation to wage war against Iran. That means the Iranians cannot tolerate a Sunni-dominated government that is heavily armed and backed by the United States. Nor, for that matter, does Tehran completely trust Iraq's fractured Shiite bloc with Iran's national security. Iran wants to play a critical role in defining the nature, policies and capabilities of the Iraqi regime.

The recent U.S. successes in Iraq, however limited and transitory they might be, may have caused the Iranians to rethink their view on dealing with the Americans on Iraq. The Americans, regardless of progress, cannot easily suppress all of the Shiite militias. The Iranians cannot impose a regime on Iraq, though they can destabilize the process. A successful outcome requires a degree of cooperation — and recent indications suggest that Iran is prepared to provide that cooperation.

That puts the United States in an incredibly difficult position. On the one hand, it needs Iran for the endgame in Iraq. On the other, negotiating with Iran while it is developing nuclear weapons runs counter to fundamental U.S. policies and the coalition it was trying to construct. As long as Iran was building nuclear weapons, working with Iran on Iraq was impossible.

The NIE solves a geopolitical problem for the United States. Washington cannot impose a unilateral settlement on Iraq, nor can it sustain forever the level of military commitment it has made to Iraq. There are other fires starting to burn around the world. At the same time, Washington cannot work with Tehran while it is building nuclear weapons. Hence, the NIE: While Iran does have a nuclear power program, it is not building nuclear weapons.

Perhaps there was a spectacular and definitive intelligence breakthrough that demonstrated categorically that the prior assessments were wrong. Proving a negative is tough, and getting a definitive piece of intelligence is hard. Certainly, no matter how definitive the latest intelligence might have been, a lot of people want Iran to be building a nuclear weapon, so the debate over the meaning of this intelligence would have roared throughout the intelligence community and the White House. Keeping such debate this quiet and orderly is not Washington's style.

Perhaps the Iranians are ready to deal, and so decided to open up their facility for the Americans to see. Still, regardless of what the Iranians opened up, some would have argued that the United States was given a tour only of what the Iranians wanted them to see. There is a mention in the report that any Iranian program would be covert rather than overt, and that might reflect such concerns. However, all serious nuclear programs are always covert until they succeed. Nothing is more vulnerable than an incomplete nuclear program.

We are struck by the suddenness of the NIE report. Explosive new intelligence would have been more hotly contested. We suspect two things. First, the intelligence on the Iranian nuclear program consisted of a great number of pieces, many of which were inherently ambiguous and could be interpreted in multiple ways. Second, the weight of evidence for there being an Iranian nuclear program was shaded by the political proclivities of the administration, which saw the threat of a U.S. strike as intimidating Iran, and the weapons program discussion as justifying it. Third, the change in political requirements on both sides made a new assessment useful. This last has certainly been the case in all things Middle Eastern these past few days on issues ranging from the Palestinians to Syria to U.S. forces in Iraq — so why should this issue be any different?

If this thesis is correct, then we should start seeing some movement on Iraq between the United States and Iran. Certainly the major blocker from the U.S. side has been removed and the success of U.S. policies of late should motivate the Iranians. In any case, the entire framework for U.S.-Iranian relations would appear to have shifted, and with it the structure of geopolitical relations throughout the region.

Intelligence is rarely as important as when it is proven wrong.

The Real Struggle in Iran and Implications for U.S. Dialogue
June 29, 2009

Speaking of the situation in Iran, U.S. President Barack Obama said June 26, "We don't yet know how any potential dialogue will have been affected until we see what has happened inside of Iran." On the surface that is a strange statement, since we know that with minor exceptions, the demonstrations in Tehran lost steam after Iranian Supreme Leader Ayatollah Ali Khamenei called for them to end and security forces asserted themselves. By the conventional wisdom, events in Iran represent an oppressive regime crushing a popular rising. If so, it is odd that the U.S. president would raise the question of what has happened in Iran.

In reality, Obama's point is well taken. This is because the real struggle in Iran has not yet been settled, nor was it ever about the liberalization of the regime. Rather, it has been about the role of the clergy — particularly the old-guard clergy — in Iranian life, and the future of particular personalities among this clergy.

Ahmadinejad Against the Clerical Elite

Iranian President Mahmoud Ahmadinejad ran his re-election campaign against the old clerical elite, charging them with corruption, luxurious living and running the state for their own benefit rather than that of the people. He particularly targeted Ali Akbar Hashemi Rafsanjani, an extremely senior leader, and his family. Indeed, during the demonstrations, Rafsanjani's daughter and four other relatives were arrested, held and then released a day later.

Rafsanjani represents the class of clergy that came to power in 1979. He served as president from 1989-1997, but Ahmadinejad defeated him in 2005. Rafsanjani carries enormous clout within the system as head of the regime's two most powerful institutions — the Expediency Council, which arbitrates between the Guardian Council and parliament, and the Assembly of Experts, whose powers include oversight of the supreme leader. Forbes has called him one of the wealthiest men in the world. Rafsanjani, in other words, remains at the heart of the post-1979 Iranian establishment.

Ahmadinejad expressly ran his recent presidential campaign against Rafsanjani, using the latter's family's vast wealth to discredit Rafsanjani along with many of the senior clerics who dominate the Iranian political scene. It was not the regime as such that he opposed, but the individuals who currently dominate it. Ahmadinejad wants to retain the regime, but he wants to repopulate the leadership councils with clerics who share his populist values and want to revive the ascetic foundations of the regime. The Iranian president constantly contrasts his own modest lifestyle with the opulence of the current religious leadership.

Recognizing the threat Ahmadinejad represented to him personally and to the clerical class he belongs to, Rafsanjani fired back at Ahmadinejad, accusing him of having wrecked the economy. At his side were other powerful members of the regime, including Majlis Speaker Ali Larijani, who has made no secret of his antipathy toward Ahmadinejad and whose family links to the Shiite holy city of Qom give him substantial leverage. The underlying issue was about the kind of people who ought to be leading the clerical establishment. The battlefield was economic: Ahmadinejad's charges of financial corruption versus charges of economic mismanagement leveled by Rafsanjani and others.

When Ahmadinejad defeated Mir Hossein Mousavi on the night of the election, the clerical elite saw themselves in serious danger. The margin of victory Ahmadinejad claimed might have given him the political clout to challenge their position. Mousavi immediately claimed fraud, and Rafsanjani backed him up. Whatever the motives of those in the streets, the real action was a knife fight between Ahmadinejad and Rafsanjani. By the end of the week, Khamenei decided to end the situation. In essence, he tried to hold things together by ordering the demonstrations to halt while throwing a bone to Rafsanjani and Mousavi by extending a probe into the election irregularities and postponing a partial recount by five days.

The Struggle Within the Regime

The key to understanding the situation in Iran is realizing that the past weeks have seen not an uprising against the regime, but a struggle within the regime. Ahmadinejad is not part of the establishment, but rather has been struggling against it, accusing it of having betrayed the principles of the Islamic Revolution. The post-election unrest in Iran therefore was not a matter of a repressive regime suppressing liberals (as in Prague in 1989), but a struggle between two Islamist factions that are each committed to the regime, but opposed to each other.

The demonstrators certainly included Western-style liberalizing elements, but they also included adherents of senior clerics who wanted to block Ahmadinejad's re-election. And while Ahmadinejad undoubtedly committed electoral fraud to bulk up his numbers, his ability to commit unlimited fraud was blocked, because very powerful people looking for a chance to bring him down were arrayed against him.

The situation is even more complex because it is not simply a fight between Ahmadinejad and the clerics, but also a fight among the clerical elite regarding perks and privileges — and Ahmadinejad is himself being used within this infighting. The Iranian president's populism suits the interests of clerics who oppose Rafsanjani; Ahmadinejad is their battering ram. But as Ahmadinejad increases his power, he could turn on his patrons very quickly. In short, the political situation in Iran is extremely volatile, just not for the reason that the media portrayed.

Rafsanjani is an extraordinarily powerful figure in the establishment who clearly sees Ahmadinejad and his faction as a mortal threat. Ahmadinejad's ability to survive the unified opposition of the clergy, election or not, is not at all certain. But the problem is that there is no unified clergy. The supreme leader is clearly trying to find a new political balance while making it clear that public unrest will not be tolerated. Removing "public unrest" (i.e., demonstrations) from the tool kits of both sides may take away one of Rafsanjani's more effective tools. But ultimately, it actually could benefit him. Should the internal politics move against the Iranian president, it would be Ahmadinejad — who has a substantial public following — who would not be able to have his supporters take to the streets.

The View From the West

The question for the rest of the world is simple: Does it matter who wins this fight? We would argue that the policy differences between Ahmadinejad and Rafsanjani are minimal and probably would not affect Iran's foreign relations. This fight simply isn't about foreign policy.

Rafsanjani has frequently been held up in the West as a pragmatist who opposes Ahmadinejad's radicalism. Rafsanjani certainly opposes Ahmadinejad and is happy to portray the Iranian president as harmful to Iran, but it is hard to imagine significant shifts in foreign policy if Rafsanjani's faction came out on top. Khamenei has approved Iran's foreign policy under Ahmadinejad, and Khamenei works to maintain broad consensus on policies. Ahmadinejad's policies were vetted by Khamenei and the system that Rafsanjani is part of. It is possible that Rafsanjani secretly harbors different views, but if he does, anyone predicting what these might be is guessing.

Rafsanjani is a pragmatist in the sense that he systematically has accumulated power and wealth. He seems concerned about the Iranian economy, which is reasonable because he owns a lot of it. Ahmadinejad's entire charge against him is that Rafsanjani is only interested in his own economic well-being. These political charges notwithstanding, Rafsanjani was part of the 1979 revolution, as were Ahmadinejad and the rest of the political and clerical elite. It would be a massive mistake to think that any leadership elements have abandoned those principles.

When the West looks at Iran, two concerns are expressed. The first relates to the Iranian nuclear program, and the second relates to Iran's support for terrorists, particularly Hezbollah. Neither Iranian faction is liable to abandon either, because both make geopolitical sense for Iran and give it regional leverage.

Tehran's primary concern is regime survival, and this has two elements. The first is deterring an attack on Iran, while the second is extending Iran's reach so that such an attack could be countered. There are U.S. troops on both sides of the Islamic republic, and the United States has expressed hostility to the regime. The Iranians are envisioning a worst-case scenario, assuming the worst possible U.S. intentions, and this will remain true no matter who runs the government.

We do not believe that Iran is close to obtaining a nuclear weapon, a point we have made frequently. Iran understands that the actual acquisition of a nuclear weapon would lead to immediate U.S. or Israeli attacks. Accordingly, Iran's ideal position is to be seen as developing nuclear weapons, but not close to having them. This gives Tehran a platform for bargaining without triggering Iran's destruction, a task at which it has proved sure-footed.

In addition, Iran has maintained capabilities in Iraq and Lebanon. Should the United States or Israel attack, Iran would thus be able to counter by doing everything possible to destabilize Iraq — bogging down U.S. forces there — while simultaneously using Hezbollah's global reach to carry out terror attacks. After all, Hezbollah is today's al Qaeda on steroids. The radical Shiite group's ability, coupled with that of Iranian intelligence, is substantial.

We see no likelihood that any Iranian government would abandon this two-pronged strategy without substantial guarantees and concessions from the West. Those would have to include guarantees of noninterference in Iranian affairs. Obama, of course, has been aware of this bedrock condition, which is why he went out of his way before the election to assure Khamenei in a letter that the United States had no intention of interfering.

Though Iran did not hesitate to lash out at CNN's coverage of the protests, the Iranians know that the U.S. government doesn't control CNN's coverage. But Tehran takes a slightly different view of the BBC. The Iranians saw the depiction of the demonstrations as a democratic uprising against a repressive regime as a deliberate attempt by British state-run media to inflame the situation. This allowed the Iranians to vigorously blame some foreigner for the unrest without making the United States the primary villain.

But these minor atmospherics aside, we would make three points. First, there was no democratic uprising of any significance in Iran. Second, there is a major political crisis within the Iranian political elite, the outcome of which probably tilts toward Ahmadinejad but remains uncertain. Third, there will be no change in the substance of Iran's foreign policy, regardless of the outcome of this fight. The fantasy of a democratic revolution overthrowing the Islamic republic — and thus solving everyone's foreign policy problems a la the 1991 Soviet collapse — has passed.

That means that Obama, as the primary player in Iranian foreign affairs, must now define an Iran policy — particularly given Israeli Defense Minister Ehud Barak's meeting in Washington with U.S. Middle East envoy George Mitchell this Monday. Obama has said that nothing that has happened in Iran makes dialogue impossible, but opening dialogue is easier said than done. The Republicans consistently have opposed an opening to Iran; now they are joined by Democrats, who oppose dialogue with nations they regard as human rights violators. Obama still has room for maneuver, but it is not clear where he thinks he is maneuvering. The Iranians have consistently rejected dialogue if it involves any preconditions. But given the events of the past weeks, and the perceptions about them that have now been locked into the public mind, Obama isn't going to be able to make many concessions.

It would appear to us that in this, as in many other things, Obama will be following the Bush strategy — namely, criticizing Iran without actually doing anything about it. And so he goes to Moscow more aware than ever that Russia could cause the United States a great deal of pain if it proceeded with weapons transfers to Iran, a country locked in a political crisis and unlikely to emerge from it in a pleasant state of mind.

A Defensive Buildup in the Gulf
February 1, 2010

This weekend's newspapers were filled with stories about how the United States is providing ballistic missile defense (BMD) to four countries on the Arabian Peninsula. The New York Times carried a front-page story on the United States providing anti-missile defenses to Kuwait, the United Arab Emirates, Qatar and Oman, as well as stationing BMD-capable, Aegis-equipped warships in the Persian Gulf. Meanwhile, the front page of The Washington Post carried a story saying that "the Obama administration is quietly working with Saudi Arabia and other Persian Gulf allies to speed up arms sales and rapidly upgrade defenses for oil terminals and other key infrastructure in a bid to thwart future attacks by Iran, according to former and current U.S. and Middle Eastern government officials."

Obviously, the work is no longer "quiet." In fact, Washington has been publicly engaged in upgrading defensive systems in the area for some time. Central Command head Gen. David Petraeus recently said the four countries named by the Times were receiving BMD-capable Patriot Advanced Capability-3 (PAC-3) batteries, and at the end of October the United States carried out its largest-ever military exercises with Israel, known as Juniper Cobra.

More interesting than the stories themselves was the Obama administration's decision to launch a major public relations campaign this weekend regarding these moves. And the most intriguing question out of all this is why the administration decided to call everyone's attention to these defensive measures while not mentioning any offensive options.

The Iranian Nuclear Question

U.S. President Barack Obama spent little time on foreign policy in his Jan. 27 State of the Union message, though he did make a short, sharp reference to Iran. He promised a strong response to Tehran if it continued its present course; though this could have been pro forma, it seemed quite pointed. Early in his administration, Obama had said he would give the Iranians until the end of 2009 to change their policy on nuclear weapons development. But the end of 2009 came, and the Iranians continued their policy.

All along, Obama has focused on diplomacy on the Iran question. To be more precise, he has focused on bringing together a coalition prepared to impose "crippling sanctions" on the Iranians. The most crippling sanction would be stopping Iran's gasoline imports, as Tehran imports about 35 percent of its gasoline. Such sanctions are now unlikely, as China has made clear that it is not prepared to participate — and that was before the most recent round of U.S. weapon sales to Taiwan. Similarly, while the Russians have indicated that their participation in sanctions is not completely out of the question, they also have made clear that time for sanctions is not near. We suspect that the Russian time frame for sanctions will keep getting pushed back.

Therefore, the diplomatic option appears to have dissolved. The Israelis have said they regard February as the decisive month for sanctions, which they have indicated is based on an agreement with the United States. While previous deadlines of various sorts regarding Iran have come and gone, there is really no room after February. If no progress is made on sanctions and no action follows, then the decision has been made by default that a nuclear-armed Iran is acceptable.

The Americans and the Israelis have somewhat different views of this based on different geopolitical realities. The Americans have seen a number of apparently extreme and dangerous countries develop nuclear weapons. The most important example was Maoist China. Mao Zedong had argued that a nuclear war was not particularly dangerous to China, as it could lose several hundred million people and

228

still win the war. But once China developed nuclear weapons, the wild talk subsided and China behaved quite cautiously. From this experience, the United States developed a two-stage strategy.

First, the United States believed that while the spread of nuclear weapons is a danger, countries tend to be circumspect after acquiring nuclear weapons. Therefore, overreaction by United States to the acquisition of nuclear weapons by other countries is unnecessary and unwise.

Second, since the United States is a big country with widely dispersed population and a massive nuclear arsenal, a reckless country that launched some weapons at the United States would do minimal harm to the United States while the other country would face annihilation. And the United States has emphasized BMD to further mitigate — if not eliminate — the threat of such a limited strike to the United States.

Israel's geography forces it to see things differently. Iranian President Mahmoud Ahmadinejad has said Israel should be wiped off the face of the Earth while simultaneously working to attain nuclear weapons. While the Americans take comfort in the view that the acquisition of nuclear weapons has a sobering effect on a new nuclear power, the Israelis don't think the Chinese case necessarily can be generalized. Moreover, the United States is outside the range of the Iranians' current ballistic missile arsenal while Israel is not. And a nuclear strike would have a particularly devastating effect on Israel. Unlike the United States, Israel is small country with a highly concentrated population. A strike with just one or two weapons could destroy Israel.

Therefore, Israel has a very different threshold for risk as far as Iran is concerned. For Israel, a nuclear strike from Iran is improbable, but would be catastrophic if it happened. For the United States, the risk of an Iranian strike is far more remote, and would be painful but not catastrophic if it happened. The two countries thus approach the situation very differently.

How close the Iranians are to having a deliverable nuclear weapon is, of course, a significant consideration in all this. Iran has not yet achieved a testable nuclear device. Logic tells us they are quite far from a deliverable nuclear weapon. But the ability to trust logic varies as the risk grows. The United States (and this is true for both the Bush and Obama administrations) has been much more willing to play for time than Israel can afford to be. For Israel, all intelligence must be read in the context of worst-case scenarios.

Diverging Interests and Grand Strategy

It is also important to remember that Israel is much less dependent on the United States than it was in 1973. Though U.S. aid to Israel continues, it is now a much smaller percentage of Israeli gross domestic product. Moreover, the threat of sudden conventional attack by Israel's immediate neighbors has disappeared. Egypt is at peace with Israel, and in any case, its military is too weak to mount an attack. Jordan is effectively an Israeli ally. Only Syria is hostile, but it presents no conventional military threat. Israel previously has relied on guarantees that the United States would rush aid to Israel in the event of war. But it has been a generation since this has been a major consideration for Israel. In the minds of many, the Israeli-U.S. relationship is stuck in the past. Israel is not critical to American interests the way it was during the Cold War. And Israel does not need the United States the way it did during the Cold War. While there is intelligence cooperation in the struggle against jihadists, even here American and Israeli interests diverge.

And this means that the United States no longer has Israeli national security as an overriding consideration — and that the United States cannot compel Israel to pursue policies Israel regards as dangerous.

Given all of this, the Obama administration's decision to launch a public relations campaign on defensive measures just before February makes perfect sense. If Iran develops a nuclear capability, a defensive capability might shift Iran's calculus of the risks and rewards of the military option.

Assume, for example, that the Iranians decided to launch a nuclear missile at Israel or Iran's Arab neighbors with which its relations are not the best. Iran would have only a handful of missiles, and perhaps just one. Launching that one missile only to have it shot down would represent the worst-case scenario for Iran. Tehran would have lost a valuable military asset, it would not have achieved its goal and it would have invited a devastating counterstrike. Anything the United States can do to increase the likelihood of an Iranian failure therefore decreases the likelihood that Iran would strike until they have more delivery systems and more fissile material for manufacturing more weapons.

The U.S. announcement of the defensive measures therefore has three audiences: Iran, Israel and the American public. Israel and Iran obviously know all about American efforts, meaning the key audience is the American public. The administration is trying to deflect American concerns about Iran generated both by reality and Israel by showing that effective steps are being taken.

There are two key weapon systems being deployed, the PAC-3 and the Aegis/Standard Missile-3 (SM-3). The original Patriot, primarily an anti-aircraft system, had a poor record — especially as a BMD system — during the first Gulf War. But that was almost 20 years ago. The new system is regarded as much more effective as a terminal-phase BMD system, such as the medium-range ballistic missiles (MRBMs) developed by Iran, and performed much more impressively in this role during the opening of Operation Iraqi Freedom in March 2003. In addition, Juniper Cobra served to further integrate a series of American and Israeli BMD interceptors and sensors, building a more redundant and layered system. This operation also included the SM-3, which is deployed aboard specially modified Aegis-equipped guided missile cruisers and destroyers. The SM-3 is one of the most successful BMD technologies currently in the field and successfully brought down a wayward U.S. spy satellite in 2008.

Nevertheless, a series of Iranian Shahab-3s is a different threat than a few Iraqi Scuds, and the PAC-3 and SM-3 have yet to be proven in combat against such MRBMs — something the Israelis are no doubt aware of. War planners must calculate the incalculable; that is what makes good generals pessimists.

The Obama administration does not want to mount an offensive action against Iran. Such an operation would not be a single strike like the 1981 Osirak attack in Iraq. Iran has multiple nuclear sites buried deep and surrounded by air defenses. And assessing the effectiveness of airstrikes would be a nightmare. Many days of combat at a minimum probably would be required, and like the effectiveness of defensive weapons systems, the quality of intelligence about which locations to hit cannot be known until after the battle.

A defensive posture therefore makes perfect sense for the United States. Washington can simply defend its allies, letting them absorb the risk and then the first strike before the United States counterstrikes rather than rely on its intelligence and offensive forces in a pre-emptive strike. This defensive posture on Iran fits American grand strategy, which is always to shift such risk to partners in exchange for technology and long-term guarantees.

The Arabian states can live with this, albeit nervously, since they are not the likely targets. But Israel finds its assigned role in U.S. grand strategy far more difficult to stomach. In the unlikely event that Iran actually does develop a weapon and does strike, Israel is the likely target. If the defensive measures do not convince Iran to abandon its program and if the Patriots allow a missile to leak through, Israel has a national catastrophe. It faces an unlikely event with unacceptable consequences.

Israel's Options

It has options, although a long-range conventional airstrike against Iran is really not one of them. Carrying out a multiday or even multiweek air campaign with Israel's available force is too likely to be insufficient and too likely to fail. Israel's most effective option for taking out Iran's nuclear activities is itself nuclear. Israel could strike Iran from submarines if it genuinely intended to stop Iran's program.

The problem with this is that much of the Iranian nuclear program is sited near large cities, including Tehran. Depending on the nuclear weapons used and their precision, any Israeli strikes could thus turn into city-killers. Israel is not able to live in a region where nuclear weapons are used in counterpopulation strikes (regardless of the actual intent behind launching). Mounting such a strike could unravel the careful balance of power Israel has created and threaten relationships it needs. And while Israel may not be as dependent on the United States as it once was, it does not want the United States completely distancing itself from Israel, as Washington doubtless would after an Israeli nuclear strike.

The Israelis want Iran's nuclear program destroyed, but they do not want to be the ones to try to do it. Only the United States has the force needed to carry out the strike conventionally. But like the Bush administration, the Obama administration is not confident in its ability to remove the Iranian program surgically. Washington is concerned that any air campaign would have an indeterminate outcome and would require extremely difficult ground operations to determine the strikes' success or failure. Perhaps even more complicated is the U.S. ability to manage the consequences, such as a potential attempt by Iran to close the Strait of Hormuz and Iranian meddling in already extremely delicate situations in Iraq and Afghanistan. As Iran does not threaten the United States, the United States therefore is in no hurry to initiate combat. And so the United States has launched a public relations campaign about defensive measures, hoping to affect Iranian calculations while remaining content to let the game play itself out.

Israel's option is to respond to the United States with its intent to go nuclear, something Washington does not want in a region where U.S. troops are fighting in countries on either side of Iran. Israel might calculate that its announcement would force the United States to pre-empt an Israeli nuclear strike with conventional strikes. But the American response to Israel cannot be predicted. It is therefore dangerous for a small regional power to try to corner a global power.

With the adoption of a defensive posture, we have now seen the U.S. response to the February deadline. This response closes off no U.S. options (the United States can always shift its strategy when intelligence indicates), it increases the Arabian Peninsula's dependence on the United States, and it possibly causes Iran to recalculate its position. Israel, meanwhile, finds itself in a box, because the United States calculates that Israel will not chance a conventional strike and fears a nuclear strike on Iran as much as the United States does.

In the end, Obama has followed the Bush strategy on Iran — make vague threats, try to build a coalition, hold Israel off with vague promises, protect the Arabian Peninsula, and wait — to the letter. But along with this announcement, we would expect to begin to see a series of articles on the offensive deployment of U.S. forces, as good defensive posture requires a strong offensive option.

Thinking About the Unthinkable: A U.S.-Iranian Deal
March 1, 2010

The United States apparently has reached the point where it must either accept that Iran will develop nuclear weapons at some point if it wishes, or take military action to prevent this. There is a third strategy, however: Washington can seek to redefine the Iranian question.

As we have no idea what leaders on either side are thinking, exploring this represents an exercise in geopolitical theory. Let's begin with the two apparent stark choices.

Diplomacy vs. the Military Option

The diplomatic approach consists of creating a broad coalition prepared to impose what have been called crippling sanctions on Iran. Effective sanctions must be so painful that they compel the target to change its behavior. In Tehran's case, this could only consist of blocking Iran's imports of gasoline. Iran imports 35 percent of the gasoline it consumes. It is not clear that a gasoline embargo would be crippling, but it is the only embargo that might work. All other forms of sanctions against Iran would be mere gestures designed to give the impression that something is being done.

The Chinese will not participate in any gasoline embargo. Beijing gets 11 percent of its oil from Iran, and it has made it clear it will continue to deliver gasoline to Iran. Moscow's position is that Russia might consider sanctions down the road, but it hasn't specified when, and it hasn't specified what. The Russians are more than content seeing the U.S. bogged down in the Middle East and so are not inclined to solve American problems in the region. With the Chinese and Russians unlikely to embargo gasoline, these sanctions won't create significant pain for Iran. Since all other sanctions are gestures, the diplomatic approach is therefore unlikely to work.

The military option has its own risks. First, its success depends on the quality of intelligence on Iran's nuclear facilities and on the degree of hardening of those targets. Second, it requires successful air attacks. Third, it requires battle damage assessments that tell the attacker whether the strike succeeded. Fourth, it requires follow-on raids to destroy facilities that remain functional. And fifth, attacks must do more than simply set back Iran's program a few months or even years: If the risk of a nuclear Iran is great enough to justify the risks of war, the outcome must be decisive.

Each point in this process is a potential failure point. Given the multiplicity of these points — which includes others not mentioned — failure may not be an option, but it is certainly possible.

But even if the attacks succeed, the question of what would happen the day after the attacks remains. Iran has its own counters. It has a superbly effective terrorist organization, Hezbollah, at its disposal. It has sufficient influence in Iraq to destabilize that country and force the United States to keep forces in Iraq badly needed elsewhere. And it has the ability to use mines and missiles to attempt to close the Strait of Hormuz and the Persian Gulf shipping lanes for some period — driving global oil prices through the roof while the global economy is struggling to stabilize itself. Iran's position on its nuclear program is rooted in the awareness that while it might not have assured options in the event of a military strike, it has counters that create complex and unacceptable risks. Iran therefore does not believe the United States will strike or permit Israel to strike, as the consequences would be unacceptable.

To recap, the United States either can accept a nuclear Iran or risk an attack that might fail outright, impose only a minor delay on Iran's nuclear program or trigger extremely painful responses even if it succeeds. When neither choice is acceptable, it is necessary to find a third choice.

Redefining the Iranian Problem

As long as the problem of Iran is defined in terms of its nuclear program, the United States is in an impossible place. Therefore, the Iranian problem must be redefined. One attempt at redefinition involves hope for an uprising against the current regime. We will not repeat our views on this in depth, but in short, we do not regard these demonstrations to be a serious threat to the regime. Tehran has handily crushed them, and even if they did succeed, we do not believe they would produce a regime any more accommodating toward the United States. The idea of waiting for a revolution is more useful as a justification for inaction — and accepting a nuclear Iran — than it is as a strategic alternative.

At this moment, Iran is the most powerful regional military force in the Persian Gulf. Unless the United States permanently stations substantial military forces in the region, there is no military force able to block Iran. Turkey is more powerful than Iran, but it is far from the Persian Gulf and focused on other matters at the moment, and it doesn't want to take on Iran militarily — at least not for a very long time. At the very least, this means the United States cannot withdraw from Iraq. Baghdad is too weak to block Iran from the Arabian Peninsula, and the Iraqi government has elements friendly toward Iran.

Historically, regional stability depended on the Iraqi-Iranian balance of power. When it tottered in 1990, the result was the Iraqi invasion of Kuwait. The United States did not push into Iraq in 1991 because it did not want to upset the regional balance of power by creating a vacuum in Iraq. Rather, U.S. strategy was to re-establish the Iranian-Iraqi balance of power to the greatest extent possible, as the alternative was basing large numbers of U.S. troops in the region.

The decision to invade Iraq in 2003 assumed that once the Baathist regime was destroyed the United States would rapidly create a strong Iraqi government that would balance Iran. The core mistake in this thinking lay in failing to recognize that the new Iraqi government would be filled with Shiites, many of whom regarded Iran as a friendly power. Rather than balancing Iran, Iraq could well become an Iranian satellite. The Iranians strongly encouraged the American invasion precisely because they wanted to create a situation where Iraq moved toward Iran's orbit. When this in fact began happening, the Americans had no choice but an extended occupation of Iraq, a trap both the Bush and Obama administrations have sought to escape.

It is difficult to define Iran's influence in Iraq at this point. But at a minimum, while Iran may not be able to impose a pro-Iranian state on Iraq, it has sufficient influence to block the creation of any strong Iraqi government either through direct influence in the government or by creating destabilizing violence in Iraq. In other words, Iran can prevent Iraq from emerging as a counterweight to Iran, and Iran has every reason to do this. Indeed, it is doing just this.

The Fundamental U.S.-Iranian Issue

Iraq, not nuclear weapons, is the fundamental issue between Iran and the United States. Iran wants to see a U.S. withdrawal from Iraq so Iran can assume its place as the dominant military power in the Persian Gulf. The United States wants to withdraw from Iraq because it faces challenges in Afghanistan — where it will also need Iranian cooperation — and elsewhere. Committing forces to Iraq for an extended period of time while fighting in Afghanistan leaves the United States exposed globally. Events involving China or Russia — such as the 2008 war in Georgia — would see the United

States without a counter. The alternative would be a withdrawal from Afghanistan or a massive increase in U.S. armed forces. The former is not going to happen any time soon, and the latter is an economic impossibility.

Therefore, the United States must find a way to counterbalance Iran without an open-ended deployment in Iraq and without expecting the re-emergence of Iraqi power, because Iran is not going to allow the latter to happen. The nuclear issue is simply an element of this broader geopolitical problem, as it adds another element to the Iranian tool kit. It is not a stand-alone issue.

The United States has an interesting strategy in redefining problems that involves creating extraordinarily alliances with mortal ideological and geopolitical enemies to achieve strategic U.S. goals. First consider Franklin Roosevelt's alliance with Stalinist Russia to block Nazi Germany. He pursued this alliance despite massive political outrage not only from isolationists but also from institutions like the Roman Catholic Church that regarded the Soviets as the epitome of evil.

Now consider Richard Nixon's decision to align with China at a time when the Chinese were supplying weapons to North Vietnam that were killing American troops. Moreover, Mao — who had said he did not fear nuclear war as China could absorb a few hundred million deaths — was considered, with reason, quite mad. Nevertheless, Nixon, as anti-Communist and anti-Chinese a figure as existed in American politics, understood that an alliance (and despite the lack of a formal treaty, alliance it was) with China was essential to counterbalance the Soviet Union at a time when American power was still being sapped in Vietnam.

Roosevelt and Nixon both faced impossible strategic situations unless they were prepared to redefine the strategic equation dramatically and accept the need for alliance with countries that had previously been regarded as strategic and moral threats. American history is filled with opportunistic alliances designed to solve impossible strategic dilemmas. The Stalin and Mao cases represent stunning alliances with prior enemies designed to block a third power seen as more dangerous.

It is said that Ahmadinejad is crazy. It was also said that Mao and Stalin were crazy, in both cases with much justification. Ahmadinejad has said many strange things and issued numerous threats. But when Roosevelt ignored what Stalin said and Nixon ignored what Mao said, they each discovered that Stalin's and Mao's actions were far more rational and predictable than their rhetoric. Similarly, what the Iranians say and what they do are quite different.

U.S. vs. Iranian Interests

Consider the American interest. First, it must maintain the flow of oil through the Strait of Hormuz. The United States cannot tolerate interruptions, and that limits the risks it can take. Second, it must try to keep any one power from controlling all of the oil in the Persian Gulf, as that would give such a country too much long-term power within the global system. Third, while the United States is involved in a war with elements of the Sunni Muslim world, it must reduce the forces devoted to that war. Fourth, it must deal with the Iranian problem directly. Europe will go as far as sanctions but no further, while the Russians and Chinese won't even go that far yet. Fifth, it must prevent an Israeli strike on Iran for the same reasons it must avoid a strike itself, as the day after any Israeli strike will be left to the United States to manage.

Now consider the Iranian interest. First, it must guarantee regime survival. It sees the United States as dangerous and unpredictable. In less than 10 years, it has found itself with American troops on both its eastern and western borders. Second, it must guarantee that Iraq will never again be a threat to Iran. Third, it must increase its authority within the Muslim world against Sunni Muslims, whom it regards as rivals and sometimes as threats.

Now consider the overlaps. The United States is in a war against some (not all) Sunnis. These are Iran's enemies, too. Iran does not want U.S. troops along its eastern and western borders. In point of fact, the United States does not want this either. The United States does not want any interruption of oil flow through Hormuz. Iran much prefers profiting from those flows to interrupting them. Finally, the Iranians understand that it is the United States alone that is Iran's existential threat. If Iran can solve the American problem its regime survival is assured. The United States understands, or should, that resurrecting the Iraqi counterweight to Iran is not an option: It is either U.S. forces in Iraq or accepting Iran's unconstrained role.

Therefore, as an exercise in geopolitical theory, consider the following. Washington's current options are unacceptable. By redefining the issue in terms of dealing with the consequences of the 2003 invasion of Iraq, there are three areas of mutual interest. First, both powers have serious quarrels with Sunni Islam. Second, both powers want to see a reduction in U.S. forces in the region. Third, both countries have an interest in assuring the flow of oil, one to use the oil, the other to profit from it to increase its regional power.

The strategic problem is, of course, Iranian power in the Persian Gulf. The Chinese model is worth considering here. China issued bellicose rhetoric before and after Nixon's and Kissinger's visits. But whatever it did internally, it was not a major risk-taker in its foreign policy. China's relationship with the United States was of critical importance to China. Beijing fully understood the value of this relationship, and while it might continue to rail about imperialism, it was exceedingly careful not to undermine this core interest.

The major risk of the third strategy is that Iran will overstep its bounds and seek to occupy the oil-producing countries of the Persian Gulf. Certainly, this would be tempting, but it would bring a rapid American intervention. The United States would not block indirect Iranian influence, however, from financial participation in regional projects to more significant roles for the Shia in Arabian states. Washington's limits for Iranian power are readily defined and enforced when exceeded.

The great losers in the third strategy, of course, would be the Sunnis in the Arabian Peninsula. But Iraq aside, they are incapable of defending themselves, and the United States has no long-term interest in their economic and political relations. So long as the oil flows, and no single power directly controls the entire region, the United States does not have a stake in this issue.

Israel would also be enraged. It sees ongoing American-Iranian hostility as a given. And it wants the United States to eliminate the Iranian nuclear threat. But eliminating this threat is not an option given the risks, so the choice is a nuclear Iran outside some structured relationship with the United States or within it. The choice that Israel might want, a U.S.-Iranian conflict, is unlikely. Israel can no more drive American strategy than can Saudi Arabia.

From the American standpoint, an understanding with Iran would have the advantage of solving an increasingly knotty problem. In the long run, it would also have the advantage of being a self-containing relationship. Turkey is much more powerful than Iran and is emerging from its century-long shell. Its relations with the United States are delicate. The United States would infuriate the Turks by doing this deal, forcing them to become more active faster. They would thus emerge in Iraq as a counterbalance to Iran. But Turkey's anger at the United States would serve U.S. interests. The Iranian position in Iraq would be temporary, and the United States would not have to break its word as Turkey eventually would eliminate Iranian influence in Iraq.

Ultimately, the greatest shock of such a maneuver on both sides would be political. The U.S.-Soviet agreement shocked Americans deeply, the Soviets less so because Stalin's pact with Hitler had already stunned them. The Nixon-Mao entente shocked all sides. It was utterly unthinkable at the time, but once people on both sides thought about it, it was manageable.

Such a maneuver would be particularly difficult for U.S. President Barack Obama, as it would be widely interpreted as another example of weakness rather than as a ruthless and cunning move. A military strike would enhance his political standing, while an apparently cynical deal would undermine it. Ahmadinejad could sell such a deal domestically much more easily. In any event, the choices now are a nuclear Iran, extended airstrikes with all their attendant consequences, or something else. This is what something else might look like and how it would fit in with American strategic tradition.

Iran and the United States, Grasping for Diplomacy
May 5, 2010

The Iraqi balance swung in Tehran's direction Tuesday when an announcement was made that Iraq's two main rival Shiite coalitions have finally agreed to merge into a single parliamentary bloc. While there is still more political wrangling to be had, including the chore of picking the prime minister, this development carries enormous implications for the United States and its allies in the region. Before diving into those implications, we first need to review the results of the March 7 Iraqi elections.

The Iraqi vote was primarily split four ways: Former Interim Prime Minister Iyad Allawi, a Shi'i leading the Sunni-concentrated al-Iraqiya bloc, barely came in first with 91 seats, while Prime Minister Nouri al-Maliki's predominantly Shiite State of Law (SoL) bloc took second place with 89 seats. In third place, the Iranian-backed Shiite Islamist Iraqi National Alliance (INA) won 70 seats, while the unified Kurdish bloc came out with 43 seats. The magic number to form a ruling coalition is 163, raising all sorts of ethno-sectarian coalition possibilities that could make or break the stability the United States created with the 2007 troop surge.

The Kurdish strategy was the most predictable in this fractured political landscape. Knowing that their Arab rivals would lack enough seats on their own to form a coalition, the Kurds positioned themselves early on to ensure their kingmaker status in the new government. An SoL-INA coalition is just four seats shy of the 163 needed to form the government, and the Kurds fully expect to fill that gap.

The Sunni-Shiite and the Shiite-Shiite divisions are where things get much more complicated. With just two seats between them, al-Iraqiya and SoL were both intent on ruling the next government. Since neither bloc could get along with one another, two possibilities emerged over the course of the last eight weeks: Either a super Shiite bloc could be formed between the INA and SoL, effectively sidelining the Sunnis in Allawi's al-Iraqiya bloc, or the INA could join with al-Iraqiya, leaving al-Maliki in the dust.

Such political wrangling may be taken as a sign of a healthy democracy in most countries, but in Iraq, coalition politics can turn very deadly, very fast. It is important to remember that when Iraq held its first democratic experiment in 2005, the bulk of Iraq's Sunnis chose the bullet over the ballot. This time around, the Sunnis are looking to regain their political voice in Baghdad, and they still have the guns and militant connections to return to if that search ends in failure.

An INA-SoL coalition is thus political poison for Iraq's Sunnis, the United States, Saudi Arabia, Turkey and anyone else in the region who is highly uncomfortable with the idea of Iraq living under an Iranian shadow. The United States did not anticipate having more than 98,000 troops in Iraq more than seven years after it toppled Saddam Hussein, and needs at least half of those troops out of Mesopotamia within the next three months. To do that, Washington needs to leave at least some semblance of a Persian-Arab balance in the Middle East, and that means ensuring a place for the Sunnis at the winners' table in Baghdad.

But Iran is not about to make things easy for the United States. The Iranians can see that the U.S.-led sanctions effort, while irritating, lacks bite. They can also see that the U.S. administration is not interested at the moment in waging a third military campaign in the Islamic world, no matter how much Israel complains. Iran is thus in a prime position. They have a super Shiite majority getting ready to rule Iraq, while the United States is left helpless for the most part.

That does not mean Iran is home free, however. In spite of the daily barrages of rhetoric emanating from Tehran on Iranian military might, the country is ill at ease with having the world's most powerful military stacked on its eastern and western borders. Iran would very much like those U.S. troops to go home, but only if it can be assured somehow that a U.S. military with more of an attention span will not show up in the neighborhood again with plans for an air campaign against Iranian nuclear facilities. For Iran to get this security assurance, it needs to set a high price: American recognition of Iranian dominance in the Persian Gulf.

Given the United States' need for a Sunni-Shiite balance in this region, this is likely too high a price for Washington to pay at this point in time. So Iran has to turn to more coercive means to capture the United States' attention. This could include the threat of disenfranchising Iraq's Sunnis, upping the ante on the nuclear issue, bolstering Taliban forces when U.S. troops are surging into Afghanistan and a resurgence of Shiite militia activity. Indeed, the same day the Iraqi Shiite political merger was announced, radical Iraqi Shiite leader Muqtada al-Sadr, who has been living under Tehran's protection since 2007, proclaimed the official revival of his Mehdi Army and threatened to attack U.S. forces should they outstay their Dec. 31, 2011, deadline. This was not exactly a subtle signal on Iran's part.

There is no shortage of reasons for the United States and Iran to come back to the negotiating table, but the process will be a painful one. Moreover, the fact that Iran is holding the upper hand in this round is a bitter pill for Washington to swallow. Many in Washington will make the case that it is better for the United States to focus on bolstering its regional allies and rely on a residual force of 50,000 troops in Iraq to keep Iran at bay until more options come into view. But Iran has a plan for that, too. If Tehran cannot get the United States to leave Iraq on its terms, then it might as well have U.S. forces concentrated in places where Iran carries influence through proxies. In other words, maintain the status quo. Either way, Iran has options.

Rethinking American Options on Iran
August 31, 2010

Public discussion of potential attacks on Iran's nuclear development sites is surging again. This has happened before. On several occasions, leaks about potential airstrikes have created an atmosphere of impending war. These leaks normally coincided with diplomatic initiatives and were designed to intimidate the Iranians and facilitate a settlement favorable to the United States and Israel. These initiatives have failed in the past. It is therefore reasonable to associate the current avalanche of reports with the imposition of sanctions and view it as an attempt to increase the pressure on Iran and either force a policy shift or take advantage of divisions within the regime.

My first instinct is to dismiss the war talk as simply another round of psychological warfare against Iran, this time originating with Israel. Most of the reports indicate that Israel is on the verge of attacking Iran. From a psychological-warfare standpoint, this sets up the good-cop/bad-cop routine. The Israelis play the mad dog barely restrained by the more sober Americans, who urge the Iranians through intermediaries to make concessions and head off a war. As I said, we have been here before several times, and this hasn't worked.

The worst sin of intelligence is complacency, the belief that simply because something has happened (or has not happened) several times before it is not going to happen this time. But each episode must be considered carefully in its own light and preconceptions from previous episodes must be banished. Indeed, the previous episodes might well have been intended to lull the Iranians into complacency themselves. Paradoxically, the very existence of another round of war talk could be intended to convince the Iranians that war is distant while covert war preparations take place. An attack may be in the offing, but the public displays neither confirm nor deny that possibility.

The Evolving Iranian Assessment

STRATFOR has gone through three phases in its evaluation of the possibility of war. The first, which was in place until July 2009, held that while Iran was working toward a nuclear weapon, its progress could not be judged by its accumulation of enriched uranium. While that would give you an underground explosion, the creation of a weapon required sophisticated technologies for ruggedizing and miniaturizing the device, along with a very reliable delivery system. In our view, Iran might be nearing a testable device but it was far from a deliverable weapon. Therefore, we dismissed war talk and argued that there was no meaningful pressure for an attack on Iran.

We modified this view somewhat in July 2009, after the Iranian elections and the demonstrations. While we dismissed the significance of the demonstrations, we noted close collaboration developing between Russia and Iran. That meant there could be no effective sanctions against Iran, so stalling for time in order for sanctions to work had no value. Therefore, the possibility of a strike increased.

But then Russian support stalled as well, and we turned back to our analysis, adding to it an evaluation of potential Iranian responses to any air attack. We noted three potential counters: activating Shiite militant groups (most notably Hezbollah), creating chaos in Iraq and blocking the Strait of Hormuz, through which 45 percent of global oil exports travel. Of the three Iranian counters, the last was the real "nuclear option." Interfering with the supply of oil from the Persian Gulf would raise oil prices stunningly and would certainly abort the tepid global economic recovery. Iran would have the option of plunging the world into a global recession or worse.

There has been debate over whether Iran would choose to do the latter or whether the U.S. Navy could rapidly clear mines. It is hard to imagine how an Iranian government could survive air attacks without countering them in some way. It is also a painful lesson of history that the confidence of any military force cannot be a guide to its performance. At the very least, there is a possibility that the Iranians could block the Strait of Hormuz, and that means the possibility of devastating global economic consequences. That is a massive risk for the United States to take, against an unknown probability of successful Iranian action. In our mind, it was not a risk that the United States could take, especially when added to the other Iranian counters. Therefore, we did not think the United States would strike.

Certainly, we did not believe that the Israelis would strike Iran alone. First, the Israelis are much less likely to succeed than the Americans would be, given the size of their force and their distance from Iran (not to mention the fact that they would have to traverse either Turkish, Iraqi or Saudi airspace). More important, Israel lacks the ability to mitigate any consequences. Any Israeli attack would have to be coordinated with the United States so that the United States could alert and deploy its counter-mine, anti-submarine and missile-suppression assets. For Israel to act without giving the United States time to mitigate the Hormuz option would put Israel in the position of triggering a global economic crisis. The political consequences of that would not be manageable by Israel. Therefore, we found an Israeli strike against Iran without U.S. involvement difficult to imagine.

The Current Evaluation

Our current view is that the accumulation of enough enriched uranium to build a weapon does not mean that the Iranians are anywhere close to having a weapon. Moreover, the risks inherent in an airstrike on its nuclear facilities outstrip the benefits (and even that assumes that the entire nuclear industry is destroyed in one fell swoop — an unsure outcome at best). It also assumes the absence of other necessary technologies. Assumptions of U.S. prowess against mines might be faulty, and so, too, could my assumption about weapon development. The calculus becomes murky, and one would expect all governments involved to be waffling.

There is, of course, a massive additional issue. Apart from the direct actions that Iran might make, there is the fact that the destruction of its nuclear capability would not solve the underlying strategic challenge that Iran poses. It has the largest military force in the Persian Gulf, absent the United States. The United States is in the process of withdrawing from Iraq, which would further diminish the ability of the United States to contain Iran. Therefore, a surgical strike on Iran's nuclear capability combined with the continuing withdrawal of U.S. forces from Iraq would create a profound strategic crisis in the Persian Gulf.

The country most concerned about Iran is not Israel, but Saudi Arabia. The Saudis recall the result of the last strategic imbalance in the region, when Iraq, following its armistice with Iran, proceeded to invade Kuwait, opening the possibility that its next intention was to seize the northeastern oil fields of Saudi Arabia. In that case, the United States intervened. Given that the United States is now withdrawing from Iraq, intervention following withdrawal would be politically difficult unless the threat to the United States was clear. More important, the Iranians might not give the Saudis the present Saddam Hussein gave them by seizing Kuwait and then halting. They might continue. They certainly have the military capacity to try.

In a real sense, the Iranians would not have to execute such a military operation in order to gain the benefits. The simple imbalance of forces would compel the Saudis and others in the Persian Gulf to seek a political accommodation with the Iranians. Strategic domination of the Persian Gulf does not necessarily require military occupation — as the Americans have abundantly demonstrated over the past 40 years. It merely requires the ability to carry out those operations.

The Saudis, therefore, have been far quieter — and far more urgent — than the Israelis in asking the United States to do something about the Iranians. The Saudis certainly do not want the United States to leave Iraq. They want the Americans there as a blocking force protecting Saudi Arabia but not positioned on Saudi soil. They obviously are not happy about Iran's nuclear efforts, but the Saudis see the conventional and nuclear threat as a single entity. The collapse of the Iran-Iraq balance of power has left the Arabian Peninsula in a precarious position.

King Abdullah of Saudi Arabia did an interesting thing a few weeks ago. He visited Lebanon personally and in the company of the president of Syria. The Syrian and Saudi regimes are not normally friendly, given different ideologies, Syria's close relationship with Iran and their divergent interests in Lebanon. But there they were together, meeting with the Lebanese government and giving not very subtle warnings to Hezbollah. Saudi influence and money and the threat of Iran jeopardizing the Saudi regime by excessive adventurism seems to have created an anti-Hezbollah dynamic in Lebanon. Hezbollah is suddenly finding many of its supposed allies cooperating with some of its certain enemies. The threat of a Hezbollah response to an air-strike on Iran seems to be mitigated somewhat.

Eliminating Iranian Leverage In Hormuz

I said that there were three counters. One was Hezbollah, which is the least potent of the three from the American perspective. The other two are Iraq and Hormuz. If the Iraqis were able to form a government that boxed in pro-Iranian factions in a manner similar to how Hezbollah is being tentatively contained, then the second Iranian counter would be weakened. That would "just" leave the major issue — Hormuz.

The problem with Hormuz is that the United States cannot tolerate any risk there. The only way to control that risk is to destroy Iranian naval capability before airstrikes on nuclear targets take place. Since many of the Iranian mine layers would be small boats, this would mean an extensive air campaign and special operations forces raids against Iranian ports designed to destroy anything that could lay mines, along with any and all potential mine-storage facilities, anti-ship missile emplacements, submarines and aircraft. Put simply, any piece of infrastructure within a few miles of any port would need to be eliminated. The risk to Hormuz cannot be eliminated after the attack on nuclear sites. It must be eliminated before an attack on the nuclear sites. And the damage must be overwhelming.

There are two benefits to this strategy. First, the nuclear facilities aren't going anywhere. It is the facilities that are producing the enriched uranium and other parts of the weapon that must be destroyed more than any uranium that has already been enriched. And the vast bulk of those facilities will remain where they are even if there is an attack on Iran's maritime capabilities. Key personnel would undoubtedly escape, but considering that within minutes of the first American strike anywhere in Iran a mass evacuation of key scientists would be under way anyway, there is little appreciable difference between a first strike against nuclear sites and a first strike against maritime targets. (U.S. air assets are good, but even the United States cannot strike 100-plus targets simultaneously.)

Second, the counter-nuclear strategy wouldn't deal with the more fundamental problem of Iran's conventional military power. This opening gambit would necessarily attack Iran's command-and-control, air-defense and offensive air capabilities as well as maritime capabilities. This would sequence with an attack on the nuclear capabilities and could be extended into a prolonged air campaign targeting Iran's ground forces.

The United States is very good at gaining command of the air and attacking conventional military capabilities (see Yugoslavia in 1999). Its strategic air capability is massive and, unlike most of the U.S. military, underutilized. The United States also has substantial air forces deployed around Iran, along with special operations forces teams trained in penetration, evasion and targeting, and satellite surveillance. Far from the less-than-rewarding task of counterinsurgency in Afghanistan, going after Iran would be the kind of war the United States excels at fighting. No conventional land invasion, no boots-on-the-ground occupation, just a very thorough bombing campaign. If regime change happens as a consequence, great, but that is not the primary goal. Defanging the Iranian state is.

It is also the only type of operation that could destroy the nuclear capabilities (and then some) while preventing an Iranian response. It would devastate Iran's conventional military forces, eliminating the near-term threat to the Arabian Peninsula. Such an attack, properly executed, would be the worst-case scenario for Iran and, in my view, the only way an extended air campaign against nuclear facilities could be safely executed.

Just as Iran's domination of the Persian Gulf rests on its ability to conduct military operations, not on its actually conducting the operations, the reverse is also true. It is the capacity and apparent will to conduct broadened military operations against Iran that can shape Iranian calculations and decision-making. So long as the only threat is to Iran's nuclear facilities, its conventional forces remain intact and its counter options remain viable, Iran will not shift its strategy. Once its counter options are shut down and its conventional forces are put at risk, Iran must draw up another calculus.

In this scenario, Israel is a marginal player. The United States is the only significant actor, and it might not strike Iran simply over the nuclear issue. That's not a major U.S. problem. But the continuing withdrawal from Iraq and Iran's conventional forces are very much an American problem. Destroying Iran's nuclear capability is merely an added benefit.

Given the Saudi intervention in Lebanese politics, this scenario now requires a radical change in Iraq, one in which a government would be quickly formed and Iranian influence quickly curtailed. Interestingly, we have heard recent comments by administration officials asserting that Iranian influence has, in fact, been dramatically reduced. At present, such a reduction is not obvious to us, but the first step of shifting perceptions tends to be propaganda. If such a reduction became real, then the two lesser Iranian counter moves would be blocked and the U.S. offensive option would become more viable.

Internal Tension in Tehran

At this point, we would expect to see the Iranians recalculating their position, with some of the clerical leadership using the shifting sands of Lebanon against Iranian President Mahmoud Ahmadinejad. Indeed, there have been many indications of internal stress, not between the mythical democratic masses and the elite, but within the elite itself. This past weekend the Iranian speaker of the house attacked Ahmadinejad's handling of special emissaries. For what purpose we don't yet know, but the internal tension is growing.

The Iranians are not concerned about the sanctions. The destruction of their nuclear capacity would, from their point of view, be a pity. But the destruction of large amounts of their conventional forces would threaten not only their goals in the wider Islamic world but also their stability at home. That would be unacceptable and would require a shift in their general strategy.

From the Iranian point of view — and from ours — Washington's intentions are opaque. But when we consider the Obama administration's stated need to withdraw from Iraq, Saudi pressure on the United States not to withdraw while Iran remains a threat, Saudi moves against Hezbollah to split Syria from Iran and Israeli pressure on the United States to deal with nuclear weapons, the pieces for a new American strategy are emerging from the mist. Certainly the Iranians appear to be nervous. And the threat of a new strategy might just be enough to move the Iranians off dead center. If they don't, logic would dictate the consideration of a broader treatment of the military problem posed by Iran.

U.S.-Iran Negotiations Redux
October 29, 2010

Discussion is picking up again in Washington and Brussels over another round of nuclear negotiations with Iran. EU foreign policy chief Catherine Ashton has reportedly issued an invitation to the Iranians to meet in Vienna in mid-November to discuss a fresh proposal aimed at containing the Iranian nuclear program. This time, the offer is supposed to be harsher than the one offered to Iran late last year, now requiring Iran to cease enrichment to 20 percent and to send roughly 2,000 kilograms (4,400 pounds) of low-enriched uranium (compared to the 540 kilograms of low-enriched uranium previously required) out of the country to compensate for any uranium enriched over the past several months.

One would assume that the United States and its allies feel they've made enough progress in pressuring Iran over the past several months to present Tehran with a more stringent set of negotiating terms and to expect the Iranians to come to the table. As one unnamed U.S. official told The New York Times: "This will be a first sounding about whether the Iranians still think they can tough it out or are ready to negotiate."

In reflecting over recent months, there are a couple of notable points to consider in analyzing the effectiveness of the U.S.-led pressure campaign against Iran. The most significant shift involves Russia, which has made a strategic decision to distance itself from Tehran in order to facilitate a broader understanding with the United States on respecting the boundaries of the former Soviet periphery, including U.S. noninterference in key states like Ukraine, Georgia and Belarus. Russia also has used its carefully measured cooperation with the United States against Iran to bring in Western companies to help fulfill the Kremlin's modernization plans. This doesn't mean Russia has fully abandoned Iran, but the Kremlin did broadcast to the world that there are serious limits to its relationship with the Islamic republic. Russia's announcements that it is no longer interested in selling Iran the S-300 strategic air defense system are most embarrassing for Tehran.

The United States also spent the summer revving up a sanctions campaign against Iran, this time going beyond weak sanctions in the U.N. Security Council and targeting Iran's gasoline trade. Even Europe made a big show of passing its own set of sanctions legislation against Iran, giving the impression that Washington was finally making headway in convincing its allies, including a reluctant Japan, to create consequences for companies that conduct business with Iran in violation of sanctions. The sanctions are believed to have some effect on the Iranians, as illustrated by significant drops in overseas gasoline shipments to Iran over the past few months and reports that

Iran is converting its petrochemical facilities to produce fuel to make up for gasoline shortfalls.

But whether these measures had a strategic impact on Iranian decision making is a different question. The European Union issued the legal provisions of its Iran sanctions this week, but that legislation contains giant loopholes to allow for the import and export of oil and refined petroleum to Iran, thereby undermining the core of the current U.S. sanctions effort. The fact of the matter is that even as Iran has found it more difficult to obtain gasoline and go about its everyday business, there are still plenty of companies willing to take risks and make a handsome profit off dealing with a sanctioned pariah state. This is not to mention the problem of getting other states to support the U.N.- and U.S.-led sanctions — especially China, which may have slowed down some energy projects in Iran but maintains a robust relationship with the Islamic republic.

If Iran is going to be compelled to negotiate seriously with the United States, it is likely going to take a lot more than the pressure tactics Washington has attempted thus far. This is something that Iran understands quite well, which is also what allows Iran to act so aloof, defiant even, in each round of nuclear negotiations. Iranian President Mahmoud Ahmadinejad spoke Thursday at a conference on Iran's 20-year Development Plan, where he repeated a commonly used Iranian line on how the sanctions can be turned into opportunities to develop the Iranian economy. More interesting to us was when he said that Iran's ability to realize its 20-year Development Plan depended on progress and coordination among international forces with the country. "Materialization of this plan depends on Iran's progress and Iran's progress depends on the progress of other nations," Ahmadinejad said. "These two issues are intertwined."

We believe Ahmadinejad was alluding to a shift in the global dynamic in which Iran's sphere of influence in the Middle East is recognized by the powers that be (namely, the United States), thus allowing for a broader understanding between Iran and its current foes to bring much-needed investment to the country. Such an understanding would entail reaching some level of consensus on the "new" Iraq, in which Shiite dominance is unavoidable, and on Afghanistan, where the United States is grasping for an exit strategy of which Iran plays a key part. So, while the very visible and contentious nuclear issue takes center stage if and when this next round of U.S.-Iran negotiations takes place, the subtler question of Iraq and the wider region is where both Iran and the United States will remain fixated, if not gridlocked.

The U.S.-Saudi Dilemma: Iran's Reshaping of Persian Gulf Politics
July 19, 2011

Something extraordinary, albeit not unexpected, is happening in the Persian Gulf region. The United States, lacking a coherent strategy to deal with Iran and too distracted to develop one, is struggling to navigate Iraq's fractious political landscape in search of a deal that would allow Washington to keep a meaningful military presence in the country beyond the end-of-2011 deadline stipulated by the current Status of Forces Agreement. At the same time, Saudi Arabia, dubious of U.S. capabilities and intentions toward Iran, appears to be inching reluctantly toward an accommodation with its Persian adversary.

Iran clearly stands to gain from this dynamic in the short term as it seeks to reshape the balance of power in the world's most active energy arteries. But Iranian power is neither deep nor absolute. Instead, Tehran finds itself racing against a timetable that hinges not only on the U.S. ability to shift its attention from its ongoing wars in the Middle East but also on Turkey's ability to grow into its historic regional role.

The Iranian Position

Iranian Defense Minister Ahmad Vahidi said something last week that caught our attention. Speaking at Iran's first Strategic Naval Conference in Tehran on July 13, Vahidi said the United States is "making endeavors to drive a wedge between regional countries with the aim of preventing the establishment of an indigenized security arrangement in the region, but those attempts are rooted in mis-analyses and will not succeed." The effect Vahidi spoke of refers to the Iranian redefinition of Persian Gulf power dynamics, one that in Iran's ideal world ultimately would transform the local political, business, military and religious affairs of the Gulf states to favor the Shia and their patrons in Iran.

From Iran's point of view, this is a natural evolution, and one worth waiting centuries for. It would see power concentrated among the Shia in Mesopotamia, eastern Arabia and the Levant at the expense of the Sunnis who have dominated this land since the 16th century, when the Safavid Empire lost Iraq to the Ottomans. Ironically, Iran owes its thanks for this historic opportunity to its two main adversaries — the Wahhabi Sunnis of al Qaeda who carried out the 9/11 attacks and the "Great Satan" that brought down Saddam Hussein. Should Iran succeed in filling a major power void in Iraq, a country that touches six Middle Eastern powers and demographically favors the Shia, Iran would theoretically have its western flank secured as well as an oil-rich outlet with which to further project its influence.

So far, Iran's plan is on track. Unless the United States permanently can station substantial military forces in the region, Iran replaces the United States as the most powerful military force in the Persian Gulf region. In particular, Iran has the military ability to threaten the Strait of Hormuz and has a clandestine network of operatives spread across the region. Through its deep penetration of the Iraqi government, Iran is also in the best position to influence Iraqi decision-making. Washington's obvious struggle in trying to negotiate an extension of the U.S. deployment in Iraq is perhaps one of the clearest illustrations of Iranian resolve to secure its western flank. The Iranian nuclear issue, as we have long argued, is largely a sideshow; a nuclear deterrent, if actually achieved, would certainly enhance Iranian security, but the most immediate imperative for Iran is to consolidate its position in Iraq. And as this weekend's Iranian incursion into northern Iraq — ostensibly to fight Kurdish militants — shows, Iran is willing to make measured, periodic shows of force to convey that message.

While Iran already is well on its way to accomplishing its goals in Iraq, it needs two other key pieces to complete Tehran's picture of a regional "indigenized security arrangement" that Vahidi spoke of. The first is an understanding with its main military challenger in the region, the United States. Such an understanding would entail everything from ensuring Iraqi Sunni military impotence to expanding Iranian energy rights beyond its borders to placing limits on U.S. military activity in the region, all in return for the guaranteed flow of oil through the Strait of Hormuz and an Iranian pledge to stay clear of Saudi oil fields.

The second piece is an understanding with its main regional adversary, Saudi Arabia. Iran's reshaping of Persian Gulf politics entails convincing its Sunni neighbors that resisting Iran is not worth the cost, especially when the United States does not seem to have the time or the resources to come to their aid at present. No matter how much money the Saudis throw at Western defense contractors, any military threat by the Saudi-led Gulf Cooperation Council states against Iran will be hollow without an active U.S. military commitment. Iran's goal, therefore, is to coerce the major Sunni powers into recognizing an expanded Iranian sphere of influence at a time when U.S. security guarantees in the region are starting to erode.

Of course, there is always a gap between intent and capability, especially in the Iranian case. Both negotiating tracks are charged with distrust, and meaningful progress is by no means guaranteed. That said, a number of signals have surfaced in recent weeks leading us to examine the potential for a Saudi-Iranian accommodation, however brief that may be.

The Saudi Position

Not surprisingly, Saudi Arabia is greatly unnerved by the political evolution in Iraq. The Saudis increasingly will rely on regional powers such as Turkey in trying to maintain a Sunni bulwark against Iran in Iraq, but Riyadh has largely resigned itself to the idea that Iraq, for now, is in Tehran's hands. This is an uncomfortable reality for the Saudi royals to cope with, but what is amplifying Saudi Arabia's concerns in the region right now — and apparently nudging Riyadh toward the negotiating table with Tehran — is the current situation in Bahrain.

When Shiite-led protests erupted in Bahrain in the spring, we did not view the demonstrations simply as a natural outgrowth of the so-called Arab Spring. There were certainly overlapping factors, but there was little hiding the fact that Iran had seized an opportunity to pose a nightmare scenario for the Saudi royals: an Iranian-backed Shiite uprising spreading from the isles of Bahrain to the Shiite-concentrated, oil-rich Eastern Province of the Saudi kingdom.

This explains Saudi Arabia's hasty response to the Bahraini unrest, during which it led a rare military intervention of GCC forces in Bahrain at the invitation of Manama to stymie a broader Iranian destabilization campaign. The demonstrations in Bahrain are far calmer now than they were in mid-March at the peak of the crisis, but the concerns of the GCC states have not subsided, and for good reason. Halfhearted attempts at national dialogues aside, Shiite dissent in this part of the region is likely to endure, and this is a reality that Iran can exploit in the long term through its developing covert capabilities.

When we saw in late June that Saudi Arabia was willingly drawing down its military presence in Bahrain at the same time the Iranians were putting out feelers in the local press on an almost daily basis regarding negotiations with Riyadh, we discovered through our sources that the pieces were beginning to fall into place for Saudi-Iranian negotiations. To understand why, we have to examine the Saudi perception of the current U.S. position in the region.

The Saudis cannot fully trust U.S. intentions at this point. The U.S. position in Iraq is tenuous at best, and Riyadh cannot rule out the possibility of Washington entering its own accommodation with Iran and thus leaving Saudi Arabia in the lurch. The United States has three basic interests: to maintain the flow of oil through the Strait of Hormuz, to reduce drastically the number of forces it has devoted to fighting wars with Sunni Islamist militants (who are also by definition at war with Iran), and to try to reconstruct a balance of power in the region that ultimately prevents any one state — whether Arab or Persian — from controlling all the oil in the Persian Gulf. The U.S. position in this regard is flexible, and while developing an understanding with Iran is a trying process, nothing fundamentally binds the United States to Saudi Arabia. If the United States comes to the conclusion that it does not have any good options in the near term for dealing with Iran, a U.S.-Iranian accommodation — however jarring on the surface — is not out of the question.

More immediately, the main point of negotiation between the United States and Iran is the status of U.S. forces in Iraq. Iran would prefer to see U.S. troops completely removed from its western flank, but it has already seen dramatic reductions. The question for both sides moving forward concerns not only the size but also the disposition and orientation of those remaining forces and the question of how rapidly they can be reoriented from a more vulnerable residual advisory and assistance role to a blocking force against Iran. It also must take into account how inherently vulnerable a U.S. military presence in Iraq (not to mention the remaining diplomatic presence) is to Iranian conventional and unconventional means.

The United States may be willing to recognize Iranian demands when it comes to Iran's designs for the Iraqi government or oil concessions in the Shiite south, but it also wants to ensure that Iran does not try to overstep its bounds and threaten Saudi Arabia's oil wealth. To reinforce a potential accommodation with Iran, the United States needs to maintain a blocking force against Iran, and this is where the U.S.-Iranian negotiation appears to be deadlocked.

The threat of a double-cross is a real one for all sides to this conflict. Iran cannot trust that the United States, once freed up, will not engage in military action against Iran down the line. The Americans cannot trust that the Iranians will not make a bid for Saudi Arabia's oil wealth (though the military logistics required for such a move are likely beyond Iran's capabilities at this point). Finally, the Saudis can't trust that the United States will defend them in a time of need, especially if the United States is preoccupied with other matters and/or has developed a relationship with Iran that it feels the need to maintain.

When all this is taken together — the threat illustrated by Shiite unrest in Bahrain, the tenuous U.S. position in Iraq and the potential for Washington to strike its own deal with Tehran — Riyadh may be seeing little choice but to search out a truce with Iran, at least until it can get a clearer sense of U.S. intentions. This does not mean that the Saudis would place more trust in a relationship with their historical rivals, the Persians, than they would in a relationship with the United States. Saudi-Iranian animosity is embedded in a deep history of political, religious and economic competition between the two main powerhouses of the Persian Gulf, and it is not going to vanish with the scratch of a pen and a handshake. Instead, this would be a truce driven by short-term, tactical constraints. Such a truce would primarily aim to arrest Iranian covert activity linked to Shiite dissidents in the GCC states, giving the Sunni monarchist regimes a temporary sense of relief while they continue their efforts to build up an Arab resistance to Iran.

But Iran would view such a preliminary understanding as the path toward a broader accommodation, one that would bestow recognition on Iran as the pre-eminent power of the Persian Gulf. Iran can thus be expected to make a variety of demands, all revolving around the idea of Sunni recognition of an expanded Iranian sphere of influence — a very difficult idea for Saudi Arabia to swallow.

This is where things get especially complicated. The United States theoretically might strike an accommodation with Iran, but it would do so only with the knowledge that it could rely on the traditional

Sunni heavyweights in the region eventually to rebuild a relative balance of power. If the major Sunni powers reach their own accommodation with Iran, independent of the United States, the U.S. position in the region becomes all the more questionable. What would be the limits of a Saudi-Iranian negotiation? Could the United States ensure, for example, that Saudi Arabia would not bargain away U.S. military installations in a negotiation with Iran?

The Iranian defense minister broached this very idea during his speech last week when he said, "The United States has failed to establish a sustainable security system in the Persian Gulf region, and it is not possible that many vessels will maintain a permanent presence in the region." Vahidi was seeking to convey to fellow Iranians and trying to convince the Sunni Arab powers that a U.S. security guarantee in the region does not hold as much weight as it used to, and that with Iran now filling the void, the United States may well face a much more difficult time trying to maintain its existing military installations.

The question that naturally arises from Vahidi's statement is the future status of the U.S. Navy's 5th Fleet in Bahrain, and whether Iran can instill just the right amount of fear in the minds of its Arab neighbors to shake the foundations of the U.S. military presence in the region. For now, Iran does not appear to have the military clout to threaten the GCC states to the point of forcing them to negotiate away their U.S. security guarantees in exchange for Iranian restraint. This is a threat, however, that Iran will continue to let slip and even one that Saudi Arabia quietly could use to capture Washington's attention in the hopes of reinforcing U.S. support for the Sunni Arabs against Iran.

The Long-Term Scenario

The current dynamic places Iran in a prime position. Its political investment is paying off in Iraq, and it is positioning itself for negotiation with both the Saudis and the Americans that it hopes will fill out the contours of Iran's regional sphere of influence. But Iranian power is not that durable in the long term.

Iran is well endowed with energy resources, but it is populous and mountainous. The cost of internal development means that while Iran can get by economically, it cannot prosper like many of its Arab competitors. Add to that a troubling demographic profile in which ethnic Persians constitute only a little more than half of the country's population and developing challenges to the clerical establishment, and Iran clearly has a great deal going on internally distracting it from opportunities abroad.

The long-term regional picture also is not in Iran's favor. Unlike Iran, Turkey is an ascendant country with the deep military, economic and political power to influence events in the Middle East — all under a Sunni banner that fits more naturally with the region's religious landscape. Turkey also is the historical, indigenous check on Persian power. Though it will take time for Turkey to return to this role, strong hints of this dynamic already are coming to light.

In Iraq, Turkish influence can be felt across the political, business, security and cultural spheres as Ankara is working quietly and fastidiously to maintain a Sunni bulwark in the country and steep Turkish influence in the Arab world. And in Syria, though the Alawite regime led by the al Assads is not at a breakpoint, there is no doubt a confrontation building between Iran and Turkey over the future of the Syrian state. Turkey has an interest in building up a viable Sunni political force in Syria that can eventually displace the Alawites, while Iran has every interest in preserving the current regime so as to maintain a strategic foothold in the Levant.

For now, the Turks are not looking for a confrontation with Iran, nor are they necessarily ready for one. Regional forces are accelerating Turkey's rise, but it will take experience and additional pressures for Turkey to translate rhetoric into action when it comes to meaningful power projection. This is yet another factor that is likely driving the Saudis to enter their own dialogue with Iran at this time.

The Iranians are thus in a race against time. It may be a matter of a few short years before the United States frees up its attention span and is able to re-examine the power dynamics in the Persian Gulf with fresh vigor. Within that time, we would also expect Turkey to come into its own and assume its role as the region's natural counterbalance to Iran. By then, the Iranians hope to have the structures and agreements in place to hold their ground against the prevailing regional forces, but that level of long-term security depends on Tehran's ability to cut its way through two very thorny sets of negotiations with the Saudis and the Americans while it still has the upper hand.

Made in the USA
San Bernardino, CA
16 December 2013